Critical Acclaim for
The Best Travel Writing

"Travelers' Tales has thrived by seizing on our perpetual fascination for armchair traveling, including this annual roundup of delightful (and sometimes dreadful) wayfaring adventures from all corners of the globe."   —*The Washington Post*

"Here are intimate revelations, mind-changing pilgrimages, and body-challenging peregrinations. And there's enough to keep one happily reading until the next edition."
—*San Francisco Chronicle*

"*The Best Travel Writing* is a globetrotter's dream. Some tales are inspiring, some disturbing or disheartening; many sobering. But at the heart of each one lies the most crucial element—a cracking good story told with style, wit, and grace."
—*WorldTrekker*

"There is no danger of tourist brochure writing in this collection. The story subjects themselves are refreshingly odd. . . . For any budding writer looking for good models or any experienced writer looking for ideas on where the form can go, *The Best Travel Writing* is an inspiration."   —*Transitions Abroad*

"Travelers' Tales, a publisher which has taken the travel piece back into the public mind as a serious category, has a volume out titled *The Best Travel Writing* which wipes out its best-of competitors completely."   —*The Courier-Gazette*

"*The Best Travelers' Tales 2004* will grace my bedside for years to come. For this volume now formally joins the pantheon: one of a series of good books by good people, valid and valuable for far longer than its authors and editors ever imagined. It is, specifically, an ideal antidote to the gloom with which other writers, and the daily and nightly news, have tried hard to persuade us the world is truly invested. . . . This book is a vivid and delightful testament to just why the world is in essence a wondrously pleasing place, how its people are an inseparable part of its countless pleasures, and how travel is not so much hard work as wondrous *fun*."   —Simon Winchester

T R A V E L E R S ' T A L E S

THE
BEST
TRAVEL
WRITING

2011

TRUE STORIES
FROM AROUND THE WORLD

TRAVELERS' TALES

THE BEST TRAVEL WRITING
2011

TRUE STORIES FROM AROUND THE WORLD

Edited by
JAMES O'REILLY, LARRY HABEGGER,
AND SEAN O'REILLY

Travelers' Tales
an imprint of Solas House, Inc.
Palo Alto

Art direction: Kimberly Nelson
Page layout and photo editing: Cynthia Lamb using the fonts
     Granjon and NicolasCochin
Interior design: Melanie Haage
Production Director: Natalie Baszile and Christy Quinto

ISBN 10: 1-60952-008-4
ISBN 13: 978-1609520083
ISSN 1548-0224

First Edition
Printed in the United States
10 9 8 7 6 5 4 3 2 1

Stand by the roads, and look, and ask for the ancient paths, where the good way is; and walk in it, and find rest for your souls.

—JEREMIAH 6:16

Table of Contents

Publisher's Preface

Urazinduka ntutanga rwuba
You may get up before dawn,
but destiny gets up before you.
—Kirundi proverb

When did you begin?

Was it when your parents had a roll in the hay? When your great grandparents huffed and puffed your grandparents into quickening? Was it back in the Neolithic, the Pleistocene? Your DNA, your constituent matter, is not only prehistoric, it is stardust—did your journey begin at the Big Bang, or before, when "before" had no meaning?

It is a cliché to say that life is a blossoming, but it is true. We are each a bloom of the ineffable, of something which has no age, and which no equation or words describe. We are all these: God's breath, the point of an evolutionary spear, the curling edge of the Void, the mid-current of the River Now, perhaps even "robots from the future," as at least one physicist has suggested. (Oy vey, I am hearing something from George Eliot's Middlemarch, "All of us, grave or light, get our thoughts entangled in metaphors, and act fatally on the strength of them.")

It is a cliché to say that life is a journey, but it is true. What shore did you wash up on when you were born? What well-worn coat of many colors will you be wearing at your end, or as Buddhists have it, your passage into the Bardo? What tools do you need to make this voyage? What wisdom must you acquire? Which companions will aid you? We all wonder where and when our journey will end, but of course it will not end, just as it has no beginning. Travel is the best metaphor for life, and can help you be ever more present at all stages of an eternal becoming.

The book that follows, eighth in a series of annual compilations from Travelers' Tales, is an orchestra of travelers plucking at the strange harmonics of the world, and each one of them showing that we are part of one humanity.

It is a cliché to say that we are all kin, but it is true. Even if we hail from different clans, travel makes you certain that kinship is true not only in sentiment but in fact. The writers and explorers herein, and thousands of others not in this volume, partake of a kind of travel that Paul Theroux wrote about recently, "of the old laborious kind, [which] has never seemed…of greater importance, more essential, more enlightening." This is especially so in a time of great upheaval, natural and political, which makes it clear once again that we never were in charge. If we seem to merely persist without volition or direction (and it's not for want of trying), and politicians and our fellows disappoint us again and again, we are still free to fall in love with one another, we can still choose to explore the luminous world, become more conscious of blossoming around and within, ply the Golden Current in our raft of cells and cosmic material.

As I sit here this spring day, I'm listening to music by Moro, whose memoir *Kin to the Wind* recounts an improbable and deeply inspiring 1960s journey around the world as a young troubadour, traveling with no money or guile but with an open mind, heart, and his guitar. A little earlier than Moro, Swiss traveler Nicolas Bouvier wrote in Turkey in an account of his 1950s travels, *The Way of the World (L'Usage du Monde)*: "I dropped this wonderful moment into the bottom of my memory, like a sheet-anchor that one day I could draw up again…the bedrock of existence is not made up of the family or work, or what others say and think of you, but of moments like this when you are exalted by a transcendent power that is more serene than love."

When did you begin?

JAMES O'REILLY
PALO ALTO, CALIFORNIA

Introduction

Seeing the World Anew

Pico Iyer

Ten people walk into a crowded room, and every one of
them comes out with a different story; the Rashomon
effect plays out in all our lives pretty much every day. Someone
sees the Donna Karan sunglasses and the Paul Smith stripes,
and reads the strange figures in the room accordingly; someone else starts to talk to as many people as possible, and learns
who they are from whether they like Massive Attack or Sigur
Rós. Someone else starts to talk about "golden" and "blue" and
"light-filled" auras. The travel writer is the one who can do all
these things at once—listen more closely, see more deeply and
bring some personal question into the room—so that we feel
that we're seeing a shadow story, a secret narrative visible to
few, and everything is at stake.

There are a hundred ways of describing good travel writing, but really they all come down to much the same thing:
does the piece make you see the world anew, while offering
you a place or a feeling you instantly recognize? Does it—as
a Jan Morris essay does—take in all the surfaces so attentively
that you catch not only the way a place looks, but the way it
thinks, and mutters, and hides from itself? Does it—as Peter
Matthiessen's writing might—take on the qualities of an allegory, the story of a soul looking for the gold it's lost? Does
it—I'm thinking now of V. S. Naipaul—have such an ache of
unsettledness that you can feel that the writer himself is on
the line? The great travel writer makes you see yourself anew,
too, by introducing you to things you perhaps never allowed
yourself to observe.

Not long ago, I was driving through the Outback with my old college friend Nicolas: the most brilliant student of our generation, thirty years before, but so individual and restless that we were sure he would end up somewhere dark (he left the university, physically, after only two years and wrote his final exams so illegibly he had to be summoned back to read them aloud to an examiner for two weeks). I hadn't seen him in a quarter of a century, but I'd begun to get to know him again through the haunted, solemn, questing books he'd started to write about the Red Continent's interior, full of Central European exiles and memories of war. On my way to meet him in Alice Springs, as I got onto the plane from Sydney, he e-mailed me, casually, that we might be meeting his "wife" Alison, too (Nicolas, a legendary classicist who had been covering wars for *The Australian* for many years, living for months on end in hotel rooms in Iraq, with nothing but his copies of Proust and Kafka, was the least marriable soul I knew).

As we scuffled about the scruffy town—a smiling young soul from Bombay checked me into my hotel, Singaporeans ran the Tea Shrine and even the fanciest place in town served mostly beef vindaloo and Nonya specialties in its restaurant—we saw huge signs for "Alison Anderson": Nicolas's partner turned out to be a significant politician, and the rare Aboriginal who went back and forth between her people and the state government (speaking six indigenous tongues). As we drove across the red-dirt emptiness to visit some "old ladies" who paint (Aboriginal artists who sit on the ground outside a shed and dab patterns on canvasses that fetch hundreds of thousands of dollars in the West), I took note of the sign at the airport prohibiting tomatoes from entering the territory, Nicolas took inner notes on a strangeness that had become his second home, as familiar to him as recent patterns in his dreams. And Alison quietly told us about the "Dreamtime" stories associated with each tree or patch of desert, and how this "dingo dreaming," amidst the cordwoods and the iron-woods, marked the place where the dingo ate the caterpillar and got separated.

The parallel paths, the disparate stories each of us began to develop as we drove along the same empty road came roaring back to me when I took the stories you're about to read out onto my thirty-inch-wide terrace in suburban Japan and, in the radiant sunshine of an early November day, lost myself in them for hour after transported hour. I wouldn't say these are necessarily the "best" travel essays of the year, because the phrase makes as little sense to me as talking of a "best" color, a "best" love, or even a "best" child. But many, many of them did what only the most memorable trips—and the most deeply felt essays—do, which is to deposit me back in my life someone different from the person who set out.

When I sat with Gary Buslik, musing on the wistfulness of old slides and long-ago lives; when I began, excitedly, to find the secret treasures of an unprepossessing part of the Lorraine (with Mieke Eerkens); as I learned about what happened in Minsk, thanks to Carolyn Kraus's hard-to-forget excavations; as I found myself in a realm of meditation and allegory, learning how to see again, in the Iceland of Cameron McPherson Smith, I felt I was touching a part of the world, and of experience, that I hadn't known was there and could no longer think of cruise-ship honeymoons, look at Belarus, even reflect back on the Iceland I knew and loved in quite the same way as I had before.

One thing that exhilarates me about this book is that so many of its writers are women (you would not have found that thirty years ago, when I began writing), and many of these women are in places that I would be afraid to go to even as a shifty male—alone in New Delhi's train station after midnight, on the edge of the Sahara with a mother and a sometime lover, in Guyana after the exodus of most white folks, or looking for mass graves in Minsk. There is a sense of personal investment, of openness and soulfulness, a heart-felt introspection in many of the pieces here that would have shamed (and surely could have taught) the "travel writers" I grew up on in my youth, mostly tight-lipped British men remarking wryly on the natives.

So many of these pieces, too, show how our world is moving as much as we are, growing multiple and diverse, newly complex, as the entire planet, so it seems, is on the road or spinning on its axis. An American and his Polish girlfriend are looking for the Mona Lisa; a Canadian and her African lover are watching her mother receive news, in a cyber-café among the mosques of Africa, of a death in the family. Women are traveling to ski resorts with their eighty-three-year-old fathers, and young men are going all the way to Hiroshima or My Lai to say sorry, after a fashion, for what their country has done. In a meticulously crafted piece like Michael Shapiro's account of rafting down the Colorado River, even that most famous of poster images, the Grand Canyon, is made human and mysterious and new.

When a piece of travel writing is truly transporting, it works a small transformation in our lives, so that we are carrying around with us not just a new pair of eyes, but a fresh heart and an awakened conscience. And many of these essays take me back to some of the great works of travel-literature, old and new, that have permanently altered the way I think about the world. I cannot hear the words "Iraq" or "Afghanistan" today without calling up the hallucinatory intensity and horror of Dexter Filkins's accounts of both in his recent work of combat reportage (and therefore travel literature), *The Forever War*; and when I try to think of how to make sense of war and the peace we need to cultivate within, I call upon the clarifying priorities and gift for essentials of the great poet laureate of journeying in one place, Thoreau.

My favorite travel writers tend to be ones whose first and foremost interest is not in travel: they're closet anthropologists, personal historians, readers of texts or even just observers of the treacherous human heart and the cycles of history (think of John le Carré or Derek Walcott). A travel writer, for me, is someone like Elizabeth Gilbert, who can at once find a wise man, a lover, and a new life in Bali, yet also take the time and trouble to excavate much of the island's bloody history of violence and slavery.

Occasionally, nowadays, you'll hear people say that travel is dead, since we can access almost anywhere from the comfort of our living rooms and find Louis Vuitton stores in the shape of suitcases in Shanghai. Pshaw! As these pieces often memorably show, travel will last as long as we have difficult loves, unsolved memories, haunting questions, restless hearts and legs. Nicolas is still tracking the empty wastes at the center of Australia; his new wife Alison is still trying to find a way though the tangles of history; and I am still revisiting the interior of their land, and of their memories, and planning how I might somehow return there. The travel writer shines a light on something we never thought to look at—"gray, moss-covered churches, and gray, moss-covered cemeteries, and gray, moss-covered monuments," in Mieke Eerkens's beautiful essay—and then the light comes on in our eyes, too, and we can see its "hidden beauty."

∼≈ ∼≈ ∼≈

Born in Oxford, England, to parents from India, raised in California and long settled in Japan, Pico Iyer has always been interested in the places where cultures collide and conspire. His first book, Video Night in Kathmandu, *explored the West playing itself out in ten countries in Asia; his second,* The Lady and the Monk, *tied together the Western dreams of Japanese with the Japanese dreams of those from the West; and his third,* Falling Off the Map, *traveled to isolated places from Paraguay to North Korea and Iceland to Bhutan. In the years since, he has been looking at what travel is doing to a world and humanity on the move, in an age of immigration and exile, as described in such works as* The Global Soul, Sun After Dark, *and* The Open Road: The global journey of the Fourteenth Dalai Lama. *His next book, on Graham Greene, will look at what fears and hopes we can legitimately carry out into the world.*

CAMERON McPHERSON SMITH

❧ ❧ ❧

The Way of the Mist

He discovers how to vanish.

I'VE BEEN KICKED OFF ICELAND'S VATNAJÖKULL ICE CAP three times—once by a windstorm that would uproot trees (if Iceland had any trees), once by a labyrinth of crevasses that remains deliciously impenetrable after thirteen days on the ice, another time by a snowstorm that all but buries me alive—but this time the dice I roll are magicked and somehow in a week of negotiations with the ice I've sneaked through the heavily-crevassed ice cap margin. My supply sled has not dragged me down and the volcano under the ice has not blasted me up. Every night when the snow is frozen solid I lean into the harness and take the first step forward with the rich glory of slugging back a glass of wine that I cannot afford. Here on the ice cap my wealth is limitless.

Like a glass of wine, though, the glory doesn't last. Traveling at night on the ice is exhausting and worrisome; it's winter, and not even mountain guides come up here after

1

October. But most of all there is a pervasive uncertainty. Maps of the ice cap interior—the best I've been able to find were charted in the 1930s—suggest that it's flat and featureless, but even here in the interior previous expeditions have encountered giant crevasses crusted over with a thin snow bridges, vast pools of sliding slush melted by subglacial volcanic vents, strange conical ice formations, and subtle magnetic anomalies that seduce compass needles and send you off-course.

So I travel in an alien world. Darkness and mist before me, ice and snow of a thousand varieties underfoot, like flour, or steel. Wind, hail, and sleet drive horizontally. There are no landmarks and I follow my compass day after day. It seems I can never be sure of anything. Once I see my face reflected in the metal lid of my cooking pot and the haggard hobo in that metal is a stranger.

Often I travel through mist. The ice cap makes its own weather, the Icelanders have told me. I inhale the mist, I feel it cool my lungs, I exhale it in thick clouds. It looks like boiling milk in the cold beam of my headlamp.

In the mist I slip in and out of exhaustion, dehydration, terror, and elation. There are also unique mental states ranging from laser-like focus to complete dissolution.

The mist is distant; yet it is right against my goggles. The mist moves; but is itself immovable. Things swim at me from the static gray-white. I cannot see anything except my ski-tips and my chest-mounted compass, but I cannot tell if this mist is light or dark; it is simply blinding. As one explorer waggishly described it, it is like "living inside a ping-pong ball."

And in—or through—this mist I see four classes of things: things I want to see; things I definitely do not want to see; things simply inexplicable; and a very few real things.

I see faint shapes that prick me up, shapes I desperately want to be landmarks I know and believe in, though I know them only from poring over my charts; they are landmarks that would confirm that I am actually moving forward.

There, that must be the Háabunga Ice Dome! But, no; just a billow of snow ambling across the ice cap, like a tumbling sagebrush.

There, now that grayish blob must be the end of this hill I'm climbing! No; just a shadow cast by the cold moonlight that has somehow penetrated the mist and shown up a low, fast-moving cloud; the slope does not level off.

Finally! The Grímsvötn Ice Cauldron, maybe two miles ahead! No; a few steps farther the dark, expansive oval is just a small depression ten feet wide, and I stand there swaying and disoriented.

Lights? No, my friend; just a tumbling grain of ice that has flashed for an instant in your headlamp beam.

Crevasses, dead ahead! No. The broad smear of gray turns out to be sastrugi, a low ridge of snow sculpted by the wind....

Rocks! What are rocks doing here in the middle of the ice cap? But they're not rocks...illusions, again, this time I find no explanation for what appear to be a pile of dark boulders.... I arrive where they seemed to be and there is nothing but snow.

The most trying illusion is that of an enormous pair of legs, knees in the clouds, striding across the ice cap ahead of me. I stop in my tracks, mouth open. The mirage lasts only a moment, but it is distinct.... I watch as the gargantuan legs take one, and then two giant steps, a mile at a stride, right across my path, then fade into the gloom! I am hallucinating!

Or...was it real? Could this have been the Frost Giant Ymir, a primordial character of the Norse mythos, up from Hell to inspect the ice cap? Ymir, the Icelanders say—and have said, and sung, and murmured in their warm sod huts for a thousand years—was formed early in the universe. He originated in a mist, he assembled within it and of it. When Ymir was killed by Odin, his body dissembled, forming the Earth. As a human being, the Sagas tell me, my relation to Ymir is intimate: humans are the maggots that squirm through Ymir's flesh. So it is a sort of recursion; my own squirming thoughts have brought Ymir back to the ice, in the vision of enormous striding legs.

I find that the only way to repress such illusions is to force myself to fear nothing and to expect nothing; to simply exist. This reduces my universe to a small bubble of perception, a small bubble of consciousness. It is not unpleasant.

Behind, only vague memories; ahead, only the vaguest expectations. I need only think of here, now, this moment, the next step converted from the future to the present in an endless loop.

Only a few times do I see real phenomena.

It is cold and clear one night, an astronomer's paradise. I tip my head back and look up into the stars feeling dizzy and light. I may as well be suspended in interstellar space. I feel far from the warmth of any star. In the black voids there is only distance, only emptiness. The punctuations of starlight are still. The void is not disheartening. It demonstrates the value of any spark of life. The enormity and improbability of consciousness appears like a terrifying mirage and I think *I do not have the maturity for this* before moving on.

Later, a fountain of amber light washes across the sky like spilled liquid, stopping me in my tracks. *Aurora!* I say out loud as a gout of flaming red bursts above me, then fades almost immediately. Then an amber swath wavers like an enormous tapestry fluttering slowly at an impossible distance. It, too, fades, replaced by dim green columns illuminated from within, their infinitely-distant tops tilting towards one another. I try to commit the fantastic images to memory. Eventually the cold nudges me; move along.

Another real phenomenon I see, only occasionally, is the expanse I am traveling across. For brief moments the mist parts and I am granted a view of the starlit snowscape leaping away in all directions. It is ruffled, like a windblown lake, but stopped in motion, and here and there diamond-like snow crystals seem to shine beams at my eyes. But cloud and mist always return, speeding in to blur and then obliterate. The mist is wet and it glazes my clothes with a cracking armor of ice.

I keep marching, heading uphill for the Grímsvötn Ice Cauldron. Around 3 A.M., just before Christmas, eight hours of uphill slogging bring me to the level ground of the ice cap plateau. I drop to my knees, sobbing with exhaustion.

I look east. The low clouds have retreated here, revealing an icy plain that falls away before me towards the three-mile wide volcanic crater.

The Ice Cauldron!

Tolkein himself could not have conjured such a diabolical scene!

Dense white vapor billows up from the center of the crater, and contacting the supercooled air it freezes into unbelievable glitter that roils and writhes—

Up!

Up!

A mile-high column of glass dust, winking in moonlight!

The vision breaks my heart. Everything I know or have done or have ever thought is shattered.

You try to create beautiful things in life, I think, *but when you encounter a natural masterpiece you dissolve, and that is right.*

≈≈≈

Cameron M. Smith is an explorer and writer based in Portland, Oregon, where he is a member of the writing group The Guttery. He has written about his expeditions for many books and magazines. An active scuba diver and paraglider pilot, he is slowly retiring from ice cap expeditions in order to explore the lower stratosphere in a specially-constructed balloon and capsule. You can follow his expedition and writing projects at www.cameronsmith.com.

❧ ❧ ❧

Fire and Water

She is a wanderer. There is no cure.

IT WAS A FULL MOON IN HOMBORI ON THE EDGE OF THE Sahara. I was drawing in the sand as Issa and I argued our love. Across the open came the laughing, playful sounds of adolescents. Above us, in the incredible rock faces I could see the markings, traces of ancient portals that had been sealed forever. I had come back to make things right, but nothing had changed. Our words were the same after six years of separation. I knew him by his words.

We had been traveling all day, speeding along the broken road, wind in the windows. The way he drove incensed me, forcing the breaks at the last minute, dancing around the potholes and coming down on the sand verge, sometimes at a tilt, half on, half off, again and again, choosing the way in his mind, never speaking, as if we weren't there. My mother and his gentle younger brother, who looked up to him, were gazing out the windows in the back, equally silent. This was our last excursion. My mother had never agreed to rent this 4-wheel drive, but he had talked me into it. After our trip to Dogon country she had wanted to go up the Niger by boat. Instead we were going to Hombori. They had not gotten along. He was lazy, she said, bossy, didn't have any drive.

I was up in the cliffs, the strange orange and black walls lit like fire in the sun, where climbing goats were just dots of white. The walls gave way to passages and other worlds unseen from the road. Crevices were filled with green. I saw how there was life in the recesses, looking for shadows and water.

I returned to the road, as if my eyes could help him to drive, my foot on an imaginary brake. He was always too fast, too reckless and it made me angry, made him angry, that I had never really trusted him.

"*Tu as peur?*" he cried. "*Tu pense que tu vas tomber?*" You're afraid? You think you will fall?

The Hand of Fatima appeared before evening, the great bluish-rose pillars rising from the white desert floor like five fingers. As we came closer the deep orange cliffs towered above us. I saw in the closest pillars the figure of a veiled woman standing with her left arm pointing to the sky. A portal. It was a holy place, ethereal, and yet I knew that travelers from my world had passed through and left their spikes and rope pinned to the fiery walls.

In Hombori I drew in the sand and it was like a divination, all the lines and waves were the years, all the love and anger, fights over money and distance, beliefs and circumstance. It was like a flower, a star, a storm, a whirlwind. And then I erased it.

"*J'ai peur de toi,*" he said. I'm afraid of you.

For twenty-five years I was pulled to Africa as if by a living rope, something made of plant fiber, tree bark, animal hair.

I can see all the initiations now, all that I had gone through.
It comes into my dreams. A certain light on a bare tree in
the Quebec hills will conjure the dust light of the Sahel. The
smell of burning kindling or sizzling meat, a crushed plant,
diesel, mulching leaves, a candle. It taught me about magic,
how to see the signs. For fifteen years I was in this relationship with Issa. Are you afraid? Do you think you will fall?
Our story traveled back well over a decade, over cattle trails
and highways, along the rivers. It lived in clay huts, among
mice and stars, divinations, ritual offerings to water, in ten-
derness and laughter, under scorching heat on Le Pont des
Martyrs in Bamako, and mango rains. It lived in the images
of a white horse, a miscarriage, malaria, a car crash, in the
phone line from a farmhouse in the snow, the failed immigration papers and business ventures, all the wire transfers,
plane tickets, emails and silence. I learned to carry it all inside,
sealed off, until I found the magic words: which way do I
go? It was inevitable that I would cross the line in myself and
come to the crossroads. My father has a saying:
    "Be strong, be brave, wait for the sign."
    The first sign was that I had to go back and that my
mother wanted to come with me. A traveler in her own right,
she has been all over the world. She had left the dark and
cold of Northern Europe when she was twenty and lived for
a year in Lagos, Nigeria, working for the embassy. And later
she moved away to Canada. But Africa was her first love.
The remnants lived in her house, hide drums, Ibo sculptures,
bronze reliefs and camel blankets. It had always been in her
heart to return. Maybe that was why I did, again and again. I
had been born into her yearning.

We traveled first in Burkina Faso. There was a village called
Ourouboro, a name that reminded me of the symbol of eternal unity, the snake that swallows its tail. It was the home of
the blacksmith, the clang of metal, the breath of fire. A mass

of white chicken feathers hung from the thick woven ceiling and the stone altar underneath was stained with blood. In Boromo we waited three hours in the forest to see the elephants. There was a great buttressed tree that my mother said looked like an elephant's foot. A stone was placed between the roots, and a carved wooden bench. She put her hands on the trunk of the tree and asked for the elephants, and they came, dark forms out of the bush, wading into the green river, trunks curling and waving, blowing water over their backs, the sound of water.

My mother lit a candle on Christmas Eve in Bobo, on the terrace of Hotel Cocotiers above the busy roundabout, and listened. I was going to transform my relationship with Issa. I wasn't going to give up. I would stay in Mali with him until the spring and make it work. A marriage procession arrived at that very moment at the City Hall across the road, a Toyota pickup filled with frenzied drummers, and bridesmaids in pink satin on the sidewalk, women in long gowns, men in pressed suits.

We floated across purple lilies in a black pirogue on Tengrela Lake and climbed up into the black Dome Mountains, a million years old, rippled by the sea.

The tiny village of Bani was known for its seven mosques that rose out of the red rock escarpment, empty, ghost-like monuments. They had come by the vision of an old village mystic. We walked up there in the evening. My mother hit her foot on a rock and the blood flowed onto the earth. But she said it was nothing so we continued up to the great tabletop of wind, a view of the Sahel on all sides, the sun like a full harvest moon in the rose-gray sky against a dark red mosque.

That night my mother was stung by a scorpion in the shower stall, in the very foot she had struck on the mountain. The young man, Ousmane was filled with reverence. His motorbike lit the way on the dark pathways to the village clinic.

A group of people were sitting by lamplight, holding vigil, the way I later held vigil outside the tent where my mother lay on painkillers with a fire burning up her leg. Ousmane sat beside me, filling my plastic cup with red wine from a box he had got from the tourists. I held the dark sugary wine in my mouth and honored the full moon over the tent and the children running in the alleyways, singing and calling down the light. The scorpion was an ancient creature, master of survival and maternal self-sacrifice, guardian of death and transition. It was also the constellation I had been born under.

The next sign was the chick that was killed at the Edbaf bus station in Ouagadougou. The chicken and her four little chicks came peeping around the passengers' feet. I saw them so clearly like light and water, the fire patterns on their little warm bodies. One ran off suddenly from the others and a man passing by lost his footing and struck it down. He stood there a moment watching as it fluttered, then he walked away. My heart was beating fast. The chick lay dead, coated with blood and sand.

On the long ride to Mali there were so many stars. I could see all of them between the constellations. It had been six years since I'd seen Issa. I had thought to drift away from him, but the pull was too strong. My heart was wide open like a door. I had a vision. Everything was in the hand, but I had to dig deeper. I had to dig around the palm, which was the heart, with a spoon, but I found it went through the back of my hand. Blood and bone; these were the essential substances. Water and earth. But there was also fire.

My love of Issa has been a strange dream, like when he told me he had taken up his father's skill of bronze casting and I never knew this was something he could do. One who works with fire is a guardian between the worlds and the fire must be fed and tended and given the ultimate respect.

A day after our arrival in his hometown in the north he brought me to the blacksmith's hut. The wailing voice of a Fulani singer came from a small radio while a little boy turned the wheel of the bellows, raising the flames. Faucets, pieces of pipe, old bracelets and locks were laid on the bed of coals. There was an explosion and we all ducked. A piece of hot metal shot over the apprentice's head. The boys smiled at me. I smiled back and shivered.

The softened pieces of metal were put into an old bent metal bowl, the outside of which was coated with clay and donkey dung. The bowl was covered with a lid and Issa's sculptures, encased in clay, were laid on the coals. Two men now took turns at the wheel that made a soft clattering sound like a sewing machine. Half an hour, an hour. I was entranced by the heat and acrid smells, by the rose-orange, turquoise, purple and bright green flames, watching the metal melt to liquid. Unlike the surface of a lake it was gleaming white, neither sky, nor sea. The boy raked sparks off its surface. He picked up the bowl with iron pinchers and poured the liquid light—some of it hitting the earth and forming beads—into the sculptures half buried in the earth. Unearthed they turned shades of color. They were alive, threads of heat glowing in them like veins.

Issa said a prayer. "This is sacred for me."

When they had cooled he gently cracked them open. Each was beautifully wrought, but one. It appeared that the foot had broken off, the left, the female side.

We talked about marriage in the night courtyard on the cane chairs, as we had talked many times before. I could not marry without losing what was sacred to me: my freedom. His father has often asked when I was going to come and "sit" in the family. Issa sat in his blue-dark purple tunic, a surface like charcoal in the darkness. The family thought that my mother had come so that the kola nuts could be given and we could be married. After his brother died he became the eldest and he was still unmarried and childless. He said his parents wanted to live in peace; living with a woman, sleeping with her in the family house was a sin. I said in the older faith the love between a woman and a man was sacred. This was the original holy fire. He said something about the spilling of seed. This was the transplanted patriarchy. Here were two elements, the sun and the moon, and they were directly opposed.

Two days after arrival, at the little cybercafé down the road my mother received an email from Europe. They had found her sister in the river a few days before Christmas. She had been healing from a broken leg for six months when she went to see the river, walking with her cane. She fell off the bridge. My mother's favorite sister, my dear aunt had left by water.

The servant brought a little stove of smoking incense into the room where my mother lay. Trails of the sweet smoldering root drifted out to us. I sat with Issa in the women's courtyard, with my journal unopened, watching the black finches in the fern tree while he carved his sun-warmed beeswax. His mothers were grilling fish for us. A mountain of clothing sat waiting to be washed by hand.

Issa called me "Lagere," favorite daughter, first and last born. I knew every one of his family and they accepted me as one of their own. Not one member of my family had ever met him until now. Issa and I had met in Kayes where the rivers meet. I had followed the river from Senegal on a white horse and rode into town where he was working at a traveler's inn. A month earlier he had lost his favorite eldest brother to water. All of this came back to me. His brother had papers, plane ticket and passport for passage to the States and drove all the way from Bamako to say goodbye. He left again by the same bridge I later crossed by horse. The high waters caught him in a current and the car slid off and sank. Issa saw it all from shore, his hand still lifted in a gesture of goodbye. He saw everything go down, his love and his life as he knew it. In that moment he took on six siblings, his aging parents, all the extended relatives, and a dark fear of Faro, Goddess of the water.

"I am lost."

My mother was sitting on the roof, wrapped in her blue desert cloth, her face bronzed by the setting sun. Her sister had been guardian of her childhood home, the last connection to her homeland.

"I'm coming back with you."

"Are you sure?"

"Yes."

Without a word to Issa I found myself with my mother booking earlier flights back to Canada, and another one for her to Europe for the funeral. We had nine days. She didn't want to stay in Issa's house any longer. She wanted to see the land.

We rented two motorbikes, packed the tents and food and set off, Issa and I, his brother and my mother, into Dogon country. As we climbed up to Nando and the most beautiful clay mosque that had fallen from the sky we picked *koronifin* under the trees, small red berries that tasted of chocolate. We ate rat in one village with a sauce of *disi*, a pale yellow stringy root like potato. Everywhere we were offered calabashes of *dagena*, a milk-like drink from *fonio*, the sacred grain of the Dogon. In another village they gave my mother bark of the *balazon*, thorn tree, for a lung infection she had developed from the dust. They call it the 'devil tree' because it withers in the rainy season and thrives in the winter. I could see she was in shock, and because I worried I did not notice my own. I gave him my decision.

"Talk to me, Issa."

"Why are you leaving?"

"I'm taking my mother home."

"What about me?"

With my arms around his waist and my eyes watering we rode through bush fires and smoke, through village pools.

Maybe the beauty of his bronzes would carry him. But it was too late. He was losing the art of fire, and there was too much water under the bridge.

We rode a donkey cart from Tuni. The man let me drive as he walked alongside, muttering and cursing at the donkey, shoving him, threatening him. He finally gave me the rope and the stick. I used them as a rhythm, with my hands out on either side high in the air, the rope in one, the stick in the other, waving a consistent motion that led me into a trance, with the 'shhh' of the tires in the sand, the trundling of the cart, the clicking of my tongue. It felt right. I was driving. I lay my hand on the donkey and closed my eyes. He was working with me. I understood then what it was to direct one's life and be in touch with the soul.

Two days after our return from Hombori my mother and I were waiting for our bus to take us home through Dogon country and on to the Burkina border. It was cold. My shawl lay wet on my back. I had dried my hair with it at dawn when Issa came to ask me for money, just enough to get his business going, just enough. He sat beside me at the breakfast stand and ordered an egg. We ate in silence. I was worrying about the bus, wondering if it would ever come. I was looking at the row of Barika soap sachets hanging behind the coffee man's head, thinking how I had to wash this tangled strand of my life, sever it. I was thinking about my aunt and how messages from the other side had led me through a door. It wasn't that I chose my mother over Issa. I chose myself.

"Zon." Issa muttered. Thief.

He was watching the commotion behind us. Two merchant women had lost their money and stood there with all of their baggage and nowhere to go.

The bus never came. A man ran up from the bus company.

"*Le bus n'est pas bon!*" The bus is no good.

He gave us back our money. My mother stared at me. Our flight left in thirty-five hours from Ouagadougou in Burkina, three hundred miles away. I had left everything too late. But then the man grabbed my hand and led us out the station door to the highway where a bush taxi sat low on its haunches, piled high with cargo and packed with people. Our man argued with the ticket seller and came out smiling with two tickets. We climbed into the back of the covered pickup, over legs and chickens and sacks of roots, and squeezed ourselves into place. Issa came to the window in his purple tunic. We looked into each other's eyes. I saw his sadness and desperation. I felt none of that pain from before, the separation I'd always had to bear when leaving yet again for another year. I felt a kind of solemn truth.

On the Bandiagara Pass the hazy band of the Sahel spread below us, luminous sands dotted with thorn trees, blue distance. We came down through the red cliffs. The Fulani man beside me was asking me the way as if I had lived here all my life. In Koro a battered white van was waiting in the heat. The owner said he now had four passengers including us, but he was waiting for ten more to make it worthwhile. Or did we want to pay the extra fare? My mother sat defiantly on the hard bench to wait it out, the sun burning the sands at her feet.

Dusty, windblown Koro. We left on the red road in an old white mini bus without windows, seven of us, the two smiling Dogon men with their sacks of onions, the Sorai in his striped tunic and white turban and sacks of salt, a young boy in lime green head cloth, and a speckled chicken at our feet. We wrapped scarves over our faces and hung on to the metal frames of the windows, bumping on the hard benches that were not fixed to the floor, as the bus rattled along and the smoke swept in and veiled us. We traveled among the great gesturing baobabs and bristly thorn trees blooming yellow flowers. We went with the camel running down the embankment, head held high, with the spotted goats moving in the bushes and a herder boy standing still against the sky. I saw my mother's face of pure joy. This was her element and mine, traveling free. The sun was setting in Mali, that golden amber sphere burning into dust.

❧ ❧ ❧

Erika Connor is an artist and writer from rural Quebec, Canada, with a love of animals, nature, myths, and culture. She has taken care of wild birds and raccoons in rehabilitation centers, worked for the Humane Society's "visiting dogs in hospitals" program in Canada, traveled by white horse both in West Africa and Mongolia, observed wild horses in Mongolia, lived with the Fulani and Bambara people of the Sahel, and continues to lose herself between the worlds.

MARCIA DeSANCTIS

≈≈ ≈≈ ≈≈

One Day, Three Dead Men

Oh Russia.

THE CONCIERGE TOLD ME IT WAS THE HOTTEST JUNE DAY on record in Moscow. In front of the National Hotel, the air was thick with a million floating seeds from the poplar tree. The Russians call it "summer snow," and in the heat, the white fluff stuck to my neck, shoulders, and legs as I drifted through the streets of the city I once had known well but now, barely recognized. I was back in Russia after a long absence and after three days, I was still hopeful I would see what I had traveled all this way to find.

It was a homecoming of sorts. Twenty-eight years had passed since I first traveled to the then-Soviet Union. I had arrived there in June of 1982 with Mom, Dad, and a brand new degree in Russian Studies. I was a wide-eyed Cold War baby who had spent the last four years reading deeply—very deeply—into the tortured Russian soul. It had been an obsession since tenth grade, when I won a school essay contest. I have no memory of the topic, but I do recall the prize: a collection of novellas by Dostoevsky. It beats me what a fifteen-year-old public school cheerleader found in *The Gambler*, but I began to devour those dark tales, and soon began to study Russian during weekends and summers.

I spent my college years in the Department of Slavic Languages and Literature, a daylight-free warren of classrooms occupying the basement of a building in the center of the Princeton campus. The language classes were crowded, but only four of us in the Class of 1982 declared Russian as our major. I took courses in politics and history to examine the centuries-old ties between the rulers—Czars, Bolsheviks, the Politburo, or whoever held the reins at the time—and the country's writers, who belonged to the Russian people. I remained obsessed with the literature—with Chekhov's stifling parlors and Gogol's lunatics, yes, but also with a couple of contemporary writers and poets, some of whom were in exile, and some of whom—through compromise or cleverness or both—survived the system as Soviet writers.

After graduation, I turned down the chance to translate interoffice memos at some Washington agency or another. Instead, I worked for tips as a tour guide for doctors on professional exchange programs. I crisscrossed the Soviet Union, starting each trip in Moscow, finishing up in Leningrad. Two years later, I began a career in network television, and as I climbed the ladder, traveled frequently to the USSR. Three times I fell in love on assignment during Moscow winters, always finding some magic of chemistry or coincidence in that barren place. In 1992, I spent two months researching weapons facilities for the American network I worked for, but it was my last trip to Moscow. I had recently married, soon would have a son, and then a daughter, and duty and domesticity curtailed my exotic travels almost to extinction. But my devotion to Russian literature remained, and I loved to re-visit my college volumes—Turgenev, Lermontov, Gorky, Aksyonov, Akhmatova, and especially Chekhov—and skim my margin notes, scribbled at a time when there was nothing on earth more important than the book in my hand.

In my forties, my old obsession began to scratch at me. I had begun to travel, write, and work again, but there was urgency in the sensation that Russia was calling me back. I started to miss, then crave, and then positively require my connection to the passion that had defined me. A classic mid-life epiphany, to be sure, where I felt a desire to stitch the known past together with the unknown future, and to soothe myself with the knowledge that I might yet be the same person after nearly three decades. My whole life was before me back then, and in a way, with two nearly-grown kids, it was now as well. So, on Memorial Day, I left my husband, my teenagers, and a couple of houseguests in the middle of a summer barbecue to catch my plane to Moscow. I was duplicating that first journey, taken right after I graduated from college. I wanted to know if, when I landed on Russian soil, it would feel like home again.

It hadn't begun well. Two weeks earlier, I had spent two full days—one of them in hurricane-force rains—standing outside the Russian consulate in New York, applying for a visa, with a restless throng of other document-waving hopefuls. I made the mistake of not hiring an outside procurement service, and spent hours on the sidewalk making anagrams in my head out of the words, *Mr. Medvedev, tear down this wall.* One advantage of traveling with a television network? I never had to get my own visa. The document came through, but I already felt done-in by the great Russian obstacle machine.

Round two greeted me upon landing in Moscow at 5:00 P.M. Passport control was interminable; it gave me severe Brezhnev-era flashbacks. I couldn't find an open bank to get rubles, so I charged a train ride to Belorussky Station, where I discovered that I left my fluent Russian somewhere in 1992.

It was pretty much gone, especially the part that might have helped me negotiate with a swarm of drivers, all clad in leather jackets, who lurked curbside ready to shake down the next sucker—in this case, me. There were no official taxis. What had I ever liked about this place? I fumed as I doled out fifty U.S. bucks to a man who ferried me to the National.

It was now a seven-star hotel. My parents had sprung for it in 1982; this time, I prepaid my stay in credit card points. In my room, the antique reproductions were high quality—crimson brocades and dainty settees. More importantly, the mini-bar was full, and I went for a double vodka, straight up. From room service, I ordered strawberries to round out my cocktail hour. The price tag? One thousand fifteen rubles. Thirty-four dollars for seven strawberries.

I put myself on a budget that made me feel more like a college student now than I had when I was twenty-one. I walked and walked, looking for a bakery where I might find something tasty and cheap. I found one on Varvarka Street, beside the Znamensky Monastery, and for pennies, I snacked on pirozhki, one filled with apples, one with potatoes, one with cheese. The lady who served me was a relic, draped with a blue baker's coat and cap atop her teased hair. Later, I bought a sack of strawberries at a kiosk, this time for ten rubles—roughly forty cents. An old friend and I ate osso bucco and gnocchi alla Romagna at a restaurant that was more delicious and expensive than anything in New York. He escorted me past an intimidating trio of doormen who were bursting out of their suit jackets. There was plenty of security because upstairs, an oligarch was throwing a lavish birthday party.

The city was changed, as I had expected—full of glitzy boutiques, and women with tan legs and towering heels—like Miami Beach of the Steppes. In the Soviet era, even young women plodded through Moscow's grim streets with their backs hunched over; now it seemed they all stood eight feet tall, their shoulders back and breasts pushed forward.

On the third morning I stopped in to see Lenin in Red Square. It had once been among the safest places on earth, patrolled by army troops and teeming with militia. Now, parts of it felt like a seedy theme park, with kiosks selling balloons and overpriced lemonade. It never seemed possible that Lenin, the tiny gray figure whom one network correspondent I knew referred to as Dead Fred the Head Red had overthrown the monarchy and set his nation on its course for almost a century. But in 2010, it seemed ludicrous. I was sad as I left the poor old fellow in his depressing permafrost.

My Russian was slowly coming back, and there were glimmers of recognition—the lady at the bakery, for one—but I otherwise felt disconnected, rudderless, like I might feel in any unfamiliar European city. The place didn't feel like mine anymore. I was a stranger now, in spite of years of work there, the love affairs, and mostly, the great trove of Russian books that had sustained me, and to which I returned again and again and again.

That afternoon, I hired a taxi which came with a driver called Pavel to take me to the Novodevichy Cemetery, to visit another grave—that of the only dead man I have a crush on. He knows my mind as if he were inside it, and grasps the confounding equation of marriage more than any writer living or dead. I hesitated before plucking two sprigs of jasmine blossoms from an overhanging tree. Then, I tossed one flower on the soil above Anton Chekhov's body, and stuck the other between two pages of a notebook in my bag.

The sky darkened and without warning split wide open—thunder, lightning, a curtain of rain that in an instant washed the poplar seeds clean off my shoulders. I took shelter against a low building, beside gravedigger tools. After about a half hour, the sky turned a blinding blue. The storm had passed, leaving puddles that I waded through in flip-flops.

As I walked towards the exit, I saw a crowd of people gathering in the main courtyard, along with eight or so television cameras. A man wearing an officer's cap and gloves stood in front of a bulky red funeral arrangement. He held a framed black and white photograph, and I recognized the image as that of the poet Andrei Voznesensky, who had died earlier in the week at age seventy-seven. I had stumbled upon his burial procession. Though I was drenched from the downpour, I decided to join it.

He was one of the great poets of the Soviet era, introduced to me by my college professors, who had the wisdom to convey that a literary tradition perseveres even—especially—when a writer is at risk, which they so often were throughout the history of the Russian, then the Soviet, Empire. With the exception of a nasty run-in with Krushchev, Voznesensky managed to preserve his humanity and his voice and not run afoul of the Soviet literary watchdogs. In the 1960s he gave readings in stadiums packed with fellow citizens who needed poetry like we in the west needed the Rolling Stones.

As the crowd of mourners swelled to the hundreds, it grew hushed. I took my place as we began to march down the tree-lined alleys, past silhouettes and gravestones and little manicured patches of grass. It was a long shuffle to the burial site, in and out of shadows, as the sun baked away what remained of the storm. His resting place was obvious—the area was festooned with a thousand bouquets draped with ribbons bearing condolences in golden lettering. Finally, the crowd, still silent, watched as the poet was lowered into the ground. Andrei Voznesensky took his place alongside Gogol, Mayakovsky, Bulgakov, and of course, Chekhov.

After the service, I found Pavel, the driver, at the appointed meeting place outside the cemetery gates. As I slipped into the passenger seat of the car, I asked him, "Who were all the mourners?"

"Just Russians," he said.

"Do you think he was a great poet?" I asked.

"Who knows?" he stopped. "But he was *our* poet." And then he said, with a low flourish as if he were alone on stage, "*Life like a rocket flies/Mainly in darkness, Now and then on a rainbow.*"

Late-afternoon sunlight poured through the open window and landed in my lap. Moscow sparkled from the thunderstorm, and Pavel drove gingerly through pools of rainwater. Finally, I broke the silence.

"Voznesensky?" I asked.

"Yes," Pavel the cab driver replied. "*The Parabolic Ballad.*"

Back at the room, I looked up the title and the line of the verse my cab driver had recited by heart. I remembered it. I had read it in college. I cracked open a $20.00 mini-bar vodka and stood by the window. The cupolas of the Kremlin were shining as they have for hundreds of years on June evenings like this one.

Finally, it made sense.

❧ ❧ ❧

Marcia DeSanctis spent years traveling the world as a network news producer and is now writing a memoir. Her work has been in Vogue, Departures, The New York Times Magazine, The Christian Science Monitor, More, Princeton Alumni Weekly, *and the* Huffington Post. *She loves to travel alone and her idea of heaven is arriving at a new place, opening the hotel room door, checking out what candy is in the mini-bar, and then heading outside to explore her new, temporary neighborhood. She tries to pinpoint a place to have her coffee every morning and always ducks into a pharmacy. She loves to bring home toothpaste or a jar of vitamins as souvenirs.*

KEVIN McCAUGHEY

※ ※ ※

How I Promised Anusha the Smile

Finding the Mona Lisa—there's nothing to it.

"THERE'S THE EIFFEL TOWEL AGAIN," I SAID. IT KEPT popping up outside the window as the tour bus bounced us around Paris.

"*Tower*," Anusha said. "I say that only one time, Kevish, *Towel*. Now you must every time say Eiffel *Towel*. English words sometime very same."

We had arrived the evening before, after twenty-seven hours on the road, fifty Poles from Gdansk and one American. The year was 1995, so for most of the Poles this was their first time in the West, first time in the City of Light. And they were willing to punish themselves to see it all. In less than twenty-four hours we'd already done the Towel, Versailles, the Musée d'Orsay, the Pompidou Centre, Notre Dame, Les Halles, and some street where paintings were sold. My twenty-six-year-old girlfriend, Anusha, had more defined ambitions. She wanted to see the Eiffel Towel, the *Mona Lisa*, and if possible, find some Polish food.

I just wanted coffee. Much of the previous night I'd spent in the hotel bar. It was afternoon now and I was flagging a bit.

"There'll be a café at the Louvre," I said.

"Eiffel Towel was my first big dream. And now, Kevish, *Mona Lisa*."

She brightened a bit, leaving her own tiredness behind. Her sunglasses were pushed atop her head, in hair that was blonder than it had any right to be.

"And you will have it. I promise."

"And after *Mona Lisa* I want eat something."

A flock of Poles and one hungover American stood in the Louvre's reception area, looking high up into the apex of a glass pyramid with its chain-link-fence pattern of panes.

Everybody's feet hurt. A hike through woods is fun; a hike through crowds debilitating. And all day we'd dodged humanity. Our pilot—that's what the Poles called our bus tour guide—announced that we would go directly to the *Mona Lisa*.

"That's kind of embarrassing," I said to Anusha. "It's not like the *Mona Lisa* is the only painting here."

"Yes, but it's big museum, and he close in two hours. So maybe we go with pilot."

"That pilot drinks too much," I said.

"So why you sit all night with him in bar? Why you didn't come to room? We are in Paris—Love City—and I am wait in bed. But you, Kevish, you in bar with pilot."

"I know. That was dumb. Look, Anusha, you don't need a pilot to get to the *Mona Lisa*. It's easy. I'll take you. I'll be your guide."

"You are certain?"

"It's the most famous painting in the world. *And* I've been here before."

She watched the pilot lead off this flock of Poles, from the central atrium to a wide stretch of stairs.

Two overpriced espressos at the museum café gave me
a boost, and though Anusha couldn't find any pastries that
looked Polish enough, her Earl Grey pleased her. So I led
the way into the museum—the opposite way that our Polish
comrades had gone.

"I have a plan," I told Anusha. "We're going to wander
around until we find it."

"That's not plan," she said.

But it was precisely how I'd done things fifteen years
beforehand. It had all been really simple. I'd made my way
to the Louvre, on foot, after spending the night in bushes
near the Eiffel Towel. I'd found the entrance—which back
then wasn't all that easy, it being in one of the many arch-
ways—and I'd wandered around until I and the *Mona Lisa*
came face to face.

What I didn't know in 1995 was that I was leading Anusha
into the Richelieu wing, which, in 1980, was not even part of
the museum, but the Ministry of Finance.

"Where we are going?" Anusha said.

"Mesopotamia," I said, reading a sign. We were on a
marble stairway, white statues in the open area below. It was
crowded down there; everyone seemed to be moving along,
executing their own game plans.

Anusha was patient in Mesopotamia. There seemed to be
a lot of statuary, and broken stuff, pieces of walls or pots with
designs on them. These were undoubtedly rare and wonderful to those who understood the context, artistry, and what
not. We didn't.

"Kevilenko," Anusha said after some time. "I want *Mona
Lisa.*" She sunk her hand into her purse and pulled out some
lipstick.

"Hey, I got you to the Eiffel Towel."

"*Tower,*" she said. "Eiffel Towel is part of bus tour. You
did nothing."

"To*wer*," I said.

"To*wel*," she said. "Now I want see *Mona Lisa*. Then, oh, Kevish, after *Mona Lisa*, we will find Polish food. Please, please.

"We can probably find, uh, that *shninki*."

"You mean *naleshniki*! You promise?"

Some promises are easy. *Naleshniki*, though I couldn't pronounce them, were just like crepes. How hard could crepes be in Paris?

But when things grew less definable, that's when it got hard. Like about the future. Anusha came into my life during a two-month summer language course in Uppsala, Sweden, just months before. We spent the first month falling in love and the second worrying about what would happen come August.

I followed her to Poland. That at least was a step towards our future, a pretty sufficient one, I thought, since I had no job and not much money. But I lived for a month in a rectangle of guest room between her and her mother's bedrooms.

Our last fling, before I would return to America, was Paris.

We moved faster through Islamic Art. People skirted to and fro, their shoes tapping, their clothing swishing.

Two girls from our group, Magosha and Kasha, found us.

Anusha asked them in Polish: Did you see the *Mona Lisa*? Of course they had. Well, where was it. They didn't know. Somewhere that way.

"Kevish," Anusha said to me, "how to find *Mona Lisa*?"

"Don't worry, we can't miss it."

She looked at her watch. "Kevish!" She showed me. It was 5:05 P.M.

We still had nearly an hour, and it took just a minute or two to look at the painting.

"O.K., let's find the *Mona Lisa*."

We left the Middle East and entered Europe: those darkish paintings of the eighteenth century, with thick light seeping into shadowed rooms. We didn't stop to look at paintings that caught our eye. We just took them all in so that our scanning glances turned a whole room into a montage.

Anusha said, "My feet."

In a small corner, she plopped down onto a bench and slung out her legs on the herringbone floor. People stepped around her.

"All this people went to see *Mona Lisa* first," she said.

"The Louvre seems a lot bigger than it did in 1980," I noted. "I mean, it was easy. I just found it, the *Mona Lisa*, in a room by itself, in a kind of box on the wall. It's actually really small."

She made a dour face, a skill of which Poles are the unchallenged champions.

"Don't worry. We're close," I said.

I really felt we were. Because I noticed that I was now staring at Rembrandt's famous self-portrait, the man coming out of a smear of shadow, angling the right shoulder toward us, his black eyes like raisins.

"I'm boring," Anusha said. "I want sleep. Polish food," she said. "And, Kevish, you promise me *Mona Lisa*."

"Wait a second," I said. I left her resting on the bench, and checked out two neighboring rooms—Rembrandt all over the place, but no *Mona Lisa*. I came back to Anusha, stood looking down at her, thinking. And a big, fairly embarrassing question climbed up in my throat.

"O.K. Did Rembrandt paint the *Mona Lisa*?"

"No. Da Vinci," she said.

I knew it had been somebody in-ignorably famous. But I was tired and these were, after all, the pre-Dan Brown years.

"Well then the *Mona Lisa* isn't going to be here. But we're

O.K. We're in the Flemish lands," I explained. "Da Vinci, see, that's Italy. All we've got to do is cut south through Belgium and France, and we're there."

"You tell me you were here before," Anusha said.

"I was."

I helped Anusha up. "Come on. We've still got time. I'll get you there."

"Why you don't ask that man who works?" Anna said. "You knew French last night in the bar."

"I was drunk when I knew French last night."

"Ask someone, Kevish!"

I knew I had to do it, although the embarrassment of such asking such a question still stings. I was an art imbecile. First, Mesopotamia and Islamic art had bored me. Then confusing Rembrandt with da Vinci. Now, to ask "Which way to the *Mona Lisa?*"—that was degrading. I could have cheerily asked for Titian's *Man Smelling Eelgrass* or something esoteric, but not the most annoying FAQ in the history of the Louvre.

"Kevish! You promise," Anusha said.

I approached a blue-suited watchman, and did it: "Excuse me, where is the *Mona Lisa?*"

He said, "You're in the Richelieu wing, not the Denon wing." He didn't go out of his way to be encouraging.

"So...how do we get to the Denon wing?"

"The museum is closing in twenty-five minutes."

"So the Denon wing, how do we *get* there?"

He pointed. We scooted, weaving through the crowd. At the Denon Wing, plaques on the walls showed a miniature Mona smile and an arrow. But now a current of bodies moved against us. Announcements came over the loudspeakers: "Closing in fifteen minutes."

We reached an elbow in the corridor. Stairs going up. On either side two escalators. Everybody was coming down, towards us. Not a soul going up.

A blue suit stopped me.

"We have come to see the *Mona Lisa*," I said in French. "By da Vinci."

"You're too late," he said. "You'll have to come back tomorrow."

"There is no tomorrow," I said. "We're bus tourists."

"*On descend*," he said again, looking away. "Come tomorrow."

"Tell him I am from Poland," Anusha said.

"She is from Poland," I said in French.

"I understand English," he said.

"We have ten minutes left. Plenty of time."

"You see that man?" the French guy said, nodding up the escalator. Another guard stood at the top of the escalator, between two waist-high poles with red laser light eyes on them. "If I let you go, he will stop you."

I didn't care. I took Anusha's hand and dragged her forward, the blue coat coming after us. We started up the unmoving escalator. The top man came down. The other came up from behind. It was a face-off half way.

"Look," I said to him. "I promised her. The *Mona Lisa*. O.K.? We don't want to examine it. We don't want to admire it. We just want to have a glance and escape."

Back in the reception area we gathered with the rest of the bus-tour Poles. They came up to us; girls offering their wrists to let us sniff the mix of perfume samples they'd sprayed at a gift shop. Some showed us postcards. Some told us they'd found a soup in the café not unlike Polish noodle soup.

And they all asked the same question: "Did you see the *Mona Lisa*?"

I put on a superior expression, conveying: *As if the* Mona Lisa *is the only reason to come to the Louvre*. But no one paid attention.

Anusha said, "No. We did not see the *Mona Lisa*. We saw Islamic Art and Mesopotamia."

~≪ ~≪ ~≪

When we were alone on the bus, she was quiet. After some time, she said, "Kevish. You promise."

"I'm sorry, Anusha."

It was really just bad planning. Or no planning. Which was usually how I traveled. But I should not have played by my own rules when it came to someone else's dream.

Our bus disgorged us somewhere in Versailles, in the vicinity of our hotel, and the entire group poured into a McDonald's.

"We're not eating here," I said. "Let's walk back to the hotel and find something really delicious."

Just up the street was a café with outdoor tables under an awning. I ordered Anusha a crepe with two scoops of ice cream and strawberries. She didn't call it a crepe though. She said, "*Naleshniki*." She ate it with a fork and knife, concentrating. The ice cream was white on her red lips.

It was probably against her will, but soon she got a trace of what might have been a smile.

I have seen the *Mona Lisa*, long ago, as I mentioned. Her smile is small, nearly flat, sly. It tells of something that has just happened, and of something that is just about to happen.

Anusha asked, "Tonight you will be with me, Kevish—or go to bar with Polish people?"

"I have a plan," I said. "Let's go directly to the hotel, up the stairs, to the room, no wandering."

"Sometimes it is best," she said, and went back to her *naleshniki*.

~≪ ~≪ ~≪

Kevin McCaughey undertook his first solo journey in 1980, at the age of eighteen. He spent three months in Europe and thirteen hundred dollars. Airfare included. Later he studied Swedish in Sweden, Polish in Poland, and Russian in Vladivostok. For the last ten years he has worked as an English language materials developer and teacher trainer in the U.S., Europe, Africa, Central Asia, and the Middle East. This is his fourth story in Travelers' Tales Best Travel Writing editions. His website of English teaching audio is English Teachers Everywhere, www.etseverywhere.com.

Ain't Ready for No Man

A woman discovers herself in Guyana.

As a child I was haunted by the "Save the Children" ad campaign. A block of simple text, a black and white photo. *In the time it takes you to finish reading this paragraph, a child will have died of starvation.* The children were my age, dark-skinned, dressed in slips, stained shorts, nothing. Babies screamed, their mouths stretched open for the food that would never come. As I began reading, a girl would stare out at me with a hungry, little smile. *Here I am,* she would say, *still alive.* And, being a literal child, when I finished reading I would think, *now she's dead.*

Children were dying in Ethiopia, hundreds of them in camps, their bellies distended so they looked fat, like they could tip over on their skinny legs. They lived with their starving mothers and fathers, starving brothers and sisters. On TV I saw them move in slow motion, too tired to wave away the sucking flies in the corners of their eyes. I cried when I heard they had to pick the grains out of animal shit just to stay alive. But when I read, *For the price of a cup of coffee a day, this child could eat for a week,* I felt the soft cushions of an armchair holding me, heard the birds singing in the backyard, my dog barking. My parents drank coffee every morning—if they stopped, how many more weeks could she live?

As I sat reading, you were running through the streets of Georgetown, sucking half-eaten candies you'd picked off the sidewalk. You were four years older than I, your worn housedress flouncing on your knees as you dodged chickens and stray dogs, trailed mango peels in the dust. When I lived in your city, I imagined that I could turn my head and see you: a phantom little girl playing in the pitted yards. Your singular look of concentration devoted to a grid drawn in the dirt with a stick, your thin brown arm poised to drop a stone, dead into the center.

When we met, I saw the shadows of this past on you, but you had little use for it by then. You were successful, college-educated, wielding the power to grant money to the poor who were no longer you. But I probed: I was still the girl who had sat in the armchair, worrying about girls like you dying. I wanted to know the end of the story. Twenty years later I had come to the country of "a child dies every thirty seconds of malnutrition." *Make me understand what happened,* I insisted. *Tell me how you didn't die. How you're alive today for me to love you.*

Guyanese do not talk loosely of the past. You tolerated my American curiosity, though perhaps you suspected it was borne of too much food. *Girl, like you love ask questions!* you teased me. Why recount a catalogue of deprivations? What could be surprising? It did not seem unique to you. When we spoke of your childhood, I felt as I did hearing Creolese, the English dialect of Guyana. I struggled to wrap my mind around this language that was so different from my own, but was, in fact, my own. I finally resorted to begging for the parts to guess at the whole. *How do you spell that?* I asked my students, my friends, the person on the phone giving me directions. And all of them would attempt the impossible, struggling to give me letters for an unwritten language. *D... O... U... W?... G?....* Their voices trailed off, apologizing. *Me sorry, Miss, me ehn't really know.*

So it was with you, humoring me with stories of the past. You gave me the facts you remembered: the crowded home, the violent father, the grandmother who hated your skin darker than her Portuguese white. But when I posed the questions, *Why? Why was it this way?* you simply shook your head. These things I had to accept: your first tongue could not be written, and your childhood could not be explained.

Still, I forged on. I pushed for the details, the off-moments, the memories you thought unimportant. I was like an investigator recreating a scene, the scene of your invention. Why did I push? Because I adored you, and thought the way to love you better lay in understanding this history. Because I wanted to know this country you sprang from where I now lived. Or maybe your life was just a peephole, a partial view into another world, where I could look on safely. Please excuse my voyeurism, my demands, my curiosity. I was young and so were you. But here is what I gathered. Here are the spellings you invented for me, and the words I made them spell.

To begin, I desired a photo of you from childhood, but none exist. I was jealous of your siblings who had known you then, in your pressed school uniform with the prefect badge. *She was always different,* your older brother Lelord told me, *even when she was small.* I envied the woman we met in Matthew's Ridge. Yes, she had known old Lam, the Chinese man who lived on the hill. *That was my grandfather,* you told her. She scrutinized your face and I watched as she located you, the little girl I would never know. *I remember you,* she nodded, unraveling the twenty years since you'd first stepped off the boat into this isolated jungle town. She smiled fondly at a girl's face I couldn't see. *You were small, small when ya come last time.*

Frustrated, I tried to shrink you down too. Your adult features on a tiny girl's head, your body loose and skinny. I flattened your breasts, straightened your hips and there you were at my waist, looking up at me, your billowing hair soft in my hand. *Strange for a child to have eyes like little coals*, I thought. *Strange,* you thought, *for a white lady to ask so many questions.*

You were born on an island named Wakenaam in the vast Essequibo River, where the family had moved for your father, Joseph, to run a logging concession. *But where exactly were you born? In a hospital, in the house?* I wanted to picture you entering the world, but you just shook her head, laughing. *Who cares, I'm here now.* Because your family did not have money for cow's milk you were weaned on coconut water, the cloudy amniotic fluid of a towering tree.

You were the last of eighteen children by your father, a fact you first told me first by the *hors d'oeuvres* table at a party. I almost dropped my paper plate. By the time you were born, you had siblings in their forties, grown brothers and sisters with their own children. Your mother Rowena, your father's second wife, already had five boys and a girl. And it was hard coming last, your father getting old, never enough powdered milk for tea in the morning. *I've had enough black tea in this lifetime*, you always told me, adding cream, spoonfuls of sugar.

Joseph was handsome, fair-skinned, half-Portuguese and half-Indian, an alcoholic at your birth. After you appeared, he stopped drinking suddenly, without explanation. He named you, as he named all his children, after characters in movies. Majestic, melancholy names: Aloma, Cordell, Rohan, Lelord, Hilrod, Gregory. You became Ardis.

Nights I stayed with you we slept together under a gauzy mosquito net that blurred the moon. We secured it to the ground with massive white dictionaries you'd bought used, excited when you found the old set with the softest onionskin paper. One morning I pulled a volume out and opened to the A's, seeking *Ardis. It won't be in there, monkey*, you said, still sleepy, *it's my name.*

It's in here, I said, flipping through pages that threatened to tear, my eyes gliding past *arctic, arcturus, arcane* to find, finally, one written fact of you. The dictionary was authoritative; you respected it. I loved telling you what your name meant.

The first, a variation, *Ardisia, a bush that gives hard, red berries and grows in East India and the West Indies.* There was a little picture with this one, lines for the branches, little berries we had to imagine red. The second, from the Greek, *point of an arrow.* And so I recognized you as hard-won, like those few small berries, and sharp, not just the arrow itself but its winnowed tip. Your father had named you well, for a future he would never know. You tried to find *Katherine* for me, but it was only a name.

Joseph was smiling in the one water-stained photo I saw of him at your brother's house on rainy afternoon. I noticed his perfectly straight teeth. *Dentures. He pulled out all his teeth once when he had a toothache,* you told me, laughing. *So he would never have a toothache again, he said.* I looked at the photograph again, tried to find his eyes through the tinted glasses. *Pulled them out himself? With what? No anesthesia?* I asked. *Don't worry about it,* you told me, *the man was crazy.* Another time he poured buckets of paint from an upstairs window on a neighbor who had crossed him. He beat you with planks and telephone cords and hands. He beat your mother, threw a bike at her, shoved a pumpkin at her head. When he locked her out of the house in the rainy season she had to sleep under the house. But he kept you in school when Rowena wanted you home scrubbing floors. You guessed it was because he thought you would support him in old age. Still, you thanked him most for that.

Rowena was your mother, a half-African, half-Chinese woman. Standing next to Joseph she is dark-skinned and plump, beaming. She balances her first grandchild on her hip, a kitchen apron tied on her waist. *I've left myself undone*, she would say at the end of the day, happy to put her family ahead of herself. *She loved her boys,* you told me when we saw the smudged faces of children on the street. You watched them gnaw the bigger shares of meat each night at dinner. *She always kept us clean and pressed*, when we saw the smudged faces of children on the street. *We were poor, but we never looked as poor as we were.*

You remember a happy childhood: cajoling your brothers to play games with you, learning to read, borrowing books from an old man on your road. Your father visiting you in the hospital when you were sick, the roar of his motorbike engine as he pulled up outside your window every day. You remember a terrible childhood: beatings, fights. Your father slapping your mother, throwing a pot of food across the backyard. Watching your dinner fly into the dirt, the pot dented, another night with an empty stomach.

Our first date was in an empty Indian movie theater. We sat alone in the high balcony by the fans, clasping our hands tightly in the dark. Later, we went to a small roadside restaurant in town, a slight breeze rippling across our legs. We touched hands and knees under the table, laughed at the fat, drunk men slamming dominoes. You looked so beautiful: our secret was hot in my mind.

Across the street we heard boys yelling at each other, beginning to fight. We were far enough away to be safe, surrounded by the light of the restaurant. They yelled threats I could hardly understand. I did not notice your face tightening until you said, *That's how my family was.* On a trip to Kwakwani, we heard a man and woman fighting outside our window, their curses getting louder and louder. I was holding you, my knees curled into your knees; I could not see your face. *My parents were like this, Mommy yelling at Daddy until she got licks.* We closed the window to shut out their noise.

Sometimes I would mine for the past, pressing my unanswerable *why*'s on you, and sometimes the past would push itself between us. The night you told me you had lived in an orphanage I thought you were kidding. *Do you think this is the kind of thing you joke about?* you whispered to me in the dark. You were not angry, just sad. *No, I just can't believe we've known each other a year and you haven't told me.* Stroking my hair: *Well, here, I'm telling you now.*

You whispered the story to me, as if ashamed. *I was young, two or three, and my parents were too poor to keep me. Reverend Sun Myung Moon had set up a church in Georgetown with an orphanage. They sent Aloma and me there to live so we would have enough food to eat. On Sundays Mommy and Daddy visited. We sang in a choir called the "Seraphim" and watched* The Sound of Music, *over and over.* There had been a picture of you singing in the angel choir, now lost. I felt this from the beginning: you were always an orphan.

You returned to your parents' home a few years later. You grew up to be beautiful and then the boys came around. One visited you on his bike, prompting Rowena to emerge from the house with a warning. *Y'all listen to dis,* she said, *Ardis ain't ready fuh no man, ya heah!* I could see it clearly: your mother's hands on her hips, you skulking back to the house, the chastened boy weaving off down the road. *What did your mother say when the boy came?* I asked you over and over. You imitated the same sing-song cadence, until finally I could hear Rowena and agree with her. *Ya ain't ready fuh no man!* I liked to say to you. But you're ready for me.

And when did you know you loved women? I asked. There had been no language for this. One morning on your way to school, you heard someone calling from an upstairs balcony and looked up, expecting what? To run to the store, maybe, deliver a message. It was the code of law to be respectful of adults; you could be beat for less. A woman stood above you wearing a sheer robe, silhouetted against the darkness of the doorway. She looked, what? Beautiful, yes. Young, but older than you, and you were no longer a child. Her robe was low between her breasts, and she seemed to be telling you something you had never heard before. *I was surprised. I had never seen a woman stand like this.* You saw her desire. And, though it would be years before it was safe to admit it, you also saw your own.

When you were sixteen, Joseph immigrated to New York City to be with another woman. *That was his true love, I think his last years were happy with her.* Rowena got cancer soon after, and you slept in the hospital bed with her every night. *She cried out for him until she died*, you said, shaking your head at this kind of love. Your father died a few years later, in your early twenties.

Now all you had was brothers and sisters, but some of them were already lost. Rohan had immigrated "backtrack" to the States, illegally; you had heard he was in jail. Cordell had tried to kill himself and then disappeared; you assumed he was dead. Hilrod always had a new business idea; you lost money believing in him. It was only through your siblings that I could imagine your childhood. They showed its liabilities, while you showed almost nothing. You showed only what you wanted to show.

I met Aloma once in your living room. She was as soft and plump as you were sinewy and strong. Girlish, quiet, mother to two boys with different fathers, she hardly spoke. She was there for money, like most other times. After your father's death she had cried to you, *he troubled me,* those few, coded words telling of years of molestation. *She was home alone with him after I went to school. He was older and couldn't find lovers as easily as before. He must have come after her then.* I paused, afraid to ask. *Never you?* I asked. She shook her head. *Why never you?* Again you won the coin toss, got your life. *Why not you?*

Of your siblings, you were the only one to pass the A-levels, studying all summer from a book a teacher gave you. I went to your college graduation in a muddy field by the Atlantic coast, your flapping robes the colors of the Guyana flag. At twenty-seven you had become the girl in the armchair, out of danger. But there was no need for black and white pictures, threatening text; you knew this story well enough already. Your nieces and nephews were those faces staring out at you from your own family photos. You watched the patterns beginning to repeat. *She likes to beat too much*, you said about Aloma after watching her with her boys. You saw that there was another girl who needed saving (there is always another girl who needs saving) and imagined that you could help her.

For Fayola, you imagined a different life. Gregory had married Hassina, a Muslim woman, and they had had nine children together. Fayola was twelve years old, the age when Guyanese children take the exam to qualify for secondary school. You decided to take her into your home, tutor her so she could pass the test. All of Hassina's other daughters had been married off young to men in the islands so they could send back money to the family. You wanted to help Fayola have a different life.

We visited them in Albuoystown on a bright Sunday afternoon in May, traveling by mini-bus from your home close to the Embassies, until we reached their sunken porch. Hassina greeted us with a child on her breast, two at her knee. The house was dark and musty with clothes piled in the corners and mattresses lining the floor. An older girl ran to buy cold drinks for us at the corner store. Fayola stood by as you and Hassina talked, and I wandered out to the back to play with the younger children. A tiny girl, two or three, kept running up to me and touching my hair then running away and laughing. She had long lashes, lovely brown eyes. When she turned to run I noticed open sores on her back and thighs.

Look at her back, I said when you came to find me. You saw your niece's wounds, her giggling, smooth face. *Should we go to the clinic, bring back cream for her?* I asked. You shook your head. *She'll get them again, there's no point.* You could only save one girl at a time.

But which girl could grow up to save herself? I glanced at the baby girl in Hassina's arms as we left. Could she be another Ardis? You had been unlikely, number eighteen. But Aloma's infant daughter would not be the one; she died of dehydration later that year. And Fayola was not the one; you soon discovered that she couldn't read. When you went to comb her hair you found a smooth layer on top, a mess of ratted knots below. It took you hours to comb down to the scalp, to find the root of the hair. She didn't want to study, wasn't serious about school. There was nothing you could do. You weren't a mother, never wanted to be. You sent her back.

I return to the ad to understand you, the black and white photo of the girl who should have died in a paragraph's time. The words told the truth. Others have died around you, or lived lives bound by suffering. The words lied; you are here today. Behind her hungry, little smile lies something else: a pure, grinding determination for a life like the reader's, sitting in her armchair thousands of miles away. Not just her food, or her pity, or her coffee money, but her chance to live as she wanted, love as she wanted.

As a child, you studied death also. After school, you went alone to the funeral parlor near your school and stood with the mourners around the open casket. You liked to be there when it was time for the viewing, to see what death looked like. You approached death methodically, unafraid; death was your rival. Poverty, abuse, disease, none of these had gotten you so far, but you knew that death was a worthy opponent.

In those days, you watched it and you mastered it, you looked back at me from the page, smiling with a different kind of hunger altogether.

≈ ≈ ≈

Katherine Jamieson is a graduate of the Iowa Nonfiction Writing Programs, where she was an Iowa Arts Fellow. Her work has appeared in The New York Times, Ms., The Writer's Chronicle, Meridian, *and* The Best Women's Travel Writing 2011. *Read more of her essays, articles, and stories at katherinejamieson.com.*

❧ ❧ ❧

The Memory Bird

Bearing witness never ends.

O N A WARM AND WINDY JULY MORNING, WE WERE headed south on the Partisan Highway out of Minsk, Belarus. Marina, the friend of a Jewish Belarusian expatriate I knew back home in Detroit, was nervous at the wheel of the little twenty-year-old Soviet-built Moskveech she'd just learned to drive, its doors wired shut and a red fire extinguisher skittering around on the dashboard. The car was coughing out smoke as we passed a six-foot-high wooden obelisk topped with a red star that marked the Minsk city limit. Farther on, the road bisected a factory district, then passed blocks of gray apartment complexes that had sprung up after the war on the outskirts of every Soviet city. Up ahead, a goatherd urged his flock along the highway beneath a sign proclaiming: "Pay your taxes. You'll feel great!" Atop many of the telephone poles lining the road, storks' nests were perched like giant straw hats.

Packed into the narrow back seat of the Moskveech were Lev, a sixty-year-old self-taught Belarusian filmmaker with intense black eyes and tufts of white hair ringing his otherwise shiny bald head, and Ina, a Belarus State University history teacher who was also curator of the one-room museum of Jewish History that occupied the corner of a basement near the center of Minsk. Jews now made up only three percent of the city's population, but given that Minsk had been nearly half Jewish before the war, the collection Ina had shown me the day before was alarmingly skimpy: a few dozen artifacts of Jewish life in Minsk that had survived—a treadle sewing machine, a matzo press resembling the wringer on an old washing machine, a lone prayer book rescued in 1944 from the smoldering ruins of the Minsk Ghetto, and a scattering of photographs including one of skulls spilling out from an upended gunny sack discovered at the site of a Holocaust slaughter.

Lev and Ina made an odd pair: the professor in her prim black skirt and bobbed gray hair; the filmmaker with his rumpled slacks and t-shirt, his solid row of gold-capped bottom teeth, and those two clownish puffs of white hair. Neither Ina nor Lev spoke any English, so for the most part, we spoke Russian, which I'd studied as a college exchange student in Moscow back in the '70s. Marina translated what I couldn't express or failed to understand.

These three would be my guides as I neared the end of a long, winding journey that had led me from my home in Detroit, where I'd raised two sons and worked as a teacher and journalist, to today's destination, Blagovschina Forest on the outskirts of Minsk, in search of my father's, my grandmother's—and ultimately my own—history. The impetus for this journey was my discovery, a decade after my father's death, of documents in a box of his papers and letters—my first solid clues to the fate of his Austrian Jewish family.

But in truth, my journey to wrest my father's history from the shadows had commenced long before I discovered the box of his papers. Growing up with a single mother scarcely out of her teens, I'd known my father only through his letters that arrived, sometimes daily, throughout my childhood. These letters revealed nothing personal about my father. Instead, they were entreaties that I renounce the materialism of my childhood world and pursue what he called "the Spiritual life." My father's letters were bitter diatribes against that slough of evil that comprised my young world—the schools, the churches, books; my mother, teachers, friends.

My father, Otto Kraus, had escaped to America in the '30s, a few years before his widowed mother and the rest of his Viennese family were exterminated. He'd given his first name at Customs as Proteus, the Greek god of prophesy and sea change. As Proteus, my father had earned a doctorate in German literature at Berkeley and had taken a teaching job at a college in Florida. After the war, in what I imagine to have been a tumult of guilt and sorrow, my father tucked Proteus the Shape-Shifter away behind an initial and, as Otto P. Kraus, embraced the rigid, ascetic personal brand of Christianity that he would preach for the remainder of his life. Denouncing this earthly swamp of mortal error that seethes below a plane of pure ideas became his obsession, ultimately replacing even his class curricula and leading to dismissals from first one university, then another.

Defrocked as an academic, my father, by then past forty, had lit out for California with the fifteen-year-old girl who would become my mother. The younger sister of one of his students, the teenager had sat in on one of his classroom sermons and had listened intently. A year later I was born, but before my second birthday, my father had wandered off to begin a new life, taking his message to the streets. I'd been in his presence only twice since I was a toddler.

Both times I'd gone looking for him in the Los Angeles neighborhood where he rented a room in someone else's apartment, I'd come upon my father scavenging through

the alley Dumpsters and piling into his shopping cart the
old sweaters, dog-eared magazines, and broken toasters that
he would later haul to the Salvation Army. During each of
these visits, my father had insisted that, despite the barrage
of letters he'd sent me throughout my childhood, given my
mother's worldly ways, he likely wasn't even my father.

When I'd tried to engage my father in conversation, he
drifted off to that higher plane, and soon—launching into the
same lecture I'd received as a child in his countless letters—he
was speaking of the life of the Spirit. "This is your true father," he'd concluded during my last visit, wagging a crooked
index finger that, I noticed, matched my own. Soon, he was
trundling his shopping cart back down the alley. With a hol-
lowness in my heart, I watched him disappear—a small, dark
figure in a cracked leather jacket and his head in a book.

Soon after my second visit to Los Angeles, my father died.
"I want my body burned," he'd stipulated in a will discovered
after his death. "I want my ashes taken out with the trash."

For years my father's instructions had haunted me, and I'd
sought in vain to uncover the source of his all-encompassing
bitterness. My first real clue was a yellow cable I found in
the box of his papers, informing my father that the money
he'd sent for a visa to enable his mother's escape from Nazi-
occupied Vienna on a boat to Cuba was forfeit, since Cuba
had just then declared war on Germany. The cable, dated
December 22, 1941, might as well have been my grandmother's death warrant. The Nazis were already rounding up
Vienna's Jews. Before finding his papers, I'd known almost
nothing about my father's life in Vienna and nothing whatever about my grandmother, not even her name.

Armed with the yellow cable and my grandparents' marriage certificate, the fruit of patient research by an Austrian
specialist at the Mormon archives in Salt Lake City, I'd set off
for Vienna, where I unearthed my grandmother's property
documents and, eventually, her 1942 deportation record. As I

held the thick ledger in my hands, I stared at the one-line notation: "Berta Kraus, destination: Maly Trostinets." I'd never heard of the place. Returning home, I could locate only a scant paragraph here and there in Holocaust histories describing events that had taken place at Maly Trostinets, named for a village outside Minsk in Belarus, then a Nazi-occupied state in the Soviet Union. Between 1941 and 1943, the surrounding woods had been the site of a slaughter that claimed more than 200,000 souls, including Partisans, Soviet soldiers, at least 60,000 Belorussian Jewish prisoners from the Minsk Ghetto and—according to wildly varying estimates, between forty and eighty thousand foreign Jews transported east from the ghettos and concentrations camps of Germany, Austria, Poland, and Czechoslovakia. Only a handful survived to tell fragments of the story.

The war ended, the Cold War froze, thawed, then froze again; the Soviet Union disintegrated; the Soviet state of Belorussia became the nation of Belarus. But the evil of Maly Trostinets has remained obscure, shrouded. Six decades later, the largest, most efficient Nazi extermination camp on former Soviet territory appears as little more than a footnote, though it ranks fourth among death camps in Europe in the number of Jewish lives it ended.

Later that summer, I returned to Vienna with a Belarusian visa, purchased a ticket to Minsk, and boarded a train, setting out on the same railroad tracks that more than sixty years earlier had carried my grandmother on an odyssey that ended in a forest trench near Minsk. Armed with my halting college Russian, I retraced my grandmother's final journey, determined to confront that tragedy from which—in sorrow, guilt, helplessness or bitterness—my father had turned away. Doing so, I hoped to reclaim a shard of my own buried history.

"Why do you want to go there?" the round-faced young man sitting opposite me in the train compartment inquired in English when I told him I was headed for Belarus. He smiled, adding matter-of-factly, "In that place is only poverty and dirt."

I shrugged. "I have friends," I told him.

That was true in a way. Through my Russian neighbors back home, I'd contacted a local community of Belarusian Jews, several of them survivors of the Minsk Ghetto. These expatriates, in turn, had put me in touch with Marina, a forty-year-old Minsk resident who'd invited me to stay in her apartment. As a Jew in an anti-Semitic country, Marina had hoped to emigrate from Minsk to America after the breakup of the Soviet Union when emigration laws had relaxed. But when both of her parents had fallen ill, Marina postponed her trip in order to care for them. Meanwhile, the window of opportunity slammed shut. Emigration laws tightened. Immigration to America became next to impossible. Belarusians could enter the U.S. only by winning permission in a national lottery. Now Marina was likely stuck in Belarus for good.

My young compartment-mate stretched his hand out to me and introduced himself as Tomás. An affable Czech with blue eyes and straw-colored hair who worked for the Subway sandwich chain, Tomás was bound for Warsaw to break ground for a new franchise, after opening forty-two new Subways in Prague that summer.

I inquired whether Subways and Golden Arches had sprung up in Belarus, reportedly the most backward country in Eastern Europe.

"One under construction in the center of Minsk," Tomás replied. "Already they have a McDonald's."

He pulled out his wallet, extracted a folded paper and waved it in the air. "This work permit. It takes me years." He frowned. "I go four times, but I always fly out the same day. If I can catch a flight." The small fleet of Belarusian-operated planes was substandard, he said. They weren't permitted to land in many European airports.

"Too loud," the Czech said. Besides, "Nothing happens in Minsk. Nothing. Economy—worst in Europe." He shook an index finger in the air. "Money—worthless." The red and blue rubles traded by the fistful were virtually play money. "No matter—it's nothing to buy," Tomás added. "They have a horrible dictator too, this Lukashenko. It's like the worst days of Soviet Communism."

A middle-aged man wearing a plaid tie and shiny brown shoes seated next to Tomás had been listening, shaking his head and smacking his lips noisily while using a jackknife to saw off hunks of a pungent salami wrapped in newspaper.

"They brought it all on themselves," he broke in between mouthfuls. In flawless English, he introduced himself as a history professor from Warsaw.

"Wasn't it a democratic election?" I asked the professor.

Brushing bits of salami from his moustache, he laughed. "Yes. Lukashenko won in a landslide. Belarus is a nation of followers. They're too scared to be without Communism, so they elect this guy, Lukashenko—he used to be the boss of a chicken collective." The professor lopped off several hunks of salami and offered them around. A brief nationalist movement had arisen in the early '90s after the disintegration of the Soviet Union, he told me. Belarusian was declared the national language, and the country set out on the road to a privatized economy.

"But they weren't ready for the breakdown of the Soviet Union," the professor said. "For them, independence was a catastrophe. They saw Lukashenko as their solution." In 1994, elections were held, and Lukashenko received eighty percent of the vote on his promise to recreate a lost paradise.

He would revive the old system, restore full employment, provide free health care, and officially reinstate the familiar Russian tongue.

"Idiots!" the professor said, shaking his head. "They were glad to return to Communism. There's no elite in Belarus to form an idea-oriented leadership. The Jews, maybe. But there aren't many now—the Nazis got most of them during the war and the rest fled. Any Jews still there want to get out."

Beyond the country's political and economic problems, Belarusians face a gruesome array of health hazards, the professor added with a look of disgust. Most of the radiation from the 1986 Chernobyl explosion blew downwind from Ukraine into Belarus, contaminating half the country's soil, possibly for the next hundred years. "Much of the food and water is probably still unsafe," he warned me.

As my fellow travelers continued their litany of Belarus's woes, the train rattled eastward, past the low hills and mist-veiled forests of the Polish countryside. Against this graceful backdrop, it was hard to picture Poland's neighbor to the east—backward, unlovely, and swept by the winds of Chernobyl. I envisioned Belarus as an island set adrift beneath a perpetually hovering raincloud.

As if reading my thoughts, the Czech stretched out both hands, palms up, his fingers spread in a gesture of futility. "Nothing there but ignorant people," he said. "The people has disappeared in their minds. They are sheep. No national identity, no history."

But, of course, Belarus does have a history, a tragic history of invasion, partition, and devastation that makes its current troubles appear not so much self-inflicted as the working out of some ancient curse. I'd caught glimpses of this past back in Detroit, while trying to flesh out a skeletal outline of events at Maly Trostinets. For four hundred years, Belarus was laid waste by a series of wars before being divided in

1919, the western part ceded to Poland, the eastern becoming the Belorussian Soviet Socialist Republic. During the Second World War, the Germans leveled more than 600 Belorussian villages and killed a quarter of the Republic's inhabitants. Not only did the Nazi army slaughter most of the Belorussian Jews, Hitler also designated the state of Belorussia as the site of a network of death camps—one vast, spreading graveyard for European Jews. Although the Nazi's grand plan was never fully achieved, one such site had been established in the forest near Minsk: the mysterious Maly Trostinets.

Transports from the ghettos and concentration camps of Europe began arriving in Maly Trostinets in 1942, the year noted on my grandmother's deportation record. Meanwhile, during a series of pogroms and transports to the forest, the entire population of the Minsk Ghetto was liquidated. The genocide ended two years later, when the Soviet Army marched into Minsk.

About this landlocked country of ten million, the news was still bad. The government was dogged by allegations of money laundering, drug smuggling, and arms dealing to terrorist groups. Yet, in the U.S. the plight of Belarus was virtually unknown outside Belarusian immigrant circles. If Americans knew anything at all about the place, it was probably that Lee Harvey Oswald had defected to Minsk and married a Belorussian before returning to the U.S. to assassinate President Kennedy.

Arriving in Minsk, I slowly came to realize that the name Maly Trostinets, so unfamiliar to the rest of the world, was also virtually unknown in Minsk beyond the city's tiny Jewish community. Neither did it show up on the area map I purchased at a kiosk in the train station.

"I'm not surprised. No one knows about it," Marina told me later when I spread out the map on her kitchen table. She herself could not locate the place, she said, observing that Maly Trostinets does not appear in Belarusian history books.

A soft-spoken woman with anxious black eyes and curly black hair, Marina had met me at the train station. As we drove off in the Moskveech that had belonged to her father, we shifted back and forth between languages until it was clear that her English was better than my Russian.

Each time the tiny car sputtered, lurched, and stalled, Marina's face would redden. Her eyes would brim with tears.

"I'm not used to driving," she whispered, as we turned onto Skorina Ulitza, the city's main street. At first glance, Minsk wasn't the shabby place I'd been led to expect by my compartment-mates on the train to Warsaw. What I saw through the fissured car window were '50s-era cinderblock buildings in a clean, though gloomy-looking city, its streets all but deserted at four in the afternoon. In another respect, though, my companions' predictions proved accurate. Minsk was a time trip back to the USSR, beginning with the scale of everything. Skorina Street was seven lanes wide and lined with hulking gray office buildings, the holdover state-run department store monopolies known by the acronyms GUM and DUM (pronounced "goom" and "doom"), and signs plastered with patriotic messages. One billboard extolled Soviet World War II heroes. Another pictured President Lukashenko with his shiny head and bushy mustache.

So, Belarus has simply exchanged one bald-headed icon for another, I reflected, recalling my student days three decades back among the streets and squares of the Soviet Union with their ubiquitous statues and portraits of Lenin. But no, Lenin was here too, towering thirty feet tall above the courtyard of "The President's Palace," as the executive headquarters was known. Other post-Soviet states might scrap their iron curtain artifacts, but in Belarus, Marina told me, gigantic Lenins still brood over every town and village.

"Do you like it?" Marina kept asking, her dark eyes begging for reassurance. I insisted I did like it. Eighty percent of its buildings destroyed during the war, Minsk had reemerged as an orderly modern city. But like Marina herself, with her apologies and her pleas for approval, the place felt abandoned. Marina parked the car before a wedding-cake-shaped "Stalin Gothic" building. Cradling my arm, she conducted me to a sundial enshrined in the center of a marble fountain in the building's courtyard.

"Here you can see the distance to *everywhere*," she said.

Etched around the sundial's face were arrows pointing toward the major cities of the old USSR and indicating their distance from this deserted sidewalk in central Minsk: "Kiev, 573 km," "Moscow 700 km." The implication that the former Empire constituted the world made the city feel even more lost. Back home when I'd told people I was headed for Belarus, their eyes would go blank.

"Belarus?" they'd say. "Where's that?"

"Is that a country?"

"Is it in Russia?"

Further on, Marina stopped the car to show me Minsk's only Holocaust memorial where it stood at the edge of a ravine surrounded by maple, chestnut and linden trees. This was the site of a particularly ghastly pogrom known as "Yama," or "the pit" that was carried out in March of 1942. Replaying Babi Yar, the infamous massacre of Ukrainian Jews that had taken place only six months earlier, the Nazis rounded up 5,000 Jews from the Minsk Ghetto, marched them to the edge of this ravine, ordered them to remove their ragged clothes, then shot them or shoved them over the drop to be buried alive as bulldozers filled up the valley.

Had my grandmother been among those murdered at Yama, I wondered? A fenced-off section of the Ghetto had been reserved for a portion of foreign Jews who were not killed immediately. "It was very terrible for these foreign

Jews," a Belarusian survivor named Galina had told me back in Detroit. "They didn't know Russian. They couldn't speak to the guards. They couldn't speak to anyone." The foreign Jews would stand, mute and starving, arms extended through the barbed wire that separated them from the larger Ghetto. "They held out watches, rings, handkerchiefs, shawls. They tried to exchange anything for food." One woman put gold earrings in Galina's hand. "She didn't realize that we, too, had no food." In winter, Galina had seen the bodies of foreign Jews beyond the barbed wire, frozen and stacked like lumber. "Some of them killed themselves," she remembered. "After a while, we started thinking it was better to be a Russian Jew."

As I thought of that scene from the past, I made out the pale ghost of a swastika on the black marble menorah commemorating the Yama bloodbath. Vandals, probably members of Belarus' flourishing neo-Nazi movement, had spray-painted it here only last month, Marina said. Elsewhere on the monument, they had scrawled: "Holocaust Now," and "Death to Jews."

Incidents of neo-Nazi vandalism had increased in recent years, Marina told me. Earlier, a 30-liter can of white paint had been splattered over the same memorial. Leaflets accusing Jews of crimes against Christianity had called for retribution. Anti-Semitic graffiti had shown up all over the city. At Jewish cemeteries throughout Belarus, memorial wreaths were often torched and headstones upended or shattered.

That night as I settled onto the red velveteen couch in the book-lined vestibule that served as a living and dining room in Marina's sixth floor apartment on Kommunistchiki Ulitza (Communist Street), I spotted a globe of the world atop a bookcase. I stretched up and traced the route I'd taken here from Vienna, my finger inching east through Warsaw, then on to the Polish border. But a chunk of colored cardboard had worn off the globe. Belarus was missing. I replaced the globe on the bookcase and scanned the titles of volumes crammed into bowed shelves. There were collected works by Tolstoy, Pushkin, Gogol, and dozens of scientific tomes whose titles I couldn't translate. Later, as we sat at a table pulled up to the velveteen couch eating dumplings and spiced mushrooms, Marina mentioned that her mother had been a radiation specialist at the National Institute of Energy. She'd worked on the cleanup of Chernobyl shortly after the reactor blew up in 1986, then on and off for years until she fell ill with the cancer that had already spread throughout her body. Marina herself had worked in "the zone' for several weeks during 1987.

Recently she'd suffered a bout of breast cancer. Her father had died of thyroid cancer the previous year. No one could prove that Chernobyl was the cause of her family's afflictions but, Marina told me, "Most of the people who worked there are dead."

The next morning Marina and I rode a bus downtown to the Museum of the Great Patriotic War of Belarus, where Marina's friend, Natasha, worked as a guide. Natasha knew the location of Maly Trostinets and had agreed to accompany me there. As we walked up the museum steps, Marina again took my arm. "I want to tell you something," she said in her gentle voice. "Natasha is Belarusian."

I didn't understand. Wasn't Marina Belarusian too?

"My country—yes. My nationality—I am Jewish," Marina explained. "Natasha is Belarusian." This was a distinction frequently drawn during my stay in Minsk. Marina wasn't religious. After generations of Communism, few Jews are. But ethnic divisions are carefully preserved. Until recently, Belarusian passports had been stamped with the bearer's "nationality." The stamp on Marina's passport had shattered her dream of attending medical school in the '80s, and she'd found work as an engineer—a meaningless title, she told me, for her job was entirely clerical.

"Natasha is old friend," Marina said. "As children, we

were in school together." But, as a Belarusian, Natasha might not understand my preoccupation with the Jewish victims of Nazi crimes. A quarter of the nation had perished during the war, Marina reminded me. Like most Belarusians, Natasha felt that Jews warranted no special place in a hierarchy of suffering. Over and over during my stay, I'd hear people make such statements with no evident malice or irony. "The War" is the dominant historical theme in Belarus, not the Jewish genocide that had taken place in the country's midst.

Natasha was a slight, pale woman with thin lips and a severe expression, which turned into a smile when she spotted Marina. We would take a taxi out to Maly Trostinets that afternoon while Marina was at work, Natasha announced in English. We would visit the monument—erected out there in the '60s, that stood on a hill above an eternal flame. "It's a lovely place," she added to my surprise.

The taxi driver shook his head when we asked to be driven to Maly Trostinets.

"*Ne zniyou*," he said. I don't know.

But Natasha gave directions, and soon we were headed south of the city on my first of two trips down the Partisan Highway. As my eyes scanned the fields of purple buckwheat and yellow cornflowers along the road, I wondered: Was this the route along which my grandmother had once been marched or driven?

Probably so, Natasha said. The old Mogolov Road, renamed Partisanski Prospect after the war, was the only route past Maly Trostinets. A few kilometers out of Minsk, Natasha directed the driver to turn off the highway and wait for us by a marshy field at the foot of a hill.

Natasha and I followed a rutted goat path up the hill past a splintered signpost that spelled out "M. Trostinets" in Cyrillic letters. From a distance, the pre-war wooden houses of Maly Trostinets, with their vanished paint and sagging ridgelines, had looked abandoned, but as we approached the village, I

spotted chickens skittering around the yards and leafy vegetables in the gardens. A pregnant goat lazed in the road.
Here and there old people sat on porches or leaned on garden
hoes. At two in the afternoon the younger generations were
at school or at work, a world away in the concrete city a few
kilometers up the highway.

"Was this the site of the killings?"

"*Nyet*," Natasha replied. No, the name "Maly Trostinets"
had come to refer to the mass slaughters that took place, not
in the village itself but in several nearby locations.

I asked some elderly villagers if they recalled the German
camp or the convoys of human cargo passing by on the highway sixty years back, but most said they'd moved here after
the war. One man with white hair bristling from underneath
a faded blue baseball cap said his wife had lived here all her
life. During the German Occupation, she had told him, villagers often heard screams in the night. But that was all he
knew, and now his wife was dead. No one else could tell us
anything.

As we walked back down the hill toward our waiting taxi,
I was startled by an ominous, loud clattering—like the rattle
of a machine gun. When I turned to Natasha in alarm, she
laughed and pointed toward a stand of wiry brown reeds
where a white stork stood, its head thrown back, breast
feather puffed up, mandibles clacking.

"This bird brings good luck," Natasha said.

With the state of things in Belarus, I thought as the stork
flapped its black-fringed wings and glided away, luck was
the most its people could hope for. But I kept this to myself.
Natasha plucked some reeds and held them out to me. These
were the hollow "trostniki" for which the village was named,
she told me, adding, "This is the plant of the bible. The baby
Moses was found among trostniki."

Back on the highway, our taxi passed stretches of birch and
pine forest and fields carpeted with dandelions and feathery

Queen Anne's Lace. Had my grandmother died on this road? I wondered. At sixty-eight, she might well have been among those too old or sick to walk, who were crammed into gas vans known in the Ghetto as "*dushagubki*," or soul killers. Survivors remembered watching from behind the barbed wire as they passed—black metal boxes on wheels marked with the letters "MAN," the name of a German truck manufacturer. Their tailpipes were rigged to spew asphyxiating fumes back up into the box.

Had this been Berta's fate? Or had she already died before reaching Minsk, suffocated in an airless freight car along the way? Or perhaps my grandmother had been among the multitudes shot at the edge of the long forest trenches discovered after the Nazis' retreat. I still hadn't seen those trenches.

"Where are the graves?"

As if in reply, Natasha instructed the cab driver to turn off the road, and we entered a clearing. At the foot of steps leading up a grassy hill to a monument sat a stone cauldron the size of a truck tire.

"The eternal flame," Natasha explained. But the cauldron held only sand.

A black marble column atop the hill commemorated "More than 200,000 victims of Nazi crimes—Partisans and soldiers of the Soviet Army and local inhabitants."

No mention of Jews.

"They were local inhabitants too," Natasha said sharply.

As I opened my mouth to protest, the clanging of a bell distracted me. A cow was tethered to a nearby pine alongside a meandering path through the woods.

"The graves were here?" I asked, gazing into the distance where a flock of goats was grazing along the path.

"*Nyet. Nyet.*" Natasha shook her head. "This monument is not in the right place." The actual site of the mass graves was "a filthy place a few kilometers down the road." Scrunching up her nose, she refused to take me there.

That evening back at Marina's apartment in Minsk, Lev, the filmmaker with the wild Einstein hair, showed me the right place. When I again smoothed out my wrinkled map on Marina's table, Lev's finger stabbed at the blue mapmaker's stamp that recorded the city's population, latitude, and other vital statistics.

"That's where it is," he said. "You think the placement of the stamp there is a coincidence? No." He turned to me, his bushy eyebrows raised. "They hide the graves, the disgrace."

Several years back, Lev had gone to the site of the graves and filmed a documentary about Maly Trostinets. But the documentary had never been shown. State-controlled television refused to air it.

When I asked him why, Lev sighed heavily. Up went the eyebrows. He would give me a guided tour of the spot beneath the mapmaker's stamp. "You will not believe it," he said in Russian, slamming his palm down with a thump on the wobbly kitchen table. "With your own eyes, you will see." Then, promising to return on Friday, he marched out the door of the apartment. Marina turned to me with the bewildered look she frequently wore. Lev's combat boots sounded on the stairs.

On the warm, blustery morning of Lev's guided tour, I was again headed down the Partisan Highway, the same road Natasha and I had taken two days earlier. Marina was driving, with Lev in the back seat. Ina the historian made up the fourth in our group crowded into the little Moskveech.

I would finally see the mass burial site known as Maly Trostinets, Lev assured me—the place where my grandmother lay buried. The place Hitler had designated as the first of what was to have been a network of mass dumps for the human trash of Europe. But, Lev added, in the same mysterious tone he'd affected in Marina's kitchen, it wouldn't be what I expected. Again, he declined to elaborate, merely repeating what he'd told me that night: "With your own eyes, you will see it."

Like virtually every Belarusian Jew, Lev had more than a professional interest in the site of the documentary I would view only later. Although he himself had survived the war and the Jewish genocide by fleeing with his mother and sister to Kazakhstan, Lev's aunts, uncles and grandmother had been prisoners of the Minsk Ghetto, as had Marina's and Ina's extended families. Their remains doubtless lay with my grandmother's in the depths of Blagovschina Forest, which was the basis of our unspoken kinship.

We passed the path to the village of Maly Trostinets, where the old man had told Natasha and me of screams in the night. Before us, beyond a field of dandelions, a fleet of canvas-covered trucks disappeared as they headed into a dip in the road, then reappeared as they climbed up the other side.

"Turn around. Look," Lev barked as the Moskveech topped the hill and headed into the dip. Peering out the car's rear window, I saw only the sloping road. "Because of this hill, a boy survived," Lev said, as the Moskveech emerged from the dip and the dandelion field reappeared. Then Lev told the only tale I'd ever hear of escape by a prisoner bound for the killing ground at Maly Trostinets.

"Two brothers were in the back of a truck. One little boy and his brother," he began. "The truck was carrying them to Blagovschina. The older boy knew they would be killed. The truck reached the top of that hill." Lev glanced back over his shoulder. "The big boy lifted up his brother. He heaved the little boy into the field by the roadside, just as the truck started down the hill." The soldiers in the truck's cab had seen nothing. The boy was found by Ghetto escapees hiding in the forest. Lev could attach no name to this story he'd heard while gathering material for his film, but if it was true, that dip in the road had provided the little boy his miracle.

The horrors of the Minsk Ghetto had been kept alive by a few thousand survivors. I'd even heard a tale of escape from the tangle of corpses in the Yama pit. But silence surrounded the gruesome events in the forest. There was only this wisp of a story. In the absence of human memories to draw on for his film, Lev had combined scenes from the present-day landscape with a voice-over narration pieced together from interviews with villagers and from a handful of uncirculated documents. These papers had been discovered by Ina's university colleague in the Belarus National Archives in 1995, a few years after Russia had turned over the records of the former Soviet state to the new nation of Belarus. But when Belarus's state-controlled television stations had refused to air Lev's documentary, the silence surrounding the forest killings settled back in.

This silence puzzled me. Maly Trostinets had been a Nazi crime, not a Russian one. The Soviet state that had sometimes collaborated in Nazi crimes against Jews no longer existed. I studied the web of splattered insect corpses on the windshield, wondering: Why would the government of Belarus be reluctant to expose the sins of another country, another era? Why would they deny the physical reality recorded in Lev's documentary? Why had the film been banned?

"Three reasons," Ina began in her professorial voice. "First, this film is about Jews. Soviets hated and feared Jews. Soviet hatred of Jews was the same as Nazis', and this anti-Semitism persists today in Belarus in both subtle and not-so-subtle ways." By "subtle" anti-Semitism, Ina meant, for example, the kind of discrimination that had ended Marina's dream of attending medical school in the '80s. "Not-so-subtle" examples included the desecration of Jewish cemeteries and the ominous graffiti smeared across the marker at Yama.

"You saw the memorial—the swastikas," Ina said. "No one was punished. The authorities ignore such things. They maintain the illusion that nothing bad happened. Lukashenko has declared that he admires Nazi order and that we can learn from Hitler."

Not until the archival material turned up in the mid-'90s had government officials conceded to Minsk's tiny Jewish community that Maly Trostinets had been a mass murder primarily of Jews. "It is time to tell the truth," Ina's colleague had written after viewing the archival documents. "Most of the victims were prisoners of the Minsk Ghetto, along with foreign Jews from the many countries of Central and Eastern Europe."

The documents also testified that the foreign Jews transported to Belarus in 1941 through 1943 had shared my grandmother's fate. Nearly all met their deaths at Maly Trostinets. Out of perhaps 80,000 Jews imprisoned in the Minsk Ghetto, "Only several thousands of Belorussian Jews survived," one report concluded, "and only a few dozen foreign Jews survived." But the documents concerning Jewish deaths at Maly Trostinets had never circulated in Belarus, and the film Lev made, based on these documents, had been squelched.

"Anti-Semitism," Ina said. "But this is only one reason Lev's film cannot be shown." She cleared her throat. "Second reason," Ina resumed in her efficient tone. "People aren't familiar with what happened at Maly Trostinets. It was hushed up." In Belarusian history, the Jewish Genocide doesn't exist." The Soviet government blocked access to information and failed to raise the matter during the postwar Nuremburg trials.

Here was another piece of the story that made no sense to me. What motive could the Soviets have for protecting the Nazis who had betrayed their trust, occupied their land, and slaughtered millions of their citizens? Why hadn't the Soviets raised the issue of Maly Trostinets at Nuremburg? Why had they protected a Nazi secret?

"Understand," Lev replied, leaning forward from the back seat, "this was not just a Nazi secret." He paused and turned to Ina, who was polishing her glasses with a handkerchief.

"The *official* number of people killed at Maly Trostinets is 206,500," she said.

"Yes." I'd heard that figure before, seen roughly that claim earlier in the week, chiseled into the monument looming above the dead eternal flame. Though Jews weren't specifically mentioned in the inscription, this number presumably included most inhabitants of the Minsk Ghetto, as well as Soviet soldiers, Partisans, and all the foreign Jews.

But according to documents unearthed in the National Archives, Lev explained, human remains in the forest told a far different story. A sheaf of reports dated July 14, 1943, just two weeks after the Occupation ended, described the uncovering of thirty-four mass graves concealed with pine boughs—some of these graves fifty meters long. After measuring the graves' grisly contents, the investigators concluded that the remains of 476,000 people were buried in the forest around Maly Trostinets, vastly more victims than could be accounted for by the ghetto dead, the transport records, and the estimates of others the Germans had killed in the forest.

"That's more than twice the official figures," Lev said, stabbing his index finger in the air. "But the Soviet government prohibited the publicizing of this information."

"But these were German crimes," I repeated. "Why would the Soviets want to hide them?"

"Because," Lev said, "this number also includes victims of the Soviet Secret Service of the '30s."

For years before the war, the territory alongside the highway on which we were traveling had been guarded by secret police, later known as the KGB. While making his film, Lev had interviewed elderly citizens of the nearby village, who remembered hearing frequent gunshots in the night during those years. Around the gravesites, Lev had found dozens of cartridges from pre-war Soviet weapons.

Ina nodded. "Stalin's police had used Maly Trostinets as a killing place in the forest, where the bodies were easily hidden. This was part of the mass extermination of the intelligentsia whom the Soviets were so afraid of. "

"You see," Lev said, "the Nazis came to a place already well-prepared for killing Jews. Stalin's police were at Maly

Trostinets before the war and killed a lot of people. The revelation of Nazi crimes would have unveiled Soviet crimes as well. So, at Nuremberg they didn't broach the subject."

Whether or not the 1944 estimates were accurate, I thought, if Blagovschina Forest had been a dumping ground for the bodies of political dissidents well before the Nazis arrived, the Soviets had a powerful motive for sealing their files on Maly Trostinets.

Lev nodded. "All during Soviet Power, no one spoke of Maly Trostinets."

"The Soviet era is over," I protested. "Belarus isn't responsible for Soviet crimes, but still, this silence persists. Why?" I turned to Ina. "You referred to three reasons why Lev's film was banned." I'd only heard two. First, the documentary would be unwelcome in an anti-Semitic country. Second, the long history of official erasure had kept Maly Trostinets out of the cultural memory. "The third reason?" I asked.

"Yes, there is something else." Ina glanced at Lev.

"As you'll see," he said, "the location of the graves would be an enormous embarrassment."

Eleven kilometers southeast of the city, we reached the section of Blagovschina hidden beneath the blue stamp on my map. We turned left at an opening in the woods and followed another convoy of trucks with canvas-covered beds, like those we'd noticed out on the Partisan Highway. As, raising clouds of dust, the trucks lumbered along a rutted dirt road through the forest, I heard the faint rumbling of heavy machinery.

Enveloped in dust, the little Moskveech rattled along, past an empty sentry box with a sign reading "Warning! No Trespassing" in red foot-high Cyrillic letters, and into the cool dimness of the forest.

I felt a surge of nausea as the thick, pungent stench hit. My hands went up over my ears as the grating and clanking grew louder.

"Shut your window," Lev barked, and I wound the handle

tight, muting the noise and reducing the stink, just before we emerged from the forest into a vast clearing where we beheld entire mountain ranges of garbage and trash. Ahead, the trucks turned left to labor up a steep path toward the crest of the nearest trash mountain.

Here was my answer. The third reason why the Belarus government still protects the secrets of Maly Trostinets. The Holocaust killing field is now the Minsk city dump.

We breathed in the thick airless vapor and stared in silence as the convoy of trucks crept up the steep incline, then tipped the city's rotten cabbage and rusted fenders and broken chairs and dead cats onto the graves of Maly Trostinets. Somewhere deep beneath those heaps of trash, along with the bones and ashes of those quarter-, maybe half-million other souls, lay my grandmother Berta's remains.

We parked near the foot of the nearest garbage heap. Marina stifled a sob. "All those people," she whispered.

I'd anticipated that I'd grieve too when I first saw the site of my grandmother's murder, but I only felt numb. The scene through the rolled-up car window felt unreal, like an abstract painting: jagged lines, grids, fractured geometric shapes, mixed with splotches and smeary curves. Muted whites, grays and browns accented here and there by glints of light and blotches of darker hues; the psychedelic swirl of an oil slick on a puddle. Splatters and webby lines of blue around the base of one slope created a mottled effect, like a canvas by Jackson Pollack. A tangle of wire spilled over a ravine. Here and there, vapor rose from the earth and drifted like smoke.

Suddenly, the air was full of shrieks and vibrating wings as a flock of gulls appeared overhead.

Ina peered up at the birds, shading her eyes from the late-morning sun. "*Surrealischeski!*" she cried.

"Hitchcock," shouted Lev, the filmmaker.

The gulls had shattered my protective shell of abstraction. As they rose in a mass and receded behind another trash mountain, the scene grew more real, more solid, my impressions specific. My stomach churned as I stared at brown liquid seeping from festering pools on the ground. Rot and dust and the sulfurous vapor of methane hung in the air. Coils of smoke rising from fires scattered over the mountains added the acrid odor of burning paper and wood to the sting of soot seeping through the car's cracked windows. Identifiable objects came into focus: twisted fenders and mufflers scattered over the clearing, a rag snagged on a piece of metal, rippling in the wind like a tattered flag.

Gradually, the people emerged. Of course, they'd been there all along, standing ankle-deep in muck near the base of the mountain—bent women in ratty headscarves and ill-fitting dresses, men in baggy trousers, one with a shirt tied over his nose and mouth like an outlaw. Farther up, other clusters of scavengers sifted through the avalanche of trash. The pronged maw of a steam shovel scooped up thick sludge. A bulldozer knocked around tires, oil drums, and unidentifiable large objects.

Lev leaned forward from the back seat and called to Marina, who'd closed her eyes and was holding her head in her hands. He gestured toward the path the trucks had taken up the mountain. Hands trembling on the wheel, Marina aimed the Moskveech toward the path, and we plowed our way up on a carpet of trash.

"*Koshmar*," Marina whispered, "nightmare."

I doubted the car would make it up the steep grade, but I kept my mouth shut. Lev was aiming for the full effect, directing the scene he'd wanted the world to witness, the memory he'd tried to snatch back from oblivion.

Marina shifted gears. The Moskveech rattled and wheezed and, miraculously, kept climbing.

A dozen yards from the summit, a tire sank into the mud. The engine stalled. Lev draped his camera strap around his neck, unhooked the door's makeshift wire fastener, and leapt out.

"Follow me," he hollered theatrically as he sprinted the remaining yards up the mountain. Turning up the collar of my shirt in a hopeless attempt to cover my nose and mouth, I stepped from the car into a welter of foul-smelling feathers and took off behind Lev, nearly tripping over the rusted springs of a mattress. Marina was soon at my side, pressing the hem of her flowered blouse to her nose, while Ina kept guard at the car like a getaway driver. We stirred up black columns of flies that settled again like soot as we passed. Here and there, gulls and yellow-billed starlings feasted on scraps of food, mixed with splintered wooden slats and leaves and paper—the whole mess strewn with ashes and chicken feathers.

The wind picked up, scouring the outer layer of trash on the summit, where machines, like mindless gladiators, kept scraping and dragging and smashing. Our presence was ignored. The ecosystem of the dump toiled on—fire and methane, machinery and scavengers—all oblivious to the invaders scaling the hill and the little car stalled on the path.

When Marina and I caught up with Lev, he was standing at the edge of a cliff paved thick with bird droppings. The cliff overlooked a half-dozen more trash mountains. Lev was peering through a veil of blowing paper and plastic bags toward the city spread out in the distance, its wedding-cake buildings shimmering in the heat.

On the outskirts of Minsk, beyond the apartment blocks, the countryside stretched to the horizon, a peaceful mosaic of deep blues and greens. With the hand that held his camera, Lev made a sweeping gesture. "The graves are all over this place." The forest around and beneath the dump was riddled with burial trenches. During his filming, he'd discovered vast caved-in gullies nearby in the forest that grave robbers had ransacked for treasure. He'd found scraps of clothing, combs, toothbrushes, and many bullet casings. Once he'd unearthed a boot with a cache of coins, provision for a future, stitched into the insole.

"How long has the dump been here?" I asked in Russian.

"After the war," Lev said. He raised his camera, snapped a photo of the vista. "Right after the war they made this dump."

"But why? Why exactly here? Right over the graves?"

Lev's bushy eyebrows shot up. He shook his head. "This site wasn't chosen at random," he said. "Remember, this was an area the Soviets wanted to keep quiet about." It was the site of many political assassinations. Locating a dump here after the war was part of the cover-up, part of the scheme to keep people out. Just after the war, the forest had been isolated, supposedly as part of a military project. It had been surrounded with barbed wire and posted with signs that ordered, STOP. NO TRESPASSING. THEY SHOOT HERE.

"That gave the impression that the place was a military shooting range," Lev said. "But no, it was already a dump. They didn't want people nosing around here."

I recalled the memorial a few miles up the road, the marble column on the hill I'd visited with Natasha.

"Is that why they set up that monument so far from the graves?" I asked Lev. "They didn't want people coming here?"

"*Da, da,*" he said, nodding vehemently. "The monument was erected in a place that's got nothing to do with the killings."

The three of us stood gazing over the city, the sun warming our backs, until Lev pointed down the slope, where a man was trudging across the path near the car, rooting out objects and dropping them into his sack. Lev jogged toward the man and called out a greeting. Marina and I tagged along close behind. As the man glanced up with expressionless red-rimmed eyes, my heart raced. The spirits of the place felt suddenly close by. Without a word the old man sloshed on across the mountain in his yellow rain cap and oversize boots.

"He's deaf," Lev said offhandedly. "I don't think he heard me."

As I watched the old man's figure receding, his yellow cap blurring into the rubble, I thought of my father, Proteus, the old shape-shifter, and my final glimpse of him vanishing down the alley pushing his cartload of relics. Although Proteus could not have known of this place, he must have understood what had befallen his mother after his failed rescue attempt. Perhaps his efforts to save my grandmother had been half-hearted. Maybe he'd waited too long. When the agent's yellow cable arrived in 1941, Proteus must have felt himself his own mother's murderer. Was this the image in the mirror that he fled? The unbearable knowledge that drove him from one protean incarnation to another and ultimately turned him away from the world?

"I want my body burned," his will had read. "I want my ashes taken out with the trash."

Shrieks filled the air, disrupting my reverie. A fresh cloud of gulls dove and receded, dove and receded, their sharp cries adding an eerie counterpoint to the low-pitched rumbling of machinery.

Lev had wandered away from Marina and me. He was snapping pictures—a box tumbling by, the clean-picked skeleton of an animal—a cat perhaps or small dog, a drift of feathers, a cart-wheeling newspaper. He scooped up a dirt-filled jar from the rubbish, shook out the dirt, and trudged back toward the summit, stooping now and then to ferret out some small fragment and drop it into the jar.

The earth was slick underfoot, and Marina slipped as we clambered down the mountain to meet Lev. I took her hand, helped her up. Her hand was cold, trembling.

"I feel it through my shoes," she murmured. Her soft voice trailed off. I felt it too. Numbness was gone, replaced by what I can only call an aching homesickness. We were standing on the horrors of history, leaning against one another in silence. There were no words for it.

Suddenly a shout rang out, and a thick, uniformed figure appeared from behind some barrels. The guardian of the dump. What had taken him so long? A nightstick dangled from the man's belt. Sunlight glinted off a badge on his navy blue shirt. Dark glasses masked his eyes. The man shouted again and hurried toward Lev, one hand hovering above his hip like a cowboy about to quick-draw.

A few yards from Lev, the guard stopped and shouted again.

Lev glared back, eyebrows arched sardonically.

The guard stepped forward, white-knuckled fists clenched above his hips, but Lev stood rooted to his spot, looking like a giant glittery-eyed bird with his beaky nose, his tufts of white hair flapping in the wind.

With one hand the guard reached for his nightstick and flourished it, lunging forward and grabbing the strap of Lev's camera with the other hand.

Still clutching the jar and his camera, trying to free the strap, Lev lowered his head like a bull and butted the guard. Marina and I hung back a few yards. I glanced down the slope, gauging the distance to the car.

The guard slammed Lev on the shoulder with his stick, but Lev wouldn't let go of his camera.

From down the path came the sound of an engine starting up. Ina had started the car, and managed to turn it around. She was backing up toward us.

Hearing glass shattering, I turned to see Lev, still clutching his camera and strap in one hand. His other hand was empty. Near the guard's feet, shards of Lev's jar of relics were scattered along with its contents—fragments of newspaper, a length of green ribbon, a twisted spoon. The guard's beefy face twisted with rage.

"Run to the car," Lev shouted, unnecessarily. Marina and I were already running, with Lev close behind, snapping pictures as he ran.

Once we were all in the car, Ina coasted down the path toward the foot of the mountain, the red fire extinguisher bouncing around on the dashboard, the wipers flapping, scraping grime from the windshield. Gasping, Lev laughed like a madman. Suddenly, we were all laughing hysterically, though at what I wasn't sure. Lev pointed at the guard, who stood on the crest of the mountain, waving his stick like a Keystone Cop.

"What does he imagine he's guarding?" Lev wondered between snorts of laughter. "What does he think he's guarding with his ridiculous uniform?"

Shoulders shaking with laughter, Lev worked the wires to secure the broken passenger door. "What the hell does he think he's guarding?" he repeated. "He probably doesn't even know!"

We laughed all the way to the foot of the mountain, where Ina stopped the car. We all fell silent then, and turned back for one final look.

"*Koshmar*," Marina whispered from the back seat. "Nightmare."

"History," corrected Ina, the historian.

As we reached the clearing and headed back toward the road, a fresh wave of gulls wheeled overhead. I turned to watch their winged shadows flickering over the mountain of trash. I still heard their cries, growing fainter and fainter, as the Moskveech bumped along past the guardhouse with its looming STOP. NO TRESPASSING sign, and on through a half-mile of sunlight-laced forest.

As we turned back onto the Partisan Highway, Marina tapped my shoulder and pointed to the cloudless sky. A stork was gliding toward us, silently, white head and neck extended, black tail feathers spread, its long legs trailing like streamers. Ina stopped the car, and we watched the stork as it coasted down to a giant nest at the top of a telephone pole, folding forward like a hinge as it landed.

"This bird is our national symbol," Marina reminded me. "We say it brings happiness."

I smiled. "Does it bring babies too?"

"Yes, we also have this story," Ina said. "There are many legends about the stork, all happy ones. The stork is the bird of hope. And, perhaps because they return to the same nest each year, there's a legend that storks brought to mankind the gift of memory."

Hearing this, Lev again burst out in laughter.

"Memory," he muttered. Then, shaking his head, he added bitterly, "Our national bird."

I considered Lev's comment as I watched the stork settling onto its enormous nest. I'd come in search of my own history to a place where there were no historical records. I'd sought a memory in a land where the campaign to vanquish memory had been waged for over six decades. Before retreating from Russia in 1943, the Nazis had torched all their records, then dug up their victims' bodies and burned them as well to destroy the evidence. For the next half-century, the Soviets had carried on that campaign, blotting out even the memory of those erasures. When the Soviet empire disintegrated, Belarus had been cast adrift, like that piece of colored cardboard missing from Marina's globe where her country should be. Now its leader clutched the helm of state with a rusty iron fist and protected the secrets of two dead empires. My journey to wrest a memory from the shadows had led me to this land where nobody remembered.

To conjure my grandmother into memory required something unshifting—a place, an image, a solid fact, yet the site of her murder had also been banished, buried beneath mountains of trash, then further obscured by the official blue stamp on the city map. My father, too, had rejected the past, even cast off his name, renaming himself after the shape-shifter of Greek mythology. To Proteus, memory had also become the enemy.

As we returned to the road and headed back toward Minsk, I watched the stork though the car's rear window until it was out of sight. I pictured my grandmother, Berta, as she may have looked as a young woman—her eyes maybe green, like mine. Maybe full of hope. But all I know of her story is that it concluded somewhere beneath those mountains of relics, layer upon layer of relics, flung away to rot or to burn or to blow, feather-light, in the wind.

❧ ❧ ❧

Carolyn Kraus is a professor of Journalism and Screen Studies at the University of Michigan-Dearborn. Her essays have appeared in Partisan Review, The Antioch Review, Threepenny Review, *and elsewhere. She has written as "Our Far-Flung Correspondent" for* The New Yorker, *and as an op-ed contributor to* The New York Times. *This story won the Grand Prize Gold Award in the Fifth Annual Solas Awards (www.BestTravelWriting.com).*

❧ ❧ ❧

Camel College

The school of life is open to all.

B Y THE TIME I MET AJIT, THE CAMEL DRIVER, I'D ALREADY
written India off.

I'd tried meditation and yoga, then yoga and hashish. I'd
read voraciously—Aurobindo and the *Bhagavad Gita*, Salman
Rushdie and *Shantaram*. I'd stayed in ashrams and hiked
through ruins, haggled in markets and took freezing dips in
the Ganges, seeking an experience of this country that everyone assured me was one of the most beautiful and amazing
places on earth. But in early 2008, after months of traveling
the subcontinent, the truth was that I *hated* India.

This should hardly be surprising. India was sickness, noise,
pollution, and death. It was barbarism, poverty, and touts,
cow shit and garbage, people pissing in the streets. Others
were always quick with advice, but the more of it I got, the
more it seemed like fortune cookie wisdom, false bits of other
people's knowledge, that I could no more use than I could

wear their shoes or eyeglasses. So it is ironic that when I finally came to make peace with India—to understand it—I owed it all to an unassuming man in pink plastic shower slippers.

That was Ajit. Stick thin, in his mid-thirties, he had the slight frame of a man who grows up poor in a poor country. A black dhoti wrapped around his legs in the cold clear desert morning, and bare feet sheathed in those pink plastic slippers like a little girl would wear to the beach, the teeth in his dark, sun-baked face were stained yellow-brown with the tar of *beedis*, which he chainsmoked continuously.

"Anyeong haseo!" he called out to the Koreans as they arrived by jeep from the desert outpost of Jaisalmer; "Shalom!" he said to the Israelis, gritty and ashen-faced in the early morning sun after a late night of partying; "Welcome, welcome!" It was mid-January in the Great Thar Desert, out in the far western margins of Rajasthan, the very edge of India, the rope of one stubborn animal in Ajit's nonsmoking hand as we padded through the landscape of scrub trees and dunes, blowing sand.

"I'm a camel man, in the bloody sa-a-and!!! Life in desert, it's fan-tastic!" he sang out to the tune of Aqua's "Barbie Girl" as we rode, spinning line after line of a hilarious desert-themed spoof. It was his wit I noticed first, the way he surprised us with his song, or the sharp turn at the end of a cuckold joke that left us laughing. It dawned on me as we rode that not only was he speaking good English to us, he was also making small jokes to the Koreans in their language, and directing the other camel drivers in rough Rajasthani Hindi. As the cold morning warmed into afternoon, Ajit began to seem decidedly wiser than just a low-caste man making a hard living humping tourists through the desert, and that night around our campfire in the undulating waves of a dune sea, I asked him about it.

"Did you study somewhere?" I asked.

"Only Camel College," he said, smiling.

"What is Camel College?"

"I am illiterate," he said to me, looking straight into my face. "I cannot even write my own name. Everything I know, everything, I know from Camel College."

"You mean, *just* doing this?"

He poked at the fire with a stick. "The desert, my life," he said, "is how I learn."

His sly smile told me that he'd said these things before, to countless tourists before me. But though I felt pity for him then, a superior pity for the poverty of his education, there remained something about the *way* he said those words that struck me, something that I couldn't place. The night wore on and the fire died, but the words kept floating through my head.

"Camel College…The desert…is how I learn."

I left that desert a day later, but the words stayed with me. They became a Zen *koan* to be unraveled, a rash that I just had to scratch. Traveling another month across northern India in my accustomed state of fear and loathing, they sat like a bolus undigested in my gut, to be chewed up and swallowed down and then chewed back up again. And it wore on like this, my mind ruminating day after day, week after week, until one random evening in New Delhi.

On that day, I had journeyed south eight hours by train from the Sikh holy city of Amritsar, and exited the train at New Delhi station, directly across from the mouth of Paharganj, the Delhi tourist ghetto.

As I walked out in the burnt-orange light of dusk, the traffic swirled around the station junction like a maelstrom, autorickshaws with horns screaming, buses groaning beneath a weight of passengers so great that they hung from the doors and windows. The fruit-sellers' tables across the street buzzed with fat black flies, skinny, sickly pariah dogs moving beneath them, searching for scraps. Cycle-rickshaws on the margins of the street detoured around cows, who stood placidly on their shit-smeared legs, munching garbage. The perfume of India hung in the air, smoke from burning garbage and exhaust, curry, incense, sewage, sweat, decay. "Cheeepest and best! Cheeepest and best!" screamed the touts in the Paharganj thoroughfare, as a legless man with filthy clothes and filthy hands, a filthy face, wheeled by on his stomach on a little ball-bearing cart.

Oh God. This scene, this *exact* moment, was everything about India that I hated and feared. It was the India I faced like an abattoir each morning as I went out for coffee, a reality in purest defiance of the sanitized brochures and postcards of the Taj. But in that moment, for the first time, faced with the things I hated, I did not turn away. I looked and, looking, saw with new eyes something exquisite in the chaos, the thousand players and dramas of the Delhi street all seamlessly meshing and mixing, animals and humans and traffic swirling balletically together.

God help me, I realized, this was actually *beautiful*. Why had I resisted this, I wondered? This mad borderless beauty, why had I hated it? I understood then how habitual my fear had become, a reaction so deeply internalized that I now hid automatically from what I had first found ugly, without ever really looking at it.

Standing and looking, the sense of peace spreading over me was immense. Bodies washed around my own, stationary like a stone in a tide. And I realized, standing there, that the resistance had completely gone out of me. This openness was the key to India, its very heart; and yet there was no class or book in the world that could have taught me this. It could only be learned through Camel College.

Oh Ajit. How misplaced my pity had been for him that night, thinking that because he could not read, his education had been lesser than my own. *That* was his Camel College, the lesson of the desert that he had smiled about so enigmatically that night: that the desert brings to you *exactly* what you need to learn.

Seeing his face grinning at me in my memory, a little smile passed my lips. He had been the perfect tutor, instructing without effort, the embodiment of his life's lesson. Smiling, I walked on through the street in the twilight, feeling in my heart like a man long gone from a place, being finally welcomed home.

❦ ❦ ❦

Writer, photographer, and part-time metaphysician, Matthew Crompton has at various times called Cleveland, San Francisco, and Seoul home, though he's most comfortable in a perpetually itinerant state. His travels have taken him through all the worst hotels on three continents, though he counts himself lucky to have caught giardia only once. His writings and photographs have been published in Asia, Australia, and the UK; it's agreed that women, zoo animals, and most Marxists find him irresistible. Follow him at goingaroundplaces.wordpress.com.

❧ ❧ ❧

Lanterns of Fear

It was a trip down memory lane—
a dark path indeed.

For our honeymoon, my wife and I took a Caribbean cruise. I don't remember much about it. It was a long time ago. I thought if the day ever came when I'd need to remember, all I'd have to do is pad over to our media room cabinet, pluck out a few slide trays, set up the old projector, and have a look-see. I thought my wife would want to put down her book, pop us some Orville Red., and join me down memory lane. I thought when the projector click-clacked and such-and-such picture dropped into place and blazed in Technicolor onto the dining room wall, she would reach over, clasp my hand, and coo, "Oh, I forgot about that! That was the day you bought me that ruby heart pendant. I forgot all about that!" And she would lean over and kiss me, just as she did that day in the St. Thomas jewelry store. That's what I thought.

❧ ❧ ❧

Undoubtedly, prehistoric showmen cast fire-shadow images on cave walls. But the known history of projectors began with sixteenth-century experiments in optics and lighting, at a time when the mystical and magical power of projected images—the Inquisition had burned Bruno at the stake for his devotion to imagistic magic—was giving way to scientific enlightenment.

The camera obscura, a device that with mirrors and lenses captured the images of external objects on a surface inside a dark box, so fascinated Renaissance Europeans that artists like Vermeer and Rembrandt included the wondrous invention in their paintings. From this obsession with capturing and casting reality came, in 1659, the "magic lantern," the first projection device using both an artificial light source and a lens—and therefore the modern slide projector's first direct ancestor.

The popularity of this invention spread around the world, resulting in its becoming, by the nineteenth century, a commercialized source of public and home entertainment—in the case of children, not always pleasant. The writer Marcel Proust, for example, recalled his childhood fear of the magic lantern slide shows his great-aunt projected on his bedroom wall: "It substituted for the opaqueness of my walls, an iridescence of many colors. But my sorrows only increased thereby, because this mere change of lighting was enough to destroy the familiar impression I had of my room. Now I no longer recognized it and felt uneasy in it."

In her autobiography, sociologist Harriet Martineau records a similar childhood reaction: "Such was the terror of the white circle on the linen sheet of the dark drawing room, and of the moving slides, that, to speak the plain truth, they sat on my heart and soul the black night through. And sometimes even morning light could not drive them away."

Thus the first slide projectors came to be known as *lanternes de peur*—"lanterns of fear."

I don't look at our honeymoon slides anymore, but I'm pretty sure we took shots of the usual tourist scenes: my wife waving in front of pastel, gingerbread Curaçao harbor facades; my wife navigating a bamboo raft down the Martha Brae River; my wife at a St. Maarten beach bar, mugging with her new ruby necklace; my wife aboard ship, leaning on the railing, back-dropped by sea and sky, her eyes wide and young and happy—the loveliest blues I had ever seen. I took a lot of pictures of my new wife—I don't recall having taken any without her in them. But I don't much remember specific shots—except the one with her at the ship's railing. She's standing there in her shorts and halter top, the most beautiful woman I ever knew, affecting a saucy smile, pointing with her seashell-braceleted wrist to a sign stenciled on the gunwale: DANGER.

That's the only one I'm really sure about. It was a long time ago.

The history of slides is, essentially, the attempt to make illusion seem more real than reality. In 1833 David Brewster invented the stereoscope, an optical device that, when viewed through lenses, made special photographs seem three-dimensional. By "projecting" an image onto the retina with the appearance of depth and texture, the device caused not only its makers but its enthusiasts to claim it provided the "perfect image of reality." Later, Daguerre's huge paintings, his dioramas, cast on transparent materials and presented in darkened theaters and illuminated from behind, imbued his landscapes with breathtaking realism. Manipulation of the light behind the pictures gave the effect of actual changing light and shade or even of complete transformation from daylight to night, and

thus an intense illusion of reality. There is a famous story of
a spellbound child observing one of Daguerre's dioramas and
declaring it "more beautiful than nature itself."

At the time of our honeymoon, cruises were different than
they are today. To eat a meal on board that did not involve
foraging for peanuts between your mattress and headboard,
you had to don a tie and jacket and enter the ship's dining
room at a specific time and sit with people you did not know.
They herded you into this immense, frenetic hall that had all
the characteristics of the Chicago slaughterhouse in Upton
Sinclair's novel *The Jungle*, in which upside-down hogs are
conveyed squealing with terror to an aproned guy who slices
their throats with a rusty knife. I don't know what women
had to wear because, to be honest, I never looked at them. I
had eyes only for my new wife.

We sat with a group of six other couples, middle-aged folks
from Nebraska who had never seen a body of water in their
lives, let alone an actual ocean, and who seemed pretty baffled
by the concept. So there my wife and I were, shouting across
the table at a bunch of devil-may-cares from the Heartland,
trying to figure out how to get our food down without chew-
ing and get back to our room to screw. Apparently our table
mates were part of a group of TV-set salesmen (and their
wives) who had won a sales contest that included all the free
liquor they could spill on themselves in a week. They talked
with their cheeks as florid and bulbous as Bavarian oom-
pah-ers, and, while spitting veal cutlet and routinely knocking over highball glasses with the maniacal gusto of a Spike
Jones routine, they barked sage marital advice to me and my
new bride that included the phrase, "Never admit anything."
They were jolly and pickled, they ate off each other's plates,
and their wives showed us pictures of their kids and snorted,
"Here's our little shits."

❧ ❧ ❧

In 1870 a Venetian, Carlo Ponti, designed the megalethoscope, a beautifully milled tabletop cabinet—itself a work of
art—in which photographs were viewed through a large lens,
creating an optical illusion of depth and perspective. Backlit
by an internal kerosene lantern, translucent albumen pictures
were colored and pierced to create dramatic visual effects,
such as stars and streetlamps. Unfortunately, the source of the
megalethoscope's power was also its downfall: its oil lantern
heart would occasionally burst into flame and destroy the
device and, sometimes, its owner's house.

The first patent for a 35mm still camera was issued in
England in 1908. The first full-scale production camera was
the Homeos, a stereo camera, produced between 1913 and
1920. Then came the big-selling Tourist Multiple, which appeared in 1913 for $175 (at today's prices, the cost of a $3000
Leica) and the Simplex, introduced in the U.S. in 1914. The
Minigraph, by Levy-Roth of Berlin, another small camera,
sold in Germany in 1915. The patent for the Debrie Sept,
a combination 35mm still and movie camera, was issued in
1918, but it was not marketed until 1922. The Furet, made
and sold in France in 1923, was the first cheap, small 35mm
camera, and looked vaguely like today's models. But it wasn't
until the great industrialist George Eastman came onto the
scene that America became, as with so many products, the
world's leader.

The moment we finished our entrees, my wife started playfully pinching my thigh to get the hell out of the dining room.
She was in a hurry to get away from those Nebraskans and
back to our room. She would take her after-dinner drink
with her. No argument from me. No need to wait for dessert.
We'd make our own.

George Eastman was born in Waterville, New York, in July 1854. His father died when George was twelve, the elder Eastman leaving his family destitute. At fourteen, George dropped out of high school to find a job. As the history of the Eastman Kodak Company attests, he managed to overcome his economic adversity. In 1884 he patented the first roll film; in 1888 he perfected the Kodak camera, the first designed specifically for roll film. In 1892 he established his famous company in Rochester, New York—the first firm to mass-produce standardized photography equipment. His gift for organization and management, his tireless work ethic, and his lively and inventive mind made him a successful entrepreneur by his mid-twenties, enabling him to lead his company to the forefront of American industry.

Before making love, my wife and I made fun of the bulbous TV-salesmen and their blustery fraus, my wife braying, "Cooked snails! Cooked snails!" and me wheezing, "Shut up and fill your purse!" Then, after we made love, feeling close enough to her to take a chance, I said, "In a weird way, I like them."

"That would be weird," she said.

"Maybe that'll be us in thirty years."

"God forbid," she said, coughing up Drambuie.

"You know, giving advice to newlyweds, pictures of kids—"

"Synchronized belching."

I realized I had made a mistake. "O.K., I get it." We were quiet for a minute, and then I rolled onto her. "And now maybe I want to get it again."

But something bothered her. She draped her arm around me and let me nibble her neck, then sighed and went limp. We had been up early that morning for muster drill. We were both tired, and I felt a little rejected. So I just sighed and also went limp.

≈ ≈ ≈

In the earliest days, photographers had to load their film into reusable cassettes and, at least for some cameras, cut the film leader. But in 1934 there was a huge breakthrough. Eastman Kodak introduced 35mm-wide, daylight-loading, single-use, *cartridge* film, principally for use in its new "Retina" camera—but, of course, adopted by competitors. In 1935 Kodak launched its 35mm Kodachrome color film. Because of its ease of use and stunning transparencies, this slide film quickly grew in popularity, becoming, by the late 1960s, the most popular photographic format. (Its lexicon remains, even if the film does not: the term *slide show* on our computer photo programs was derived from Kodak's innovation.)

Our first slide camera was a Kodak Automatic 35R4, which I bought for my wife as a wedding present, in honor of our many future trips together. I didn't have much money; this sturdy little slide-taker cost under a hundred bucks. What's more, unlike expensive Leicas and Nikons, our honeymoon Kodak was very simple to use. When it comes to photography, I'm kind of stupid. Stupid, stupid, stupid. I never did understand, nor had the patience to learn, the meaning of f-stops or shutter speed or focal lengths or ISO numbers or aperture settings or the dozen various dials and buttons that were the hallmark of upper-bracket cameras.

I don't recall if on our honeymoon cruise I told my wife how lucky I felt every time we sat on the Lido deck in the moonlight or walked together down one island Front Street or another. I wish I had told her more.

As the years rolled along, we traveled a lot. We took a lot of pictures. We would carefully pack our film in lead-lined travel bags, so it wouldn't be corrupted by airport X-ray scanners, and once home we raced to the camera store to get it developed. Ten days was a long time, but that's how long it took. Ten days seemed long. We had an agreement. If we didn't pick up the slides together, we wouldn't peek at them until they were in the projector, so we could view them at the same time. We would cuddle on the couch with a tub of popcorn and relive our recent experiences. I knew she cheated. It wasn't in her not to sneak a look at the pictures before she got home. Sometimes I would notice a number out of order or a slide upside down coming out of the package, or if she had loaded the tray, a slide would appear on the screen upside down or backwards, and I knew she had broken her promise. But I never said anything about it.

In his final years, George Eastman was plagued by a degenerative disorder of his spine. He had trouble standing, and his walking became a slow shuffle. In intense pain and frustrated at his inability to maintain an active life, on March 14, 1932, when he was seventy-seven, he shot himself in his heart.

Sometimes I will be sleeping, other times I will be lying awake in the dark, watching imaginary bursts of light, listening to the *click-clack* of a nonexistent slide projector. *Click-clack*. Here is a picture I took while kneeling on the deck of a chartered sailboat, my wife, wearing a scarlet two-piece, smiling against a backdrop of billowing sails and lapis sky. She is very happy. The breeze washes wisps of her silky blond hair across her smile. The warm, clear sea is in her azure eyes, a morning beach in her high, smooth cheeks. She is very happy. In the slide's outsize projection, colors are so vibrant—reds bursting, magentas pulsing—the images are almost living, breathing beings—three-dimensional creatures hovering long into the night.

I can't recall now if this was one of our actual pictures or just in my head. I don't remember.

❧ ❧ ❧

Clack-click. The slide projector sounds like a semi-automatic weapon. You load a tray like a clip, insert it into its receiver with a sturdy, satisfying *clack*; you press a button, and, *click*, a "shell" drops into place and explodes onto the screen. The original Kodak projector trays were rectangular and held only forty rounds. But the projector my wife and I owned, we didn't have to reload as often. The trays were circular, similar to that of a World War I machine gun's bullet magazine, and they held 160 pictures.

In the bursts of color and dust-swirling blasts from the projector's muzzle, there is something else about slides different from ordinary pictures. If they, with their bigger-than-life, dazzling images that, as in Proust's childhood bedroom, block out the familiar world and blur the distinction between imaginary and real, they might well render the image *more* real than the original, the actual events inferior to the memory. Slides, then, may create a world where false memory—the illusion of an idealized past—replaces the true experience they represent. A frozen smile, a colonial facade glinting in the sunlight, expensive jewelry, the happy glow of sand-smooth cheeks, become billowing sails of illusion.

Clack-click. Here is a picture of my wife, hair and halter top drenched, leaning against the owner of the plantation inn where we often stayed in St. Thomas. They are standing under an eave of the great house, rain bullets slicing behind them. They are holding onto each other, half-mugging, half-in-earnest, as Hurricane Lenny mows down the Eastern Caribbean. In my wife's eyes you can see the strain we all felt, holed up for four days, watching our roofs billow, listening all night to their timbers' ghostly wails, wincing from the far-off surf crashing thunder-like against the town. In the horizontal rain, denuded palm trees bend like jackknifed legs, their nesting birds long dead. A torrent of brown runoff roils down the stairs and mountainside, down, down. For once the Kodachrome is lusterless, soaked gray, as if the developing process had broken down. But the soddenness is not the film. It is in the deluged earth. In the slide's absence of color you can feel the utter wetness, the oxygen-starved, muted red of my wife's bathing suit, the winter brown of her hair, the cistern gray of the owner's shirt and beard. He hugs her shoulder, my wisp of a wife, preventing her from being sucked into the storm. He smiles, she frowns. She wants to go home. We have run out of food. There has been no electricity for three days. The only drinking water is what guests collect from the great-house roof. In front of my wife and the owner sits a large cooking vat, which they had just filled with rainwater, each holding a handle, before I told them to turn and face the camera. I do not like this picture. There is something primordially evil about hurricanes, something that suggests original sin. When we found ourselves trapped on island, I thought it might be an interesting experience, something to tell our (future) children. But it did not work out that way. Now I remember something else. When I shouted above the wind for the owner and my wife to put down the vat and turn around, when I snapped that picture, how hard it was to breathe.

Because digital photography is the new technology, it is virtually impossible to get 35mm slide film anymore. The truth is, for all of its magic, Kodachrome was doomed. It was a difficult film to manufacture and even more complex to process. There is only one remaining photofinishing lab in the world processing Kodachrome: Dwayne's Photo in Parsons, Kansas. And that will last only until either Dwayne's chemicals run out or he does.

I haven't bought a digital camera yet, but one day I might. In the meantime, my original Kodak 35R4 sits on my closet shelf, collecting dust. I thought I might one day show it to my kids, just as those Nebraskan partiers must now be showing their grandkids pictures of that long-ago cruise. That's what I thought. But it's just in the closet. It may still have a partially exposed roll of film in it. Maybe someday I'll throw it away.

❦ ❦ ❦

Gary Buslik writes essays, short stories, and novels. He teaches literature, creative writing, and travel writing at the University of Illinois at Chicago. His work appears often in Travelers' Tales anthologies. You can visit his latest book, A Rotten Person Travels the Caribbean, *at www.arottenperson.com.*

❧ ❧ ❧

All in the Same House

Saints come in all kinds of strange disguises.

THE RAIN PELTING THE GLASS WALLS OF MY PHONE booth woke me at dawn, still a hundred miles from Hiroshima. I was sitting on my backpack, legs cramped against my chest, head cushioned against the glass by a dirty t-shirt. Overnight while sleeping in the booth, my body had curled into the shape of Japanese Kanji character, I thought perhaps the symbol for "back pain."

I had been searching for a home, both figurative and literal, for some time in Japan. For six months as an exchange student, I studied the language and culture in an effort to fit into this very foreign land. But it was difficult to feel like I belonged. Even a simple question about my birthday could create trouble. Whenever I told older Japanese my birth date of August 15, they would suck in their breath, hiss it out between clenched teeth, and tell me it was *"Haisen no Hi"* ("day of defeat,") the date in 1945 when the Japanese surrendered to the U.S. to end World War II after the atomic bomb attacks.

While on break from my studies, I had decided to hit the road, hitchhiking solo across the country to mix with the Japanese. But it was slow going, as rides were scarce, some cars stopping only to take pictures of the funny foreigner on the highway.

The prior night, I hitchhiked as far as the Okayama train station, hoping to sleep in the terminal to stay out of the rain. But an insular gang of homeless Japanese men kicked me from my space next to the pornography vending machine. The only other dry, unoccupied spot I could find was a phone booth.

I worried about my reception in Hiroshima. I planned to visit the ruins of the nuclear blast, to experience how the city had been reborn in the generations after the war. But I wasn't sure if the natives were friendly. I hoped my pathos would be my protection. Perhaps a skinny, soggy, solo nineteen-year-old would pose no lingering threat to the locals.

After a full day waiting by the roadside, I met a trucker who drove me the rest of the way to Hiroshima station. I exited the truck into growing darkness. The neon signs above dingy alleyway storefronts gave the derelicts and street vendors an ominous red glow. They alternately stared at me and ignored my presence. It was time to look for lodging, and I knew the station held no hope for me.

My guidebook mentioned a youth hostel in the hills above town. I cut through alleyways, empty noodle stalls, and gravel parks, but the twisting dead ending, unsigned roads kept bringing me back to the station. Already 10 P.M., with no sign of the hostel, my back twinged at the thought of another night in a phone booth. I shivered in my still damp clothes, scanning trees for rain cover.

I stopped in a convenience store to buy a candy bar for dinner and vainly asked for directions. Exiting the shop, I nearly collided with a thick elderly woman carrying a heavy sack.

She turned her head up to stare directly into my face, her punch-permed hair jiggling as she looked me up and down. With her large cloth bag, flowered smock, and solid posture, she looked like the Japanese wife of Santa Claus.

"You!" she barked in English, "You! Where you go?" She leaned forward, head practically touching my chest, eyes squinting, lips pursed.

"I go Youth Hostel. Yoooos Hostelu," I added, trying the Japanese pronunciation of the English word.

"No Yoos Hostelu. No!" She crossed her arms to make an "X" shape, like a basketball referee signaling a flagrant foul.

I wasn't sure if this meant I shouldn't go there, or I couldn't go there. Did it exist at all, or was I just hopelessly lost?

"Yoos Hostel full! All full! No room!" She took a step back and put her hands on her hips, daring me to contradict her. My face must have dropped, realizing my plight.

"You stay my house! House!" She shouted, laughing and slapping her thigh at this apparent witticism. "You! Wait! Here!" She pointed at a spot underneath a street light. "Car come. You wait." She picked up her sack and walked away, looking back once to make sure I had obeyed orders.

About ten minutes later, a rusting brown Toyota compact car rolled to a stop in front of me. The head of a wizened old man barely poked above the dashboard. When he saw me, he smiled and began nodding vigorously, waving his bony hand downwards to indicate I should come.

"House?" he asked me.

"Um, yes, house."

He cackled with glee, repeating "house," his head bowing so deep with laughter that I could no longer see it through the window. He popped up to say, "Yes, yes, you come house. Very good. We are friends. Friends!" He thrust his thin hand toward me, causing me to self-consciously flinch, imagining a karate attack from an ancient master. I sheepishly shook his offered hand, and hopped in the car.

We drove to a trash-strewn gravel parking lot behind a two-story concrete bunker of an apartment complex. It looked like a parking garage invaded by squatters. We walked up a back stairway, the old man surprisingly spritely on the dark steps.

He reached for the door handle, and stopped. He turned to me, trying to suppress the grin on his face, like a little kid trying to hide a whoopee cushion. He turned the handle slowly, then flung open the door, shouting "HOUSE! HOUSE!"

Mrs. Japanese Claus sat tucked under a low table in the middle of a cluttered room. She shrieked with laughter as a terrified terrier dog dove into a box in the corner, causing the couple to laugh even harder. I remained in the doorway ready to flee this crazy scene.

"That, the dog house," the woman said, pointing to the box. She stood to lift the trembling dog, and we had formal introductions. They were the Yamadas, and the dog's name, amazingly enough, was Santa. Now soothed, Santa trotted to the table, looking for scraps of food.

"HOUSE!" She shouted again at Santa, who tore the tatami mat with his claws in an effort to speed back to his "house," the dog box.

"Santa speak English. Bilingual dog, yo," said the proud teacher, arms folded across her chest.

"Our house, your house," said Mr. Yamada, gesturing around the small one bedroom apartment, "You stay, you eat!"

I joined them for an extended meal of soups, fried noodles, and fish. I learned that Mr. Yamada worked long hours as a street sweeper, his wife in a laundry. The economic miracle of Japan had somehow left them behind. Yet they provided me food and shelter as if they were mayors of the city. He spread a futon for me in the corner of the room, and rushed to the end of the hallway to prepare my bath.

We shared a jolly chat in broken English about the weather, about my studies in Japan, my skills with chopsticks, everything except the obvious. Perhaps sixty or seventy years old, my hosts may have been teenagers during WWII. Most older Japanese tend to remain in the same area they were raised. Thus, they were most likely in the vicinity when a pilot from my country dropped the bomb that killed over one hundred thousand of their neighbors.

When I did bring up the war, after many shared cups of sake, they both nodded and were quiet a moment. Mrs. Yamada said the city was "like this," she waved up to the cloud of smoke in the room, but "it blow away, long ago. We together now. All in same house."

The next morning they sent me on my way with coins for the subway, and directions on how to visit Peace Park, the cherry blossom-covered site of Hiroshima's ground zero. I promised to write the couple, send them pictures of my journey, to share anything I could with my two new friends.

But the rigors of the road caused me to lose many of my belongings, including my address book. I could never thank them fully, could never find them again among the mazes of that city. So I write this story as my delayed thank you, to honor their spirit of forgiveness, and to spread their message that even after the most bitter of battles, different people can share their lives in an open house.

☙ ☙ ☙

Bill Fink is a freelance travel writer based in California. He writes about his adventures around the world for the San Francisco Chronicle, Chicago Sun Times, Islands Magazine, *and a host of other assorted magazines, guidebooks, websites, and newspapers. He also appeared in* The Best Travel Writing 2006. *You can check out more of his stories at www.billfinktravels.com.*

꙳ ꙳ ꙳

Femme in the Vosges

This is how place can put a key in your hand.

I HAVE COME AS A WOMAN TO THE LORRAINE REGION OF France, to the Vosges department more specifically. This is no Provence. There are no lavender fields and sunny squares, no late-afternoon pastis and Brie next to a babbling fountain of frolicking cherubs. This is the Vosges. There are gray, moss-covered churches and gray, moss-covered cemeteries, and gray, moss-covered monuments bearing the names of villagers lost to World War I.

What kind of woman am I, who comes to this ominous, dark landscape, this agrarian and watery culture which is on the verge of total abandonment, half of its homes now vacant and crumbling? I am beginning to question. Americans do not come here. Even the French do not come here. They leave here. It is a ghostly and forgotten place, notwithstanding the quiche. And you don't travel halfway across the world for some quiche. Do you?

I am a woman who lost my relationship. Then I lost my nonprofit job to the California economy. Then I lost my home. I was tethered to nothing. There was nothing to take stock of. I did not know what to do or where to go. Then my aunt in Holland, who was very much like a second mother to me, died of cancer. Several years ago, she and my mother bought a three-hundred-year-old stone house together in this rural area of Lorraine, in the wooded rolling hills of les Vosges. The house normally stands empty in the winters. Now it stands even emptier.

Lorraine is like a weary child of divorce; it has stood in the middle of countless gruesome and bloody custody battles with Germany for centuries, unsure of where its allegiance lies, deep in identity crisis. Steeped in a mish-mash of Gallo-Roman, Catholic, and Pagan traditions, it is awkward and gawky. With a shift away from small-farm agriculture and a decline in the mining industry in the early half of the twentieth century, its economy collapsed in a mass exodus of its population to Paris and the sunnier climes of the south. Now, most of the villages are deserted and still during the mist of fall and the sleet of winter. There are a few local farmers who eek out a meager living from their cattle or sheep, and laborers in the building trade who restore vacation houses for the Dutch and Germans. In the summer, the villages mirror the landscape and spring back to life. But in the winter, people do not come here. Except for me, because I decided that deep in my own identity crisis and depression, coming to a frozen stone home with no telephone or internet in a tiny village in the middle of nowhere somehow would be a good idea. I admit that I romanticized it, and I realize my error the moment I arrive. But in a way, this gray landscape holds a perfect mirror to my heart in its weary state, and I stay for months.

My mother and aunt's house is in a village called Serécourt and sits on a road just above the village called "Haut de Fée." Literally, this is translated as "High Faerie," but I soon

discover that it signifies a "faerie mound," which has pagan
folklore surrounding it. The only neighbor on the Haut de
Fée is the cemetery around the bend. There are no other
houses on the road, which winds from the church to the
cemetery before disappearing between cow pasture and into
the woods. This may be because, as I discover, faerie mounds
are burial mounds, magical places where the veil between
the living and the dead is thin, and in a superstition-soaked
region, one is not supposed to build houses on faerie mounds
because it generally upsets the faeries. I guess whoever built
my mother and aunt's house didn't get the memo. As my
fertile imagination begins to run at night while I sleep in my
recently deceased aunt's bedroom, I am both comforted by
that thought, as well as spooked when I begin to hear faint
voices and singing in the house late at night. I start to doubt
my sanity, but the sound is unmistakable.

The nearest neighbors, an older, reserved Dutch couple
named Hans and Elizabeth, walk by the house one day, and I
strike up a conversation. I tell them about my experience, and
they sheepishly admit that yes, they have heard some singing
too, that they too have heard voices late at night in their house,
and that Elizabeth has even seen what she thought was a group
of nuns late one night in the footpath between their house and
the former convent, now the summer home of a wealthy
Parisian publisher. Hans and Elizabeth live in a 400-year-old
house that has seen many ill-fated occupants. In World War
II, a Jewish butcher lived there. He was taken away to the
concentration camps. During the French Revolution, their
house was used by the church, and the inhabitants wiped
out along with most of the other villagers during the Reign
of Terror, which sent to the guillotine Catholics who refused
to pledge allegiance to the government's control over the
church. Before that, the plague swept through the village. If
ever there were a house predisposed to ghosts, theirs would
be it. However, we all agree somewhat noncommittally that

of course there must be a plausible explanation for the voices, not wanting to sound irrational or prone to flights of fancy. "I think I was just over-tired, hallucinating," says Elizabeth. Yet I see in her eyes that she is not fully convinced, and I find myself entertaining the possibility of ghosts, in the spirit of the folklore upon which this village was built. So I talk to the faeries just in case, and ask them to please take it easy on me, and when I pass the cemetery on my walks, I stop at the gates and call in to the centuries worth of bones buried there. "Rest easy, spirits of Serécourt. I am your friend!"

Initially, I sleep a lot and spend my days indoors, reading, crying, feeding log after log into the wood stove, and drinking wine. I am in my late thirties, and I try to figure out where my life veered off the tracks. I had imagined I would have a fulfilling career by now. I had imagined my life with a partner who stayed, who would be next to me drinking wine and asking me for crossword puzzle help. I always imagined I would have a child, have children. My future children had become so real to me that their perceived loss stings almost as much, if not more, than the loss of love. When I first got to France, I cocooned myself in the safety of the house, extracting myself from a world I no longer felt like playing with. I loved intensely, I was loyal, I did my job, but those didn't seem to be the rules of the game after all. So I don't want to play anymore. But I eventually run out of wine, notice the rapidity with which I am burning through logs during the day, and so begin to venture out, taking walks and visiting nearby towns. And as I immerse myself in the history of Lorraine, I find more than quiche. I find other women. I find strong women, women pushed out by society, following their own paths, thumbing their noses at convention. Women who found their way in this landscape. I find Joan of Arc, who I learn grew up in a village nearby. I find hundreds of women who were unjustly burned at the stake as witches, one of the highest concentrations in Europe, thanks to the leading

demonologist's residence here in the sixteenth century. I
find goddesses worshipped in a culture of Celtic, Roman,
and Catholic tradition in this area, melting together in this
muddy, rain soaked ground. Damona, the Roman goddess, has her name carved in many of the stones recovered
from the Gallo-Roman ruins here. Epona, Rosmerta, and
Nantosuelta, goddesses of fertility, also feature prominently
in the artifacts they dig up here and take their place alongside the Catholic Virgin Mary. I find a long line of women
who wove their way into this landscape. There are very few
weak women in this culture.

  This is a region famous for water, the source of several
large rivers, the site of hot springs which have fostered a
spa culture famous in all of Europe for centuries, millennia
even. In the fifth century B.C., a tribe of female Celtic druids
settled here, at the source of the Saône River, in worship of
the river goddess Sagona who brings forth the springs from
the earth. I am living in the middle of a triangle of three large
spa towns: Bourbonne les Bains, Vittel, and Contrexeville.
These spa town clocks seem to have been set permanently
on 1890 while the rest of us moved on to Pilates and Power
Yoga, acupuncture and chiropractors. Sunday afternoons,
the spas even put on civilized "tea dances" in the ballroom. I
find myself suddenly plunged into a Jane Austin novel when
I go to these towns to visit their farmers' markets. Amazed,
I wander through groomed rose gardens where "curists" sit
in antiquated Pavilions and on benches along the promenade,
in between their water cures for rheumatism or perhaps, one
begins to wonder, for their tuberculosis or polio, quaintly
unaware of the vaccines and antibiotics that exist outside the
walls of this time capsule. Reading the advertisements for the
magic spring waters that'll cure what ails you, it would not
entirely surprise me if leeches and bloodletting were also on
the menu. I find myself wanting intensely to believe, wishing

I could wash clean my afflicted spirit, but when I drink the special waters, I am not cured.

One afternoon in Lamarche, the closest town where I can do grocery shopping, I pull over when I see a beautiful gothic steeple rising up from behind a tall stone wall. It appears to be a chapel of some sort. I find a place where the wall has crumbled and push through the brambles to make my way in, then stand, mouth agape, at the scene before me. I am standing in thick, deep mud, on the expansive property of an imposing chateau with two wings. With a large black thundercloud hanging ominously above it, this is exactly what a "haunted house" looks like in every child's imagination. There are several magnificent outbuildings, including the spectacular gothic chapel. But the property is now a morass of mud and junkyard and cow pasture. I climb over old motors and rusted washing machines to get a better look at the gothic chapel, its spires piercing the gray and threatening sky above. It is adorned with intricate carved stone flourishes. Through its crumbling arches, it is stuffed full of hay. The hay is propped up by marble gravestones from the cemetery next door. A cow lies in the muck beneath the chapel, lord of the most stately hayloft in the world. Other white cows stand about, up to their bovine knees in thick black mud, lowing at my arrival. We stand for many minutes, staring coldly at each other, each finding the other an equally unwelcome intrusion. A second outbuilding with a round turret decomposes in abandonment, its stone wall collapsed in on itself. It's a disturbing scene, this forsaken estate which clearly was once quite majestic. Certainly once upon a time, horse-drawn carriages rode up this lane to deliver ladies in their Parisian fineries to this country estate. The image is incongruous with this swampy junkyard overrun with stray cats and dirty cattle. It's a tragedy. How could they let it get this way? When did they stop caring? But then, one could easily ask me the same question. I imagine it crept up on them, just as it crept up on me. I snap photographs, then leave.

I only go to Domrémy-la-Pucelle, Joan of Arc's birthplace, because that's what one does as a tourist in this region. I figure I'll pop in, check it out, check it off my list. But it shifts something in me. Watching a video about her life in the small museum adjacent to her house, I feel deeply connected to her isolation, the sense of her difficulty as a woman. She spent her childhood a loner and a dreamer, walking through the woods. Later, after she left her family and went into battle, she spent nights alone, always in armor and male clothing against a sea of dark figures who tried to sexually assault her while she slept. I taste her loneliness. I walk through her tiny childhood home, put my hands on the modest walls of her bedroom, see the hearth where she sat with her family. Somehow, I never really grasped her as a real person before. I saw her only as a mythical icon. Seeing where she actually lived changes all that. I go inside the village church where she heard the voices of angels that told her to fight for France, to don armor and lead an army of men to defeat the British and take back her country. Whether or not it was divine intervention or mental illness that produced the voices, I marvel at the injustice she endured and her unwavering resolution, even when her former allies offered her up on a platter after she led them to victory. Sold out by the very people she had saved, imprisoned and sexually harassed in her cell by guards, sleep deprived, forced to endure months of twelve-hour days of relentless interrogation in a trial designed solely for the purpose of tripping her up in semantics and trick questions, she never capitulated. They called her "witch, soothsayer, false prophet, sacrilegist, idolator, apostate, scandalmonger, rebel, troublemaker," but no matter what, Joan knew who she was. I envy her conviction and try to summon her strength. Even after having come through the trial without a single slip-up in her carefully worded testimony, after they ignored the lack

of proof and convicted her of the ridiculous charges of witch-
craft and heresy anyway, even then, as she was tied to a stake
and burned alive, she stayed strong. Something about Joan
triggers my fighting instinct. A pilot light re-ignites inside
me. "Hold the crucifix up before my eyes so I may see it until
I die," Joan told them, even as the flames licked at her feet.

In the weeks that follow, I find myself noticing more and
more the hidden beauty of this place, behind the imposing
grim façade which is there to frighten off the fickle, it seems.
This place is for those made of stronger stuff, for those who
refuse to capitulate. Its rewards come out of hiding only for
patient eyes. One day on my walk in the woods, a red fox
leaps across my path, its tail a proud streaming flag behind
it. And on the front steps as I come home one evening, I
disturb a hedgehog descending. He curls in on himself, nose
tucked in, playing dead. A hedgehog! I am beside myself
with satisfaction at this development and set a dish of milk
next to the little ball of prickles, but it is committed to the
bluff, and remains motionless, fleeing the moment I turn my
back. The woods here are brilliant golds and crimsons, and
odd new mushroom clusters sprout from the mossy ground.
And the people here are salt of the earth people, but I find a
delightful streak of twisted humor behind their weathered
"visages de terroir," their "faces of the land." The doctor in
town, whom I see for a kidney infection, is decked out in full
western gear—leather vest, bolo tie, and cowboy boots—so
that I have to check the name plate on his office door to make
sure I am in the right place. He writes me a prescription with
a smile and saunters out of the office in his clacking boots as
though he's exiting through the swinging door of a saloon.
The pharmacist has a Weimariner dog that sits beside him
in the small village pharmacy. "*C'est mon fils*," says the pharmacist. His son. He produces a felt fedora, which he places
on the dog's head, and the dog walks around the pharmacy
patiently adorned. This is a place of contrasts, warm against

cold. It melts my icy view of the road before me. These are
people enjoying the only life they have and what is before
them, and their lives are hard work. Yet they find simple
pleasures. And I find my rhythm, and the baker learns that I
am here, so he stops his truck before my little house at 11:30
every morning except Sunday and Monday and honks his
horn. I come down and he opens the side of his truck to expose the glass cases of pastries and baskets of baguettes. He is
a jolly plump fellow, just what you expect a baker to be, and
he sing-songs "*bonne journée*" when he leaves. "Maybe tomorrow, a brioche!" I say as he drives off, and he honks again
and waves. In Monthureaux, I visit the butcher and order a
pork pie and a bottle of wine. He notices my sniffling, and I
tell him I have a cold from the frigid damp that won't let up.
Ah! Mon dieu! Sick! Lucky for me, he knows what to do. He
tells me I must drink much more hard liquor, that the French
never get sick because the alcohol burns the germs right out
of them. He laughs heartily as he packs up my pie in crisp
paper and makes a motion of tipping back a phantom glass to
his lips. I eat my pork pie, which must have a pound of butter
in the flaky crust alone and a pound of cream in the filling,
on the steps of the town square, and drink straight from the
bottle, and it is good. This is a place one learns to love slowly,
I discover. And maybe my life is not over yet.

　　I begin to write in the evenings, and I begin to like what
I write. A tiny idea is beginning to form, a dream I had once
and discarded because it wasn't practical and I didn't believe
I was worthy of it. I decide I am going to apply to M.F.A programs in Creative Writing and try to become a writer. After
years of writing press releases and articles in communications
and marketing jobs, I've learned to forget about writing
what *I* wanted to write, that I even have my own voice. The
fantasy alone gives me a secret thrill. The thought of being
among writers, of living as a writer, being back in academia,
teaching even, feels like a naughty thought. But it feels good.
It feels rebellious. It feels like I'm taking up arms against my

circumstances and finding a new way into my life. It's thumbing my nose at the past and deciding that I can start over at thirty-seven, that I won't capitulate, that I won't let myself go to ruin, but that I will renovate. And I spend the next weeks writing words that will become applications. I take walks in the mornings and drive into town in the afternoons, then write in the evenings until the middle of the night. I go to the library in Bourbonne les Bains to use the Internet, and I dare to ask three people across the ocean to recommend me to be a writer. I dare to write a statement of intent and proclaim my worthiness to be a writer. And I send the applications off to nine universities, asking them to help me to be a writer. And then I wait.

One morning, I am awoken early by the distinct sound of a man's voice *inside* my house, calling out. I bolt up in a panic and rush out to the kitchen to confront the intruder. The front door is wide open, but nobody is there. Confused, I go to it just in time to see a man get into his Renault and drive away on the road below. I'm puzzled and alarmed, but I scan the room and see nothing out of place, so I close and lock the door before crawling back in bed. Fifteen minutes later, as I am drifting off again, there is a frenzied knocking at the front door. Again, I get up and go to the kitchen. I open the door, but there is nobody there. The same Renault from before is idling down on the road, the doors flung open. "*Oui, hallo!*" I call out into the wet gray morning. I hear knocking at the back door now. So I walk to the back door and open it. Nobody. I call out again, "*Hallo!!!! Oui?!!!*" So I return to the front door. And from around the side of the house the neighbor Hans appears with the same man I had seen drive away earlier. "Oh! Thank God you are O.K.!" Hans says. The man begins to speak excitedly in French, grabbing his head, pointing at the front door.

Hans translates, as the rapidity with which the man speaks is too much for me to follow. It appears that he had passed my house on his morning stroll and had seen the door ajar. It had bothered him, so he returned with his car after his walk and saw that it was still open. He had come up to the house and poked his head in the door, called out for me. When there was no response and he saw that my car keys were lying by the front door, he became convinced that I had been kidnapped and murdered by an intruder. Afraid to go further into the house, he left quickly to get help. Asking around the village, he ended up at Hans's house, where Monsieur Moreau, a carpenter, was working on the facade. He informed Monsieur Moreau that I had been kidnapped and murdered by intruders. *Zut alors!* Together they raced to the front of Hans's house and banged on his door. Hans appeared and together they told him I had been kidnapped and murdered by intruders. Hans jumped into the car with the man. They raced back to my house and ran up the stairs, leaving the car running, where they finally encountered me, befuddled and sleepy and not murdered. And here we stand. The man is very embarrassed. But I am deeply touched by his concern. I had not thought anyone in the village was paying much attention to me, but it turns out they have been keeping a quiet eye on me all along, looking out for their American neighbor. I thank him for his concern, and assure him I am fine. It's likely that the door had been left open absentmindedly the night before, when I had gone out to the barn to get more wood for the stove.

The next morning, while I stand in the kitchen making coffee, I see the man who had sounded the alarm the day before loading his glass into the recycling containers in the street below. Or at least, it really looks like the man from the day before. Nibbling at my croissant, my heart is warmed, and I am moved to thank him again. Opening the top half of our Dutch door, I call out to him in bad French, "*Je vivre!*" An attempt at a little joke, calling out "I'm alive!" The man squints at me and stands up from his glass bottles. "*Hallo! JE VIVRE!!!!!*" I call again, thinking he hasn't heard me. He nods vaguely, looking befuddled. I yell it again when he still doesn't laugh. "*Oui, d'accord...*" he says uncertainly before he gets in his Peugeot and drives away. Standing in the doorway, I suddenly realize that it is not, in fact, the man from the day before. I laugh, and the laughter grows and radiates until there are tears in my eyes and I spend several minutes shaking with deep belly laughs in the kitchen. I cannot imagine what he and the other villagers he will undoubtedly gossip to must think of the American shouting from her front door that she's alive, she's alive, she's alive!

My mother's house on the Haut de Fée has not had a house number since she and my aunt bought it in ruins years ago and restored it. So the mailman delivers my mail to the neighbors, knowing that in this small village, it will eventually make its way to me. But I want a mailbox. I want an address. So one weekend I go to the town hall to talk to the mayor. The town hall is only open from 9 to 10 A.M. on Saturdays. I wait in line behind farmers, and then it is my turn, and in broken French, I introduce myself and ask the mayor for a house number on the Haut de Fée. "We have no number," I say. "*La poste n'arrive pas.*" He nods. He explains that nobody has lived in the little house for many decades, that it has never been assigned an address. He spreads out a blue parcel map of the village on his desk and points out that we are the only residence on that road besides the cemetery. He puts on his glasses and studies the map closely. Even numbers are on the left, odd numbers on the right. The cemetery is on the left. We are on the right, odd numbered. "O.K.," he says finally, straightening and removing his glasses. Deal. We can have a house number. I smile, triumphant with my accomplishment. "*Merci,*" I say. "So, what number is our house?" He sticks his thumb in the air. "*Numéro un.*" Number one. We shake on it.

Walking back up the faerie hill to the house that overlooks the village and the valley beyond, I feel strangely powerful in the realization that I can just walk into the mayor's office and change the map. Who knew you could change the map? I feel the triumph of my small victories.

After the winter, I return to California. The letters are there.

Be a writer, they say.

∼✺ ∼✺ ∼✺

Mieke Eerkens was born in Los Angeles, California to Dutch parents and has spent her life divided between the United States and The Netherlands. She has a B.A. in English-Creative Writing from San Francisco State University, and an M.A. in English Literature from Leiden University in The Netherlands. For the last seven years, she lived in the San Francisco Bay Area, where she worked in Communications and Marketing for the nonprofit sector. She is currently delighted to be working on an MFA in Creative Writing at The University of Iowa.

Beneath the Rim

Our boats are four in number. Three are built of oak, stanch and firm (with) water-tight cabin.... These will buoy the boats should the waves roll them over in rough water. The fourth is made of pine...built for fast rowing.... We take with us rations deemed sufficient to last for ten months.

—John Wesley Powell, *The Exploration of the Colorado River and Its Canyons*

WHAT A DIFFERENCE 140 YEARS MAKES, I THINK AS we pump up our inflatable Hypalon boats and fill our coolers at Lee's Ferry on the eve of a 297-mile journey down the Colorado River through the Grand Canyon. John Wesley Powell's rations on his 1869 expedition included flour for unleavened bread, bacon, dried apples, coffee, and whiskey. The basics. For our twenty-four-day trip, we pack pasta and pesto, fresh organic broccoli and carrots, homemade apple and pumpkin pies, and a whole turkey, frozen in a block of ice, for Thanksgiving two and a half weeks after our launch.

Powell, a geologist, explorer, and Civil War captain who lost most of one arm during the Battle of Shiloh, set out in 1869 with nine other men to attempt the first descent of the Colorado. Among Powell's fleet were boats called *Maid of the Canyon* and *No Name*; the boat I'll help steer down the river is the *Black Pearl*. We learn from Johnny Beers, of Canyon REO, the company renting us the boats, that the *Black Pearl* was recently washed out of a Canyon camp by a flash flood and floated forty miles downstream. When found, it was upright, a map book was still atop a cooler, Johnny said. An auspicious story, the kind of tale that whether true or embellished is calming on the eve of a river trip down one of the most ferocious whitewater rivers in the world. Much more reassuring than the blown-up photos on Canyon REO's wall showing a 1983 fatal flip in Crystal rapids.

Unlike most trips down the Canyon, we're guiding ourselves rather than relying on a commercial outfitter. We have sixteen people in five boats; rowing is shared but each boat has a captain responsible for rigging and getting the raft safely through the most fearsome rapids. But no one in our group, other than me, has been down the Colorado through the Canyon before, and I've only done it once, twelve years ago at a different water level. It's a river whose hydraulics are unlike any other, with pounding waves higher than our sixteen-foot boats are long, and sucking holes that can flip a raft and hold on to its passengers, recirculating boats and humans like a washing machine. It's called getting Maytagged.

As the sunset turns the canyon walls golden red, we finish packing our provisions. I wrap duct tape and cardboard around our bottles of tequila, gin, and Jack Daniel's to protect our good soldiers from the rollicking rapids ahead. After sleeping fitfully through a frosty November night, our group leader Kristen, a twenty-six-year-old Outward Bound guide from Moab, Utah, calls us together and we meet with a Grand Canyon ranger. He makes sure we have all the necessary equipment: maps, ropes, and other safety gear, and a "groover" for human waste.

Why is it called a groover? Back in the early days of white-water rafting, the groover was nothing more than a large metal ammo box lined with a Hefty bag, so after sitting on it, rafters would have a long groove on each cheek and thigh. Modern groovers have toilet seats but the name has, well, stuck.

After months of planning, preparing and provisioning, we're off. The Canyon is wide at Lee's Ferry, and the early afternoon sun illuminates the sculpted rust-colored walls. I share a boat with Owen, an Englishman in his early forties with a dry sense of humor who came to the western U.S. to teach snowboarding and do some tech work. Owen, our boat captain, takes the first pulls on the oars.

The euphoria of the journey's first moments, especially on a naturally flowing waterway, is palpable. We hear hoots and cheers from our companions upstream as we hit our first rapids. Powell had similar feelings of exultation when he navigated the first whitewater of his trip: "We thread the narrow passage with exhilarating velocity," he wrote, "mounting the high waves, whose foaming crests dash over us, and plunging into the troughs, until we reach the quiet water below."

We wake before the sun tops the rim on Day 2 and see our fully laden boats on the beach, high and dry. The river has dropped precipitously, a result of timed releases followed by curtailed flows from the Glen Canyon Dam upstream. Without the dam we probably wouldn't have enough water to be boating in November. But I'd trade that in a second to get rid of the blockage that inundated a canyon many believe was as beautiful as the Grand, but in a gentler, more seductive way. Former Sierra Club president David Brower called the 710-foot-high, 300-foot-wide dam "America's most regretted environmental mistake." The reservoir the dam created is called Lake Powell, which I'm certain would make old Captain Powell, who reveled in the beauty of this place, wince.

We know that eventually the water will rise and allow us to get our boats back in the river, so we wait. "That's what I like about there not being other groups around," says Lynsey, an easygoing outdoor leader and flute player. "There's no one to laugh at us," she says. "We can laugh at ourselves."

> *The sun is going down and the shadows are settling in the canyon. The vermilion gleams and roseate hues, blending with the green and gray tints, are slowly changing to somber brown above, and black shadows are creeping over them below; and now it is a dark portal to a region of gloom—the gateway through which we are to enter on our voyage of exploration to-morrow. What shall we find?*

Powell's description shows not just apprehension about the monstrous rapids he expected downriver, but his appreciation of the natural beauty of the Southwest. Unlike the dour explorers of his time, Powell appreciated the glory of the landscape.

Consider what his contemporary, Lt. Joseph Christmas Ives, who attempted to navigate the Colorado in 1857, said about the Grand Canyon and the river that runs through it: "The region...is altogether valueless. It can be approached only from the south, and after entering it there is nothing to do but leave. Ours has been the first, and will doubtless be the last, party of whites to visit this profitless locality. It seems intended by nature that the Colorado River...shall forever be unvisited and undisturbed."

Today several million people visit the Canyon each year and about a million of those hike into it, according to the National Park Service. About twenty thousand people raft the Colorado River each year, mostly on guided commercial trips. The figure would be far higher if the park didn't restrict the number of boaters with a lottery permit system. Until a few years ago, there was a waiting list to get permits for non-commercial trips, like ours, down the Colorado. When the list stretched to more than twenty years it was phased out and replaced with the lottery system. If boaters can't use a permit, they can cancel, which happens with some frequency for cold-season trips—that's how we got our winning lottery ticket.

On Day 2 we catch an eddy and pull over to scout House Rock Rapid, our first real test, seventeen miles down from the put-in (starting point) at Lee's Ferry. To scout we hike above the rapid to see it. Unlike Powell, we have a detailed map that suggests routes through the rapids. But the river is ever changing. Boulders tumble into it and can make formerly safe routes hazardous; the powerful current can rearrange rocks, and a rapid can be easy at low water but frightening at higher flows—or vice versa. So we scout and understand the name of this rapid: the current plunges against a rock the size of a house, creating fearsome hydraulics.

In the rapids a fast funnel of waves coerces our boat to the left, toward the canyon's south wall. Lateral waves push the boat sideways. Owen pulls at the oars with all his strength—we get just right of two mammoth waves and a hole that could flip a boat. I peer into the churning maw of the rapid's recirculating hole as we clear it, the dark waves crashing in upon themselves.

We celebrate that evening at House Rock camp, just below the rapid, with gin-and-tonics and feast on fish tacos and fresh organic salad with goddess dressing. That evening I read of Powell's reliance on "flour that has been wet and dried so many times that it is all musty and full of hard lumps." Hanging off the side of each of our boats is a mesh bag filled with beer, staying cool and ready in the fifty-degree river water.

The next morning we scramble up eggs with spinach and cheddar. I overhear Kevin, the youngest member of our group at twenty-two, say "I don't need the hot cock this morning." Startled, I see Victoria, a nurturing soul who's become our camp mom, reach across the table, grab a bottle, and say, "I'll take the hot cock anytime of day." They're talking about the Sriracha chili sauce, with its proud and upright rooster on the label.

In the evenings, Powell's party dispelled "the gloom of these great depths" by sharing Civil War stories around a campfire; many of his crew had fought in the conflict. Though we cook on propane stoves, we too build fires and share our "war stories" of prior river adventures, love gone awry and the misguided exploits of our youth. We brighten the cold, dark evenings with tiki torches and strands of battery-powered twinkly colored lights that we drape around our chairs, adding a note of festivity to our home for this one night.

And we sing songs like The Band's "The Night They Drove Old Dixie Down," and Bob Dylan's "Wagon Wheel," tunes that would have been as timely and at home in the nineteenth century as they are in the twenty-first. Our voices are leavened by Lynsey's plaintive flute and Kevin's acoustic guitar, toted on the river in watertight cases. Kevin, who just completed college, is considering a career in outdoor education, like his older brother Steve, a trip leader for Outward Bound and one of our five boat captains.

Powell wrote that his men would occasionally "shout or discharge a pistol, to listen to the reverberations among the cliffs." We blow off steam with pyrotechnics, setting an open can of collected bacon grease on a grill atop our campfire.

"Is everyone at least ten feet from the fire?" Steve shouts as he fetches water from the river. Neil, a mellow river ranger and one of our boat captains, says "No, they're about two feet away." Steve: "Then get the first aid kit!" Steve has attached a pail of water to ten-foot-long oar and moves toward the fire. Some in our group start chanting: "Ba-con bomb! Baaa-

con bomb! Baaaaa-con bomb!" Steve yells at us to back away
and pours the water into the can of bubbling bacon grease. It
explodes, sending a plume of flame fifteen feet into the air, as
we leap away and howl.

In November, only one group is allowed to start a trip down
the Colorado each day, compared to five or six in midsummer.
We have the glorious feeling of having the entire Canyon to
ourselves. And while our coolers and bar are extravagantly
stocked, we've made a point to leave behind most of modern
society's distractions. We don't bring a boom box—our music
is homegrown—and cell towers are beyond our reach. One
concession is a satellite phone in case of emergency.

Powell's party had its share of technical equipment too,
most notably barometers for measuring altitude. Early in his
exploration, before reaching the Grand Canyon, Powell's boat
No Name was dashed to pieces, its hull caught in a turbulent
rapid. The crew survived, but Powell's treasured barometers
were in the stranded *No Name*. The captain sent two men
into the river to rescue his instruments. "The boys set up a
shout, and I join them," Powell wrote, "pleased that they
should be as glad as myself to save the instruments." When
the men returned, he saw they also salvaged a three gallon
keg of whiskey. "The last is what they were shouting about,"
Powell noted dryly.

Drink is what we shout about when we reach camp the
next afternoon. As the sun disappears it gets cool, so we attach a propane tank to a camp stove and make some hot but-
tered rum. Over a dinner of pesto pasta with spicy sausage,
I consider how decadent our trip is compared to Powell's
expedition, whose members ate the same drab food every day
and often huddled under cold, wet blankets. Until they lost
blankets after one of their boats capsized, leaving some men
shivering in the frigid night with nothing more than a canvas
tarp to cover them.

We flick a Bic and have a cook fire, our waterproof sacks keep our compressible zero-degree sleeping bags dry, and our inflatable boats can navigate even the Canyon's most ominous rapids, sparing us the torture of carrying boats over crumbly canyon walls around the biggest drops, as Powell's party did.

Yet we share Powell's appreciation of the Canyon. We see the "cathedral-shaped" buttes, towering monuments, and "grandly arched" half-mile-high walls reflected in calm stretches of the river, and the polished ochre spires that tower above it all. Our spirits soar as we float through Marble Canyon, with its pink and purple hues and "saffron" tints.

At a bend in the river, we find a deep oval opening scoured into the rock by millions of years of the river surging into it. Powell estimated that if it were a theater it could seat 50,000 people. Now called Redwall Cavern, it's a perfect spot for an impromptu game of soccer, and we exhaust ourselves chasing a ball over the sandy beach. A Frisbee gets pulled out and flung towards the water. We dive off the boats attempting to catch it, plunging into the chilly eddy like eager dogs.

Just downstream we pull over to explore a delicate waterfall spraying from peach-colored rocks. Lush green vegetation surrounds the cascade; the sunshine lights up the misty veil with all the colors of the rainbow. Powell named this place Vasey's Paradise for a botantist who had previously traveled with him through the Southwest. Downriver we hike into Nautiloid Canyon—I expect to see fossils of chambered nautiluses preserved in stone but we find evidence of yard-long creatures with tail fins for propulsion that I learn were ancestors of squid.

Every day my sense of wonder grows. I appreciate the perfect balance of water, desert, cliff and sky, and find myself agreeing with desert gnostic Edward Abbey who wrote: "There is no shortage of water in the desert but exactly the right amount, a perfect ratio of water to rock, of water to sand, insuring that wide, free, open, generous spacing among

plants and animals, homes and towns and cities, which makes
the arid west so different from any other part of the nation.
There is no lack of water here, unless you try to establish a
city were no city should be."

We take a day off from paddling and spend a layover day
at Nankoweap, the first place we'll camp for two nights. High
above us native peoples built granaries to store their grain. I
hike a few hundred feet above the river to explore what appear to be windows in the Canyon walls. I sit alone among
the ancient spirits and feel gratitude for this trip, the bounty
in my life, and the now famous vista of the Canyon as it bends
to the right and the river disappears from view.

With limited rations, "an unknown distance yet to run"
and "an unknown river yet to explore" the mood of Powell's
party turned serious at the Little Colorado. For us, the Little
Colorado is another gorgeous canyon feature to explore. The
sky-blue river is brightened by chalky mineral deposits which
have ever so slowly created tiny (a foot or two high) travertine
falls, little steps in the river over which the shiny water fans.
I sit mesmerized by the sounds of dozens of these falls and
their gentle music accompanied by the song of canyon wrens
overhead.

Back on the water, upstream gales hit us full force. The
strength we've built during a week of rowing helps, but still
we make only 1 mile per hour, compared to our average speed
of 4 or 5 mph. At camp we play bocce among the stones,
thickets and sand, the terrain adding new elements to the
old Italian game. That night we make s'mores from graham
crackers, chocolate bars and toasted marshmallows. River
guides say most accidents happen on land and that night is the
closest I've come so far to injury. As Jason, who is Kristen's
boyfriend and so pretty I call him "Boy Band," tells a story,
he excitedly gestures and a flaming marshmallow vaults off
his stick and leaps across the fire, landing on my leg. But the
burn is mild and easily remedied with cool water.

As we break camp on a rainy cool morning, I put on my Neoprene hood for the first time—it's a wetsuit for the head and makes me look like a dorky aviator from the 1930s. I can't picture Powell or his rugged men in one of these, but I'll gladly put vanity aside and don the hood, my fleece top, nylon splash jacket and Neoprene booties to stay warm.

After ten days I feel in tune with the cadences of the canyon, but our isolation is interrupted by a stop at Phantom Ranch near the bottom of the Bright Angel Trail. This is a popular lodge and campsite for those hiking deep into the Canyon, and it's where we bid farewell to three members of our party, who hike out to return to commitments above the rim.

Though I'm tempted to eschew Phantom Ranch's conveniences, I go to its pay phone for two reasons: to tell my girlfriend and mother that I'm having the time of my life, and because it's my birthday and I want to hear the voices of my loved ones. It feels strange to touch a credit card and money. When an operator asks for my zip code to authorize the card, I can barely remember it. I reach my mother and she recounts the story she tells me every year: how at my first Thanksgiving, when I was a week old, I was placed on the table as the centerpiece and the turkey was bigger than me.

On the way back to the boats I catch the eye of a mule deer, a young buck who lets me get within a few feet of him. The deer doesn't seem to fear people, perhaps because in this park deer can't be hunted. I meet a couple of tourists from South Korea, who are astounded that we're in the midst of a twenty-four-day voyage. The young woman touches my shoulder in farewell; it seems that a part of them wants to connect to our journey. We refill our big plastic water jugs and get back on the river.

There is a descent of perhaps seventy-five or eighty feet in a third of a mile, and the rushing waters break into great

*waves on the rocks and lash themselves into a mad, white
foam. We step into our boats, push off, and away we go,
first on smooth but swift water, then we strike a glassy
wave and ride to its top, down again into the trough, up
again on a high wave, and down and up on waves higher
and still higher until we strike one just as it curls back,
and a breaker rolls over our little boat. Still on we speed…
until the little boat is caught in a whirlpool and spun
around several times.*

The Colorado welcomes us back with some of the most technical and scary rapids on the river. Most rivers have a rating
scale of Class I (flat water) to Class VI (virtually unrunnable),
but the Colorado is graded from one to ten. Today we have
several Class 10 rapids, the first being Horn, a mess of towering waves, rocks, chutes, and holes. While Owen scouts, I put
on my dry top with rubber neck and wrist gaskets to keep the
water out. In the rapid we get knocked sideways, then slide
backwards for a minute before Owen pulls the boat away
from a gaping hole and into the calm water below.

Next is Granite. We spend more than half an hour scout-
ing, searching for a route through it. As arduous as carrying
the boats around the rapids would be, gazing at Granite almost makes me consider portaging. But that's not an option.
Steve, only twenty-four years old, has volunteered to be lead
boat. A true outdoorsman, Steve has been nonchalant leading
us through all the rapids during the past few days.

But Granite is different from what we've seen so far: it
has more hazards than we can count. The only possible run
is a thread-the-needle along the right wall: if you get too far
left an angry set of waves will probably flip you, too far right
and you'll be slammed into the north wall. Steve's eyes blaze
with fierce determination as he enters the river. He eludes the
biggest waves, pulls back hard on the oars to stay off the wall
and he's through. Up close, as we run it, Granite is faster and

harder to read than from the river bank, and we get bounced around near the bottom, but with some strong, well-timed tugs on the oars, Owen pulls us to safety.

Hermit has a twenty-foot curling haystack wave in the center, is even bigger that Granite. But it's a straight shot down the center. Just hit it hard and enjoy the ride. The wave is higher than our boat is long, but we keep the boat straight and have a clean roller-coaster run. We float to camp to the celebratory sounds of cheers and beers being popped. My birthday celebration has begun.

On a sandy beach that evening I'm offered the camp throne, a reclining nylon chaise longue. My other chair, battered by the river, is missing an arm—we name it the John Wesley Powell because he'd lost his arm before his Canyon journey. I dig out the bottle of Herradura tequila I've brought for this night, passing it around the campfire circle for all to swig. The group presents me with a blueberry muffin cake baked in a Dutch oven, a large, covered cast-iron pot that's set on coals for baking.

When I first considered a twenty-four-day Canyon trip, it seemed like a long time. At the halfway point, I feel time slipping away. There's so much to see every day in the side canyons: the fern-shrouded waterfall at Elves Chasm where Kristen and others leap naked into the pool below, Blacktail Canyon with its magical concert-hall acoustics, and Deer Creek Falls, a thundering 100-foot-high cascade next to the river. I'm in no hurry to return home, but I am ready for some rest.

We take a layover day at Galloway Camp where we enjoy a warm solar shower (the water heated in a dark bag attached to a hose and shower head). A drove of about eight bighorn sheep stroll right through camp, scampering up an impossibly steep hillside as we approach. We wash our clothes in buckets of river water and drape them over the spindly desert trees.

I sink deeper into the Canyon's natural rhythms. I put away my watch and tell time by the progression of Pleiades,

the Big Dipper and Orion across the night sky. We've become
a resourceful group—we fix broken chairs with extra straps,
we patch boats if they spring a leak, and erect shelters with
tarps and oars when it rains. I appreciate this sense of self-
containment and the group's confidence that we have the
ability to handle almost anything that comes our way.

As we travel deeper into the crucible, past rock walls more
than a billion years old, the Canyon gets steeper and narrower.
Our sense of isolation intensifies. "It seems a long way up to
the world of sunshine and open sky," Powell wrote. And it
is: in the heart of the Canyon the walls are 6,000 feet—more
than a mile—high. The sun shines through the sharp, narrow
slot for an hour or less each day this time of year; we warm up
when the river bends to the south and catches the late autumn
sun in the southern sky.

By late August of 1869, Powell's crew had traveled for three
months since beginning their journey at Green River City. By
the time they reached the deepest part of the Grand Canyon,
Powell wrote, their canvas tent was "useless," their rubber
ponchos lost, "more than half the party are without hats, not
one of us has an entire suit of clothes, and we have not a blanket apiece." When the rain pours down, "we sit up all night
on the rocks shivering, and are more exhausted by the night's
discomfort than the day's toil."

At Ledges Camp we sleep comfortably atop Thermarest
pads on shelves of shiny black gneiss. I fall asleep to a column of stars visible through the Canyon's slot, the occasional
meteor shining brilliantly for a flash before being consumed
by Earth's atmosphere. I dream of a tiger in a cage, so lonely
it's going crazy. It needs to roam. Then I dream of traveling
across the U.S. entirely by water with my brother. Perhaps the
inescapable Canyon is taking an emotional toll after all.

"Are we running Lava tomorrow?" Nathan, a wiry and
strong former collegiate soccer player, shouts to our campfire
circle. "Because if we are," he announces as he puts down his

beer, "I need to stop drinking right now!" A few miles down-stream, Lava is the most intimidating rapid on the river, with a precipitous fifteen-foot drop that tumbles into a recirculat-ing ledge hole and ferocious lateral waves that seem to upend boats for kicks.

The mood the next morning is serious, quiet. We tighten lines on the boats so if we flip we won't lose our gear. Without a word we start stretching, we want to be limber, ready, in case we swim in the frothy madness. As we row downriver, the steep red walls widen slightly. Layers of basalt give way to black volcanic rock, the river's descent gets steeper. The water picks up speed. We hear the rapids' roar before we see Lava and pull over at the scout point just as two boats from the trip ahead of us are about to run the gauntlet.

At this water level the forgiving left chute is too shallow to run. The center hole must be avoided at all costs. So we'll run right. The first of the other trip's two rafts, a solo boater on a catamaran, drops in. The boat is buried by a crashing wave; when it emerges, its pilot is gone, swept out by the rushing waters. The next boat gets slapped sideways by the first couple of grinding curlers, by the third its downstream side starts to rise and we watch helplessly as the boat flips, dumping everyone on board into the hammering current. We exhale when we see everyone flush out safely below.

At each of the life-threatening rapids we've run, Owen has rallied us by sounding his kazoo-like horn, a sort of Cavalry rallying cry. Each boat captain taps the top of his or her head, river sign language for "O.K." and "Ready." Owen blows on the kazoo but there's no sound—it's waterlogged—an omi-nous sign. He blows the water out and tries again—nothing. Then he shakes it out; the third attempt yields a warbled call, enough sound to give us superstitious guides inspiration for the run ahead.

Our map-guide says running through Lava takes twenty seconds. But we all know how long twenty seconds can be if things don't go well. And if they don't, it will take much more than twenty seconds to pick up the pieces and put everything back together again.

Steve, in our lead boat, drops in—we can't see his run from above—but Boy Band stands atop his boat and shouts: "one boat through!" Nathan follows and gets slapped around—he looks a bit sideways and one side of his boat starts to rise, but then it comes down and he's through. Kristen and Neil roll into it; we drop in just after them. It's hard to see exactly where we planned to enter—the frothy green and white maelstrom makes it almost impossible to chart a course.

But Owen is on target and hits the first wave hard and straight, just like you're supposed to. We break through the first hurdle, hit the V of the second wave right where we want to and punch through. Several fifteen-foot curlers break over our boat then we hit a wall of whitewater. The *Black Pearl* seems to stop, suspended above the mighty Colorado in slow motion. Then the river grabs us and drags us through the final drops. We're through the worst of Lava Falls. From here it's a roller-coaster of waves to the bottom of the rapid. We pull over at Tequila Beach, named for post-Lava celebrations, break out the Sauza and Hornitos, and pass the bottles around. The group that had the flip and swimmers is there too. We compare notes, borrow their hula hoops and whirl as ecstatically as dervishes.

We've made it through the big rapids; all we need to do now is find a beach to sleep on. Kristen pulls us over about a mile below Lava, but the beach is tiny and covered with prickly shrubs. The group revokes her status as trip leader for the rest of the day. Owen, the only sober one among us, is given command. He locates a fine camp, and we play bocce on a spit of beach so close to the river that we sink up to our ankles in the watery sand.

Powell's journal suggests his party portaged the boats around Lava Falls and had a clear sense that they were near the end of the journey. They too celebrated after Lava, stumbling upon an Indian garden with ripe green squashes. Powell excuses his "robbery" by "pleading our great want." After so many meager meals, the captain is exultant: "What a kettle of squash sauce we make! True, we have no salt with which to season it, but it makes a fine addition to our unleavened bread and coffee." Powell estimates his team covered thirty-five river miles that day. "A few days like this," he writes, "and we are out of our prison."

Canyon veterans warn that trips can fall apart during the final few days. Once Lava has been run, the theory goes, all the pent-up and buried resentments surface, and group cohesion suffers. But we're a companionable, easygoing group. We know we won't fall prey to petty disputes.

After a festive spaghetti dinner we gather round the campfire to chart the rest of the trip. Because we're a bit behind schedule and have a set take-out date, Kristen suggests floating over the flatwater at night. Steve is dead set against a night float, his emotions amplified by alcohol. He conjures visions of bodies in sleeping bags rolling off the boats, never to be seen again. "I'd rather run Lava ten times than do a night float," he exclaims. Kristen gives him a look that says "Whatever," and suggests we talk about it in the morning.

With the return of daylight and sobriety, all is forgiven. At Granite Park Canyon (Mile 209) we find an expansive beach, set up a badminton net and prepare our Thanksgiving feast. A solo boater floats by. His name is Jake and he's hungry for company, so we invite him to join us. We put the turkey in a metal drum and cover it with charcoal. Hours later it's burnt to a crisp, but we scrape off the black crust and savor the feast of tender poultry, mashed potatoes, warm stuffing and unheated green beans—we didn't have any more pots—straight from the can. For dessert we tuck into Martha's home-baked apple and pumpkin pies, perfectly fresh after three weeks on ice, and toast one another with wine and beer.

Thirty miles downstream, a wide side-canyon opens to the north, seeming to offer a way out of the Grand Canyon. At this juncture, O.G. Howland asked Powell to abandon the river and end the journey. Howland said that he, his brother Seneca, and William Dunn were determined to leave. Powell took out his sextant and found the party was about forty-five miles from the mouth of the Rio Virgen, their destination, the end of the Colorado's course through the Grand Canyon.

"All night long I pace up and down a little path," Powell wrote. "Is it wise to go on?" he wondered. "At one time I almost conclude to leave the river. But for years I have been contemplating this trip. To leave the exploration unfinished . . . is more than I am willing to acknowledge, and I determine to go on."

In the morning Powell asked Howland, Howland, and Dunn if they still wanted to leave. The elder Howland said they did. Powell sadly accepted their decision and left them his boat, the *Emma Dean*, in case they reconsidered and wanted to meet the party downstream. The men were never seen again. They may have died at the hands of Indians or Mormons; they could have perished from lack of food or water; no one knows.

This place, at Mile 239, is named Separation Canyon, and we hike up to see a plaque in memory of the three lost explorers. We make camp here with deepening awareness that our journey is nearing its end. From Separation to the take out, the water is virtually flat, save for one nasty rapid caused by human intrusion into the river. It sounds strange to say it, but the river has been drowned, submerged by Lake Mead. The rapids are gone, buried by the tepid backwash from Hoover Dam downstream. The water here is stagnant and fetid. "Bathtub rings" from the rise and fall of the reservoir blanch

the Canyon's walls. Helicopters with sightseers from Vegas
buzz overhead; motorboats storm upstream past our rafts,
their passengers pointing cameras at us and gaping.

Just two days after leaving Separation's beach, Powell's party
triumphantly concluded their journey. They had navigated
and documented the entire run of the Colorado River through
the Grand Canyon, and Powell could not contain his glee:

> *How beautiful the sky, how bright the sunshine, what
> "floods of delirious music" pour from the throats of birds,
> how sweet the fragrance of earth and tree and blossom....
> Now the danger is over, now the toil has ceased, now the
> gloom has disappeared, now the firmament is bounded
> only by the horizon, and what a vast expanse of constel-
> lations can be seen! The river rolls by us in silent majesty;
> the quiet of the camp is sweet; our joy is almost ecstasy.*

As we paddle against the wind on Lake Mead, the Canyon
widens. It's more open here, and I feel we've been released
from its magnetic grip. By late afternoon, the incessant hum
of the planes and motorboats ceases, and vestiges of the
Canyon's magic reappear. Lynsey plays her flute, the sweet
music conjuring native visions. At night a gibbous moon rises
over our Hypalon boats, which make soothing whale-like
sounds as they rub against one another. As tired and eager
for comfort as I am, I savor this final night in the Canyon,
caressed by the muted lullaby of the rippling river.

❧ ❧ ❧

Michael Shapiro is the author of A Sense of Place: Great Travel
Writers Talk About Their Craft, Lives, and Inspiration, *and
wrote the text for the pictorial book* Guatemala: A Journey
Through the Land of the Maya. *His article on Jan Morris's*

Wales was a cover story for National Geographic Traveler *and won the prestigious Bedford Pace award. He also writes for such publications as* Islands, Hemispheres, American Way, Mariner, The Sun, The Washington Post, The New York Times, *and* San Francisco Chronicle. *He works as a freelance editor and has helped his clients get published in* The New York Times, Los Angeles Times, *and* Huffington Post.

Shapiro volunteers as a guide for Environmental Traveling Companions, an outfitter that takes disabled people on whitewater rafting and sea kayak adventures. He lives with his wife and cat in Sonoma County, California, and can be reached through www. michaelshapiro.net or by email at shapiro@sonic.net.

❧ ❧ ❧

It's the Sauce

In life you never know where the spice
is going to come from.

THE SMALL RESTAURANT ON THE ISLAND IN LAKE PETÉN
was so dark I thought it was empty. As my eyes adjusted,
I saw the Drafter, the only diner, sketching on lined paper with
a pencil bearing chew marks, beneath the unblinking stare of
an antlered deer's head. The waitress, a young, dark-haired
woman wearing a light cotton dress, stood at his table holding
a menu glued to a tablet of wood. The Drafter did not look up.
He gently waved away the plank, all the time shading something on the paper with the side of the graphite point.

"Armadillo," he said.

"*Si, señor,*" said the young woman.

She turned to me and indicated a place a couple of tables
away. I sat beneath another antlered head. She approached
with the oversized menu.

Behind her in the dimness, high on the opposite wall, I
saw a jaguar's face taking shape. His body sliced away, the

head and broad neck came out of the wood paneling like a creature emerging from dark foliage. He roared silently, tongue rich pink, amber eyes open forever. Waiting next to my table, the waitress seemed small and waif-like among the jungle animals.

"Uh, give me a moment," I said, taking the plank off her hands. "*Por favor.*"

"Take all the time you need," she said.

The great Mesoamerican rainforest once called Gran Petén has never been known as a gourmet's paradise. On the other hand, the continuous tropical land that spreads across parts of three countries was a gastronomical democracy. Whatever might be plucked from trees or picked from the jungle floor, or brought down with gun or bow, is what landed on all plates from southern Mexico's Chiapas across Guatemala's northern Petén region to Belize. Beans and rice might accompany the deer, rodent, nuts, or bird, but roughly the same meals appeared on the laps of indigenous Maya, and after the sixteenth century, the plates of conquering Europeans. By the 1990s, things had not changed much.

"*Tepesquintle*," I said when the waitress returned.

From the corner of my eye I saw the blond Drafter lift his head and regard me. He seemed to be in his mid-thirties, younger than I, but not too young. I figured he knew I had been staring at him, so I did not return his full-on look. He flipped a page of his notebook and began to draw anew.

The waitress served our meals. Mine looked like pot roast in thick, red-brown sauce, but the light was so poor anything might have looked like stew. *Tepesquintle* is a forty-pound rat that roams the jungle at night. I knew it was edible. Old books about Petén wrote of the animal as the occasional food of *chicleros*, men who tapped jungle trees for chewable sap, boiled it into blocks and sent it by plane to the Wrigley gum factory in Chicago.

I pushed the food around on the plate, cut a small piece. It didn't taste like chicken. It wasn't gamey or beefy. It tasted like nothing I had ever experienced, rich without being heavy, meaty but light. The aroma was delicious, herbaceous. Finishing, I told the waitress to give my compliments to the cook, and asked for the sauce recipe. She hesitated as if she didn't understand, but my Spanish is pretty good. She walked toward the kitchen.

"You're absolutely right," said the Drafter from his table.

"I beg your pardon?"

"It's the sauce," he said.

(Of course, I did not know his name then. Later, when he told me it was Edwin, I told him I'd rather call him the Drafter, which to me fit him better. "Yes, it calls up 'Drifter,'" he said. "It calls up 'Daft,'" I said.)

The lithe waitress returned, followed by a portly woman in a grease-spotted apron. Wisps of salt and pepper hair bristled out from her blue headscarf. The cook, for that's clearly who she was, placed her hands on wide hips and recited the ingredients for the sauce. Like the most competitive international chefs, she wouldn't, or couldn't, give their precise measures.

"Write it down," said the Drafter.

"What?"

"Write it down."

I took out my notebook and asked the cook to repeat. I thought she might be annoyed, but instead she seemed proud that what she said was being registered, taken down in words. I wondered whether, like many women in these parts, she had never learned to read and write. This time she gave the recipe a title.

Tepesquintle Rodent Sauce

Thyme, laurel, cumin, black pepper, garlic, green or red pepper, tomato, onion, V-8 juice, white wine, cinnamon, honey, consommé, Saborin (like Accent).

She looked over at the Drafter, who was listening intently. Turning to me again, she winked and whispered, "For armadillo, replace the wine with vinegar."

When I left the restaurant, heading for my hotel, the Drafter followed, catching up and speaking as if he were continuing the thread of a conversation we had begun somewhere, but I had forgotten. "They can be farmed, you know," he said. "Those raised domestically are indistinguishable to the palate from those in the wild, when prepared in the same sauce."

He went on about seasoning and spits, chattering in a vaguely public school accent embedded in origins I could not exactly pinpoint. India? The Caribbean? His light skin argued against them, but he didn't seem British either. I negotiated puddles on the road. I felt confused. My face must have been saying, "What in bloody hell are you talking about? Why are you even talking? Who are you?"

Rounding a corner, he saw my expression, and stopped. At first, his look said the problem was mine, then slowly, his deep brown eyes lost their sparkle. "The *tepesquintle*," he said. "I thought you'd be interested."

That's when I made my mistake. Or set the course for one of the most memorable weeks of my life. We faced each other on the walkway that runs a ring around the island, which is only a mile across. Modest old houses with pastel color walls were turning luminous in late sun. Waves lapped softly against the *malecon*.

"Look, let's have a coffee, shall we?" I said, feeling apologetic about my snooty attitude.

Travelers tend to skip the thousand small steps that begin the journey of social communication, because they already share the road. In Petén, they know they also share interest in, or a need for, a place off the tourist path; the rainforest ruins of fallen civilizations; an atmosphere on the edge of isolation. When travelers meet in Petén they already know a lot about each other, before either says a word.

"I haven't seen Ceibal or Altar de Sacrificios," I said, "but I want to go because it means traveling the river that runs past them, the one with the wonderful name, Passion, *Rio Pasión*."

We sat on a pier drinking tea laced with the local rum called *Zacapa*, not the cheap stuff but the aged honey-colored kind, in the bottle encased with woven sisal. The toddy was his idea. I told the Drafter I had been coming to Petén annually for five years, enamored of Maya ruins since I first saw the grand site of Tikal. Stepped temple pyramids rising into hot, blue sky. Carvings of sacred animals, and of lords dressed in fine feathers and jaguar hides. Glyphs, dots, and short lines that once spoke to men and women in a language only now being decoded. And jungle, threatening at any moment to hide again the fallen rainforest cities.

"After two weeks I go back to the office feeling like I've really *been* somewhere, you know?"

"Right," he said, staring straight across the water into the setting sun. It burned orange-red in color, like the circular bands on ancient Maya pots. Only when a boat approached did the Drafter drop his eyes to the lake.

The skipper tied the bow to a piling and jumped from deck to dock. He walked past us toward shore with a friendly *Buenas tardes*. Empty, the wooden craft left behind rocked slowly in the water, red hull with chipped paint, a faded look to its striped canopy that sheltered passengers during the day.

"I've walked to El Mirador, three days from the nearest settlement," said the Drafter. He was the first I'd met who had been there, the largest ancient Maya city yet discovered, far to the north against the border with Mexico's Yucatan.

"Wow, and three days back," I said.

"Not if you are continuing on to Mexico," he said.

Before I could respond another boat pulled close, but its skipper merely called out, "San Jose? Lake tour?"

"No," said the Drafter, which suited me fine.

By the next day we were traveling companions. We discovered we both liked going to Tikal, about fifty miles north of the lake, even though we each had seen it before. He knew things, and I knew things. For instance, I knew how we could travel at one tenth the cost of the Tikal tourist shuttle. Just cross the causeway on foot from the island to the mainland, and grab the twice-daily local bus that runs to the village of Uaxactun, where the gum tree tappers and *xate* gatherers live. Before the bus heads into deeper rainforest on a dirt road, get off at Tikal, and, *voilà*.

Once at Tikal, the Drafter knew how to avoid the ticket kiosk, where a hefty entrance fee was levied on foreigners. The bus stopped on the old runway, unused for thirty years since archaeologists decided the rumble of propellers was destabilizing the thousand-year-old temples. We left behind the bustle of visitors arriving by vans and private cars. The Drafter led me around a pond with a sign warning *Beware of the Crocodile*, up a narrow path through giant *matapalo* trees, past a corrugated metal house where the resident sha- man lived, and beyond, through a palmy grove once home to a family of indigenous Maya Lacandon. Emerging from the steamy forest, we saw the Temple of the Great Jaguar before us, rising into the sky. We were in.

By the end of the day I felt rather bad about not having paid an entrance fee, reckoning the money went to a good cause—keeping up the lawns, fixing stairs on lofty temples so ascending visitors depended less on grabbing tree roots for balance. When the Drafter wasn't looking, I slipped the amount of the ticket into a donation box near the park's exit. No use telling him, I thought; we were, after all, almost per- fectly compatible for strangers who met on the road.

On the return bus, we watched another foreigner—French, I think—plunging one tortilla after another into his mouth, smearing each first with a dark substance from a small jar.

"I hate it when travelers make an exhibition," I whispered. "I take it personally."

"It's the sauce," said the Drafter.

The young man wore a shirt made from a *huipil*, embroi- dered in a dozen colors and typically Guatemalan-looking, but, please! *Huipiles* are women's clothing. His jeans were fashionably ragged with holes at the knees. Even the poorest peasant farmer dons his single decent pair of pants to travel.

"He can't help it," said the Drafter. "Nutella."

That's the way the Drafter was, as perspicacious and forgiving as I could be critical. In the next days, waiting for meals, for buses, for sleep to come, he drew, and I read. We didn't talk about where we came from, or how we earned our livings, not from lack of curiosity, at least not on my part, but because such details would have pushed the conversation to a different plane. We were quite satisfied, I suppose, with the air we breathed.

Anyway, it was clear enough we had grown up in different places. He never put his knife down when he ate. Discussing the classic Maya Ball Game, where players re-fought the transcendent battle of the Hero Twins of the *Popol Vuh* against the Lords of the Underworld, his metaphors came from soccer, mine from football. At night he placed his shoes—they were leather, not canvas boots like mine—outside the room wherever we stayed, as if he expected to awake to them clean and buffed. It never happened. He blew dust from the shoes in the morning, although the pale powder of Petén paths covered them again once we were outside.

We departed by a local bus from the area of Lake Petén, heading for southern Petén, a remoter region with less rainforest, where fewer tourists ventured. We would see the Passion River, but we were unlikely to find surprisingly good restaurants like the one on the island that had served the delicious *tepesquintle*.

"From here on any meat is road-kill," said the Drafter. "'*Road-kill*,' right?"

"Very good, very colloquial U.S.A.," I said, and watched him smile.

That night, the evening of the fourth day, I caught myself looking at the Drafter in a certain way, as he bent over pencil and paper in a crummy cantina in Sayaxche, a town on the Passion River. We were waiting for our food.

I looked at his blond hair falling over his forehead, in the low-watt light of a bare bulb hanging from the thatched ceiling, and I wished him to raise his face. I wished him to give me that smile again, the one I had seen on the bus in the morning.

I stared at his hands. I couldn't help it. Their daytime pale-ness was gone, replaced by an olive cast that seemed to take over in dim light, a tone so warm to the eye and attracting I lifted my fingers from the table, but stopped. If I touched him, the pencil would slip, and I could ruin the picture.

The waiter delivered two plates of the daily special. I was glad to hear it contained no meat. Just squash flowers on melted cheese.

"It's the sauce that makes this one rich," said the Drafter. The special gravy was neither thick nor thin, slightly lumpy, black as tar. Liquified corn fungus. Tasty.

When the table was cleared, the Drafter took a few draw-ings from his bag and spread them before me. They were impressively detailed, but carried something other-worldly, too, as if my friend saw not just shape and line, but the pos-sibilities of his subjects, their other selves. An antlered head looked alive even missing its body, not hung on a wall but suspended in mist, not trophy but forest lord. A canopied boat, unmanned, self-contained, floating as if at will. A candle and mosquito coil like those we placed on the cement floors of rooms where we stayed, the smoke of each join-ing the other in the air to create a vision serpent with open jaws.

Before dinner, I supposed, he had made the drawing of the vintage juke box standing near the bar, all chrome strips and rounded shoulders, with colored lights (you knew they were colored, even rendered in black and white). You could almost see those lights flashing on the bass tones, almost hear the

ranchero songs. And the old *corridos,* given we were so close
to Mexico.

On the last day I would see him—had I known it was the
last I would not have enjoyed myself so much—we drove
toward Laguna del Tigre, another lake, near the border with
Mexico. We rented the car in my name because the Drafter
didn't drive.

By this time I knew his German father had died in a flying accident in the Guatemala mountains, and his mother
was half-Kekchi, one of two dozen Maya indigenous groups
whose roots reach back more than a thousand years. "That's
why I don't like to pay to enter the sacred sites," he said,
meaning, I supposed, Tikal. "They should not belong to the
government, but to the Maya."

It was the closest to a political statement I ever heard
him make. I knew "German" in the mountains could mean
someone who was not German at all, but light-skinned
Guatemalans whose families had lived in the country for
more than a century, since the government invited Europeans
to plant coffee on Kekchi land. The invitation had been an
official effort to enter world markets, which worked, and
to "purify" the race at home, which didn't. In his case, the
Drafter said, English came from British tutors in Belize next
door, and two years studying art in America.

"I'm Guatemalan enough so they won't give me another
visa," he said. "I don't own a house or a business, and we
don't have bank accounts." No collateral to ensure he would
return. I guess the Drafter could not say to the consul at the
U.S. Embassy, *Of course I won't stay there forever. My mother
lives here.*

I liked the idea of knowing he would be in the country
when I visited, year after year. I didn't think to ask how he
received permission to live in the United States when he had.
Didn't cross my mind.

What was important was seeing a world foreign to me,
alongside him. We watched porters offloading boats on the

beach in Sayaxche, stripped to the waist, carrying covered baskets, square tin boxes, squealing pigs. A girl dressed in white, seated on the back of a motorcycle, miraculously un- sullied by splattering mud, like old Maya royalty whose feet never touched the ground.

About midday, on the way to Laguna del Tigre, Lake of the Jaguar, some time before we crossed the San Pedro River, I stopped the car in front of a house with a painted sign, *Comida,* the rural promise of cooked food. In the door- way stood a Kekchi woman, recognizable by her full cotton blouse, loose and lacy where most indigenous women wore heavily woven *huipiles* tucked tightly into wide cumberbunds. Many Kekchi Maya migrated to Petén when they lost land in the Verapaz highlands, the Drafter's home. The woman served us a dish I never thought I would eat: beans, rice, and spaghetti heaped together in a bowl.

"I know," I said to the Drafter. We sat at a plain table out- side the house. "It's the sauce that will make the meal."

"It's true," he said, as the woman spooned it over the food. "It makes the ordinary memorable."

Homemade tomato sauce, fresh of course, thickened with flour, tarted up with half-inch slices of hot dogs. "Not bad," I said.

We crossed the San Pedro River on a hand-cranked ferry, driving from the boat onto a badly pocked road, still on the Guatemala side of the border but not far from Mexico. Wetlands, inundated in the rainy season, now appeared as low forest and open savannah. Slim, elegant egrets walked on their stilts of legs among tall grass. The road's poor condition meant we drove slowly. In my romantic period, when I had read everything D.H. Lawrence had ever written, I vowed to myself I too would become familiar with the names of flowers and trees, as the master had. I did not, but I wished I had gone at least as far as the primitive palms, to know what to call the myriad kinds swaying now on all sides, so different one from another in heights, fronds, trunks, capacities to bend.

In an hour, when we could go no farther by road, we walked the rest of the short distance toward the lake under double canopy forest, dark and cool. Somewhere the border ran nearby, but in this wild land there were no markers or fences, no sign of other visitors. As we followed a curve, a dashing movement rustled low foliage just off the trail. We stopped. Probably it was not a jaguar—although that would have been thrilling—because the big cats are nocturnal. Perhaps a peccary, or a brocket deer.

At the lake we lay on our backs, unspeaking, but communicating, it seemed to me, our ease with the moment and place. We didn't point or cry out to each other when we saw the pair of scarlet macaws fly overhead, electric red and blue with fine yellow collars, their long tails like fiery rays in the pale sky. But I heard the Drafter take the same deep breath as I.

More birds cried softly and flapped their wings in passing, but I don't know what they were because I had shut my eyes, keeping them closed despite some curiosity. I liked more the dreamy feeling of experiencing the forest through its sounds.

I thought I heard a deep human voice calling from a few feet away. I jumped to my feet in a single move, startled. The Drafter stood too, saying, "Don't be afraid."

He waved to the caller, who waited at the forest's edge with two young indigenous men, and a woman with two children, a boy and a girl. The woman and girl wore pants. This struck me as unusual, because here females wear dresses or long skirts.

"You know that man?" I asked.

"The leader, *coyote,* guide," he said.

Figure it out, I thought. Figure out what is happening.

"I could not change all these moments, these good moments, by telling you," he said. "The road is safe. You'll be all right."

From his bag he drew out a piece of paper rolled like a tube, tied with a thick blade of grass, handing it to me as he turned to join the others. Understanding flooded my mind as fast and overwhelming as a tidal wave, and I felt helpless against it. For the next weeks this small group would traipse through Mexico and sneak across borders, aiming for destinations in America. The Drafter would walk through my country's back door, since he had been turned away from the front.

I watched him walk across twenty feet of marshy shore to join the band. I heard him speak to one of the young men in a language I did not understand. He turned and called, "Kekchi!," smiling, waving, but missing not a step, melting into the forest with the others.

I gazed for a while at where he had been, but saw only trees, huge and brooding. I felt no sense of betrayal, because there had been no promise. I did feel that something of value was disappearing, but whatever it was had never been mine, so I could not say to myself he stole it away.

Inside the car I took the grass tie from the paper tube and unrolled it. I saw myself at a table in a dark room, the head of a great deer on the wall, the figure of a woman looking more sensuous than I had ever believed myself to be. I tossed the paper in the back seat, too brusquely. I drove so fast the tires raised a cloud of dust. I ignored thin figures waving me down, hoping for a ride.

Like a survivor tossed upon shore, I felt whole, but shaken. I was not the same person who—was it only a week before?—had stepped into a dark restaurant on an island floating in a deep blue lake.

That night I returned the car and went back to the cantina in dusty Sayaxche, even though I was not hungry. I did not want to be alone, even though I talked to no one. Black flies studded a sticky yellow strip hanging above the table.

I ordered meat—why not?—picking it slowly from the bone. It tasted dry. There was no sauce.

❧ ❧ ❧

Journalist Mary Jo McConahay is the author of the travel memoir, Maya Roads, One Woman's Journey Among the People of the Rainforest. *She was a war correspondent in Central America, a reporter in Saudi Arabia, and her work appears in more than thirty journals and periodicals. She will eat anything she is served. Once.*

❧ ❧ ❧

Jimmy the Natural

Ireland is rich in many things, including the unexpected.

WHEN I WAS IN MY MID-TWENTIES I SPENT SUMMERS fly-fishing rivers and lakes for salmon and sea trout in County Donegal in the north east of Ireland. The area had wonderful, wild scenery and a spectacular Atlantic coastline. One summer, I rented a cottage high on a hillside, two miles from Killybegs, a small, busy fishing port. The cottage overlooked barren hillsides, dotted with stone ditches and sheep and the views towards the ocean were heart stopping. At the end of each day, I walked into the village of Killybegs for a pint or two of Guinness and a chat with the locals, many of them men who had spent their lives working on trawlers in the treacherous waters of the Atlantic. They told fascinating stories of heroism and tragedy but some stories got taller in the telling. Of all the people I met, two brothers, Declan and John, intrigued me the most. They shared a house on the outskirts of Killybegs and worked a small plot of land on which they had some goats and sheep. In the evenings they frequented local bars and had a pact never to be in the same bar together. According to Declan, they spent so much time "within a hand's breadth of each other during the day," it was unthinkable they should have to suffer one another's company at night when "the demon drink took hold," and besides, they were destined to "spend enough time together in eternity." In the meantime, a recipe for harmony was to patronize different bars and if possible go home alone. As a rule, after a long, drunken walk home each was too tired to argue.

Declan was the most instantly recognizable. He wore a heavily soiled, cream-colored cap, claiming it was a gift from a famous American whose name he had long forgotten. I learned a lot about Killybegs from him, but only after I bought him pints of "the black stuff." He claimed his love affair with Guinness began when he realized the color of the "head" on a pint resembled the color and texture of female breasts.

One evening, he asked if I had ever seen or met "a strange one" on my late night walks back to the cottage. I told him the only creature I had ever seen on the winding, two-mile journey was a badger that once crossed my path. Anyway, there were no street lights and it was impossible to see much beyond the beam of the torchlight I carried. It helped me walk a straight line to avoid falling into ditches on either side of the narrow lane to my cottage.

"So you've never seen The Natural?" he whispered.

Before I could ask him who The Natural was, he went off to retrieve a pint someone else had bought him. I walked outside into a cool night and strolled to the harbor to admire the fishing trawlers and enjoy the heavily scented sea air and smells of freshly gutted fish. Five minutes later, I was at the outskirts of Killybegs, walking into the dark countryside with hundreds of insects dancing in the beam of my torch. I had walked about a mile when the torch batteries died. Had it been a familiar west of Ireland night when the sky and its myriad stars were visible, I would have felt comfortable walking the rest of the way without artificial light. But this was an overcast night and I was suddenly plunged into darkness. I continued my journey at a much slower pace, hoping to stay in the center of the lane. I was confident if I did that for twenty minutes I would eventually reach the part of the lane where tarmac gave way to a stone path. At that point, I would know to veer right onto a grassy, elevated path. From there it was 150 yards to my cottage but I now kicked myself for not having the foresight to leave lights on in the cottage. My real concern was if I missed the cut I would find myself heading for cliffs overlooking the ocean.

Suddenly the eerie silence was broken by the faint sound of someone approaching from the direction of the cottage. I called out but no one answered. I began walking again and after several minutes I heard footsteps, this time coming from behind me. I swung round and the footsteps ceased. Bracing myself for an assault, I got into a fighting stance and remained like that for several minutes. Convinced the threat had passed, I walked on a step at a time, my fists still clenched. Suddenly, I was frozen still by the sound of a person or animal rushing through undergrowth. Then something brushed me gently in what seemed like a split second. I was beginning to think I was going out of my mind when all of a sudden a face appeared several feet from me. It was a grinning face lit by a torch illuminating only the nose and eyes. The face seemed to belong to a grown man but the eyes had the wondrous expression of a child. The person staring at me was slim and about 5 feet 8 inches tall. The weird apparition lasted only seconds because the torch was switched off and I heard the person running ahead of me. I waited until the sound of his footsteps was replaced by the buzz of insects and sat on the tarmac, trying to make up my mind whether it was better to retrace my steps or continue walking to the cottage. I chose the cottage because it was closer than Killybegs. I could lock the doors, close the windows and wait for the dawn. There was no phone but I was confident I could hold off an intruder until I was sober enough to drive to the local police station. I got to my feet and began walking as fast as I could only to discover I had overestimated my navigational skills. I veered slightly to my left and fell off the side of the road into a water-filled ditch. When I climbed out of it I felt like a drowned rat. The remainder of the walk to the cottage was slow and painful. When I got inside, I lost no time locking up. I then sat on a worn couch with an axe by my side and a fishing knife in my lap. Whether it was alcohol, stress, or a combination of both, I fell into a deep sleep. I was awakened at dawn by a rhythmic tapping on the kitchen window. I jumped up and the sound ceased. Ever so cautiously I crept to the window and gazed out at the nearby hillsides. To my great relief, all I could see were grazing sheep and goats but two donkeys were munching dried grass next to the cottage door so I quickly surmised the sound I had heard was probably one of them disturbing a patch of gravel.

Daylight made me feel confident so I unbolted the front door and gingerly stepped outside. It was a beautiful morning and there was no sign of anyone as far as the eye could see. I was about to walk back into the cottage when my eye was drawn to an object on the kitchen window ledge. On closer inspection, I found it was a wet, rolled up newspaper. I knocked it to the ground and three fresh mackerel rolled out of it. It was only then I noticed a small, open cardboard box on the gravel. Inside it, nestled on a bed of straw were four small, speckled chicken eggs. I spun around, expecting to see someone watching me from behind a hedge or stone ditch but there was no sign of a human presence. Nor was there a note from the donor of these gifts.

I took the food indoors and was pondering my next move when Patrick Dempsey, the farmer who had rented me the cottage, drove up in his car with a large bag of turf for my fire. I offered him a cup of tea and he readily accepted. He was a big, red-faced man with hands the size of dinner plates and thick, wavy gray hair. I liked him but always felt he was a wily character, innately suspicious of city dwellers. Any time I questioned him about the locals he shrugged his shoulders, yet he thought nothing of asking me endless questions about city life. He also had a habit of inquiring if I truly liked Donegal and who I had talked to in Killybegs on my pub trips.

As he loaded the turf into two large wicker baskets beside the fireplace, I wondered if it would be wise to mention the apparition on the road. I feared he would think I was a crazy drunk and stupid for not carrying extra batteries for my torch. He was definitely not the type of man to find himself without replacement batteries or for that matter to be walking the lane in the early hours. He locked up his house and outbuildings every evening at ten o'clock and did not venture out again until dawn to milk his cows and let the chickens out of their coop. He was a hard working, conservative farmer prepared for every eventuality.

His wife was a brusque woman at the best of times. Like her husband, she was big-boned and strong as an ox. She wore a headscarf which was often pulled down to the tops of her eyebrows and she tied her hair back with a black ribbon. Her daily ensemble was a woolen cardigan, a long skirt partly covered with an apron and rubber knee-length boots spattered with hardened mud. Her callused hands matched the deep lines in her face and testified to decades spent working outdoors with her husband. She was a fine cook and her specialty was a chicken and leek soup. The first time I visited them, the smell of her soup reached me when I came within sight of their house. After she poured me a bowl of it, I remarked how I met Declan and his brother the previous day and they were colorful characters. She fixed me with a stern look before she spoke.

"Those two fellas aren't the full deal." She tapped her temple with her left index finger. "If I was to be kind to them, I'd say they've haven't been right since their parents died and that was over twenty years ago. If that Declan fella and his crazy brother had gone to a match maker as I suggested to them years ago, two good women would've sorted them out and they wouldn't be having drunken fisticuffs in bars and be staggering out the road from Killybegs plastered in the dead of night. I don't know how many times they've missed being run over, not to mention the numbers of times they've both fallen off that wee bridge over the river near their place. There's hardly a trout in that river that doesn't know what they look like."

I refrained from laughing, because neither she nor her husband thought what she said funny. I was nevertheless intrigued by her reference to match making. I had once listened to a radio program about the role of match makers in remote parts of Ireland. Traditionally, children worked on the family farm until their parents died, by which time they were in their fifties or sixties and had a house and land and no one to share it with. It was an acute social problem and, in many instances, middle-aged men and women lacked the social skills to form relationships. Often, they turned for help to men known as match makers. The late Irish playwright, John B. Keane, a renowned matchmaker in the West of Ireland, claimed he had made hundreds of matches. If a woman in her sixties sought his help finding a partner, he asked her three basic questions. If she answered all three positively, his task of finding her a mate was made easier. First, he would ask if she was happy to marry a man "with a baldy head." Then, he would inquire if she would be content with a man with no "bars in his grate"—teeth. Last, and what he deemed the critical question, was whether she could marry a man who would not consummate their marriage. Many men were not interested in sex and just wanted companionship and a woman to cook and clean like their mothers and sisters had done.

"If a woman answers yes to my third question I have no problem finding her a match," John B. Keane would say.

The apparition on the road more than matchmaking was on my mind as I poured Patrick Dempsey a second cup of tea and thanked him for the turf. I was still reluctant to tell him about the apparition so I asked him if he knew who left the fish and eggs outside the cottage. He glanced out the window and smiled.

"Those were probably from Jimmy the Natural. I should've told you about him," he said, staring at me over the rim of his cup. "Sure it slipped my mind, didn't it? But you've no need to worry. The Natural means you no harm. If anything, I'd say he's taken a liking to you. He can be a wee bit like a child, you see, and he doesn't look at the world the way others do."

He removed a pipe and a worn leather tobacco pouch from his trouser pocket. While I waited anxiously, he methodically filled the pipe with tobacco and, using his right thumb firmly pushed the tobacco down into it until it was flattened beneath the rim. Then he held a lit match over it until it nearly burned down to his fingers. With a smile of satisfaction, he gripped the pipe between uneven teeth stained by years of stale tobacco smoke and inhaled until the tobacco glowed like a tiny volcano. Slowly removing the pipe from his mouth, he exhaled with a contented sigh.

"You mustn't worry yourself about the Natural," he added, casually placing the pipe in his mouth and pressing his teeth against its stem like it was a well-used prop. For the next ten minutes, he talked non-stop about The Natural, pausing at times to re-light the pipe until he tired of it and put it aside.

He explained that Jimmy the Natural was in his forties and lived with his elderly sister in a small stone house off the lane leading to the cliffs. Jimmy and his sister were born there and had worked all their lives helping their parents who died in 1956. Now in her sixties Jimmy's sister was like a mother to him. They had four goats, a dozen sheep and some chickens and their water supply was from a cool, crystal stream fed from the surrounding hillsides.

From an early age, Jimmy was never allowed to stray far from the cottage because everyone knew he was not like other children. Patrick pointed to the small fields and hedgerows overlooking the cottage.

"Sometimes, I would be working up there and I would hear a little yelp like a goat and realize it was little Jimmy but I would never see him. He had no words and communicated with gestures. Believe me, he's smart and knows more about the land than any of us. He's a great help to his sister and looks after their livestock. I never tell tourists about him because they wouldn't be likely to see him. On the other hand, they'd be on the lookout for him and might take pictures of him if they spotted him. Their kids might even make fun of him as kids do when they come across somebody strange. He leaves his house only at night or before dawn. In the early mornings, he likes to sit on the cliffs and lower a hand-line into the surf with feathered hooks attached to it and a big weight at the end. He lets it sink into deep water under the cliffs and jerks it up and down in a jigging motion. That way he catches lots of mackerel and Pollack and sometimes big conger eels. During the day, his sister keeps him close to home. At night, he knows never to stray from the lane. That's his boundary as it were."

Patrick paused long enough for me to describe the events of the previous night and laughed when I told him how I readied to repel intruders. Now I had his attention, I asked him how Jimmy acquired the Natural moniker. He glanced at me somewhat perplexed and nervously ran his hands through his hair. It was clearly a question he had never had to answer.

"I can't really say I know the origin of his nickname," he replied, nervously. "I think...but I wouldn't swear to it... Jimmy's parents were the ones who called him a Natural and, after a while it stuck. You see, he was strange but then maybe no stranger than some of the other folk in this part of the country. I remember my father telling me Jimmy was described as a Natural to stop other people being cruel and saying he was mad, crazy or a nutcase. Maybe Natural just seemed to be a natural thing to call him back then, if you know what I mean. Jimmy was purer than the rest of us in some way. He was innocent like the nature God created. I guess he's always been a little closer to God than the rest of us."

A week after my encounter with Jimmy, I met Declan on my way to Killybegs. He was striding along confidently, a slight swagger in his step. I stopped my car and got out to talk to him. When I told him I had met Jimmy the Natural, he nodded with reverence as though my knowing about The Natural conferred on me a particular status and responsibility. He stepped to within an inch of me, and grabbing my arm pulled me close.

"Whatever you do, don't go telling any of the rowdies in town about Jimmy. We don't want them going out the road when they're drunk to play some prank on him. He's one of ours and his secret is our secret. The Natural's what we would all like to be. Am I right?"

I nodded and he let go of my arm.

"The best way to get rid of a hangover is to walk it into the ground," he shouted as he strode off. He was on his way to sample the hair of the dog. "Keep the faith," was his parting comment as he disappeared from view.

After the initial apparition, fishing trips took me to other parts of Donegal and I got home too late to walk into town for a pint. Nevertheless, when driving I never exceeded fifteen miles per hour on the lane for fear Jimmy might suddenly appear in my headlights. He never showed up but I felt deep down he was hiding behind a stone wall or hedge watching me. Without fail, each morning I awoke to find gifts of fish, eggs and sometimes freshly baked wheaten bread wrapped in a napkin, with goat milk in a small pot covered with muslin.

On the last day of my vacation, I awoke at dawn with a deep sense of regret I was leaving a place where I was happy and at peace. I knew in twenty-four hours I would be waking up in N. Ireland where daily killings and bombings would once again cast a dark shadow over my life. I wanted to say goodbye to the Natural and his sister to thank them for their generosity but Patrick Dempsey and his wife advised against it. They said Jimmy and his sister were very private people.

After a final breakfast of small, boiled eggs and fried eel, I walked out into the fresh, crisp air. Out of habit I scanned the surrounding fields, as well as the laneway and hillsides, hoping to see The Natural but I was disappointed. To end my vacation on a happy note I decided to visit the cliffs and gaze over the ocean. When I stepped onto the lane below the cottage, Patrick Dempsey drove towards me from the direction of the sea, stopping in front of me.

"If I was a betting man, I'd say you're on your way to see a friend of ours," he said with a big smile.

I replied I was on my way to have a last look at the ocean. He reached out, took my hand and shook it warmly.

"Look here Martin, I know I told you not to call at Jimmy's but it's really up to you…. I was just being defensive. I told Jimmy's sister all about you and I'm sure she'd be happy to see you, if it was just to say a quick goodbye. Don't expect to see Jimmy. Even when I visit, he always hides like he's playing hide and seek."

He paused, revving his car engine.

"Now, away with you. You'll want to get back soon to all those fine city folk, won't you?"

He grinned impishly and drove off, waving until his car disappeared from view. Minutes later, I was making my way along a tiny, grass-covered path to Jimmy's place, marveling at high hedges heavily laden with blackberries that almost hemmed me in. Unexpectedly, the path widened and I found myself at a wooden gate to a clearing that dipped towards a dark two-storey stone house with two adjacent outbuildings. The smell of a peat fire filled the air in smoke rising from a brick chimney above a dark, slated roof. A cockerel and a dozen hens were picking through bread crumbs scattered on a grassy, gravelly patch of ground in front of the house. On a window ledge, a scrawny black cat hissed at me and arched its back. In the blink of an eye, it jumped to the ground, shunted sideways and vaulted over the bottom half of the door into the kitchen. It was at least a minute before I saw Jimmy's sister standing inside the door, the black cat clutched to her breast. Our eyes met and for a moment, I thought she was going to remain where she was. But, with a smile and a nod at me, she moved the lower section of the door aside and walked towards me, shooing away the cockerel and the hens.

She was a small, wiry woman with jet-black hair plaited at the back. Her eyes matched the color of her hair and her face was ruddy, with deep lines running from high cheekbones to her neck. Like Patrick Dempsey's wife, she wore a woolen jumper and a long skirt covered with an apron which stretched from neck to halfway below her knees and ankles. Her legs were wrapped in heavy brown stockings and she had brown boots laced high above her ankles.

"You're Martin, aren't you?" she asked, almost in a whisper, her right hand outstretched. As I shook it, the cat jumped to the ground and ran back to the house. I still had her hand in mine. Hers was long and slender but it gripped mine tightly. Black eyes were her most striking feature and they shone with warmth and sincerity. She was a little nervous and made no effort to hide it. I began to thank her but she brought her left index finger to her mouth to silence me. She then slowly retreated from the gate. As she walked back to the cottage the cat ambled towards her, his tail erect in the shape of a question mark. She picked him up and took him indoors. I gingerly turned to make my way back to the canopy of blackberry bushes when something compelled me to look back at the farmhouse one last time. An arm was slowly reaching out from behind the front door. As it extended, I saw it held a mackerel, its head pointed towards the ground. Ever so gently, the hand was moving the mackerel back and forth in a swimming motion like a child playing with a toy. Suddenly, a face appeared above the fish. It was the face from my apparition. It was a smiling Jimmy the Natural wearing a tightly-knit woolen hat. His face resembled a moon one might see on a bright night and his eyes were wide as saucers. As quickly as he appeared, he vanished. It was the last I saw The Natural.

A decade later, I met a fisherman who frequented Killybegs. I asked him if he had ever come across Declan and his brother. He told me he had known them well and they were "great craic" (great fun) but something horrible had happened to them. They were burned to death in their sleep after a night out drinking in Killybegs. Police believed the fire was caused by a discarded cigarette butt. The brothers, who never drank together died in the same bed and were buried in the same grave, he claimed.

Looking back, it is hardly surprising that Jimmy the Natural comes to mind when I think of beauty, lost innocence and the kindness of strangers. I often reflect sadly on how Patrick Dempsey and other locals felt they had to protect him from a cold, cynical world that too often shunned diversity and inner beauty. Some details of this story, including names, were altered for the reasons I have just expressed, namely I would not wish anyone going in search of The Natural.

※ ※ ※

Martin Dillon worked for the BBC in Northern Ireland for eighteen years and has won international acclaim for his nonfiction books about Ireland, including The Shankill Butchers, God and the Gun, *and* The Dirty War. *He is often called on as one of the foremost authorities on global terrorism.*

꙰ ꙰ ꙰

Flyover Country

It's too big to grasp—but that doesn't mean it's not worth trying.

Between Back East and Out West, in that obscure sweep of green you glimpse from the airplane window before you close the shade and put on your headphones, roads roll out across the fields like shiny gray ribbons. The sun rises over tiny rivers that you can drive across in a fraction of the time it would take to pronounce their names. It sets over cities you never think about dominated by mountain ranges you never knew existed. During the years I lived in Missouri and almost everyone else I knew lived between New York and Boston, I drove back and forth many times across this unappreciated expanse of America.

Usually I took the Interstates, which were their own world, divorced from whatever was going on in the unseen towns beyond them. The presence of civilization was indicated by watchful cows and by truck stops, which periodically appeared in the distance like miniature cities. I drove along-side lumbering big rigs. I was forever passing them, and they were forever appearing in front of me again. I sometimes felt like the only person in a sea of things, all kinds of things being busily carried to and fro. It was an odd vantage point, I was unused to seeing so much commerce with so few consumers.

For entertainment there were billboards: "Avoid Hell. Repent. Trust Jesus Today." "Where will you spend eternity? Jesus Christ is the answer!"

For reassurance there were Lewis and Clark Trail markers, which momentarily overruled the doubts I had about the sanity of my decision to move. I told myself that in leaving New York I was not giving up or stepping down. I imagined that I was better suited for another era, a time when West was the direction everyone in America wanted to go. Also comforting were the national forests, which reminded me that it didn't matter if I couldn't decide whether the East or the Midwest was my home; they belonged to the same country, after all, and I could claim that all of it was mine. Sometimes I was the only one driving through a national forest—not just mine, but mine alone.

Sometimes as I drove I forgot exactly where I was, which may have been because only those who lived there considered it a definable place. More than once, after an hour spent coaxing my car uphill, sure that I was crossing some grand and storied range, I looked at my map and saw that the peaks which I had just struggled to summit merited nothing more than a nameless green blob.

I spent too many nights in a dot on the map called Triadelphia, West Virginia. For a long time I thought it was Wheeling; I think *it* thought it was Wheeling. I learned it was Triadelphia because I got out the phone book in a hotel and checked. In Triadelphia hotel lobbies, surrounded by burly plaid-shirted men, I blended into the walls, so out of place I paradoxically became invisible.

When I didn't stop in Triadelphia I stopped in St. Clairsville, which was technically in Ohio but seemed to also want to be Wheeling. It appeared to have been built as a repository for cheap chain hotels. St. Clairsville was prone to intense fog, which confused the birds. They flew strangely, slow and lower than usual. Once one slammed its tiny body against my windshield. I was sure I'd killed it, but it left no mark.

At first I was surprised by the distances I had to cover. Ohio, a state I had never previously deigned to consider, was *huge*, its size all out of proportion to its importance. I learned to look out for particularly Ohio-like things: boats inexplicably stranded on the left shoulder of the highway, and barns brightly painted to commemorate the state's bicentennial. Once in Ohio on a snowy morning I saw a line of cars along the left shoulder of the road. Police cruisers, their red and blue lights eerie in the white almost-dawn, surrounded a little car, parked; an eighteen-wheeler, facing the wrong direction; a Brinks truck, lying upside down in the little grassy ditch of a median; and a second Brinks truck, waiting patiently to collect the loot.

Sometimes time zone changes were posted on signs, and sometimes they weren't. Sometimes they popped up where I wasn't expecting them. I drove across Tennessee, which looks small on a map but in reality goes on and on, and was surprised to find that I'd driven an hour in a second. I was vaguely confused for the rest of the day. The time zone changes in the middle of Kentucky too, but I never noticed it there. I once managed to drive across Kentucky and only step out of the car once, for three minutes. In those three minutes I was called "Hon" by two separate strangers.

Occasionally I would glimpse from the highway a gilded dome, of a church or a courthouse or a town hall, and think about how almost every place that had ever been built thought, at some point, that it was going to be spectacular. I thought about its inhabitants and investors, who must have dreamed of glorious futures, and bet on that one imposing structure, and eventually realized the whole thing would never pan out.

Mostly what I saw from the highways, though, was fields—soybean fields and cornfields and fields of crops I couldn't identify. In Illinois I was once stuck in traffic in a cornfield, a thing I hadn't thought possible. Also in Illinois, but not while stuck in the cornfield, I looked up and saw streaks of pink and blue, like a daytime sunset, stamped with a herringbone pattern of clouds. In the distance they stretched as far as I could see, their interlocking V's reminiscent of a pair of tweed pants. As I got closer, the pattern became larger, until, above me, there was nothing but a series of lines.

I encountered a tornado only once, in Paducah, Kentucky. I hid in a highway rest stop which was like no highway rest stop I'd ever seen, a stately historic building that became, for a few hours, a shelter for travelers from all directions. In Paducah, for the first time, I met grown men who openly proclaimed their fear of weather. In Manhattan, weather had never seemed to stop anyone, and real New Englanders laughed at blizzards. It was like learning a new culture in a foreign land, one where weather was far deadlier, and people had less to prove, than anywhere I'd lived before.

When I had time I left the highways and took the little two lane roads through towns that showed up on my map as the tiniest of black specks.

Here the billboards were often homemade: "Life is fragile—Handle with prayer." "Smile! Your Mom chose life!" That one was illustrated with a smiley face. "Got Faith?" That one had a picture of a faucet dripping wine.

These towns usually fit in one of two categories: Perfect, with a strip of narrow buildings like an unfurled red and white ribbon, or Unfortunate, with many churches, many cars in various states of disrepair, and sometimes a lonely-looking dog roaming around, in search of a human. When I

passed one of these I would ponder why towns with popula-
tions of less than two hundred always have a thrift store. Did
the clothes simply rotate through all the inhabitants until they
either fell apart or made it back to their original owners?

On the little roads, life unfolded beside me in blurred snip-
pets, and I wrote them down so I wouldn't forget them. If
writing made me drift towards the oncoming lane, it didn't
matter: there was nobody there. I'd take the notes later and
type them up, a compendium of Midwestern Things:

*An old man in a plaid shirt and a straw hat drives an ancient
tractor down the road. The cars behind him slow down, then carefully inch around.*

*A tiny bird runs across the road as fast as its miniscule legs can
carry it, so afraid of the oncoming traffic that it forgets it can fly.*

*Abandoned railroad tracks parallel to the road. Disused rail-
road bridges, narrow and rusted and gracefully curved.*

*A church in a field, just across the street from a store selling
guns and ammo.*

*A plump woman at a gas station strains to remove the large
plastic numerals displaying the price of fuel. She hoists a pole to
the top of the sign and detaches the numbers one by one, lowering
them to the pavement. Then she reaches up again and sticks on the
new numbers, and the cost of gas goes up.*

Little plumes of flame shoot up by nodding pump jacks.

*A girl on a the back of a motorcycle spreads her arms wide into
the wind, holding on with just her legs, like she half wants to fall
off, to see if she could fly.*

I saw other things and doubted that I'd seen them at all:
was that really a drive-thru convenience store?

I saw Ohio's smallest church, painted clean white, in which
one or maybe two people could fit. It stood on a patch of grass
near a rest stop in Coolville. In an empty parking lot under a
bright blue sky I said incredulously into my cell phone, "I'm
in *Coolville*."

Also in Ohio, I drove past the towns of Fly and Antiquity. In Indiana I stopped at an intersection which offered me a choice between towns named Pleasant and Patriot.

I drove along and let impatient pickup trucks pass me. I listened to traffic reports that originated in cities whose geographic relation to me I could not fathom. With the greatest of urgency, they described road conditions in places I had never heard of. I watched the local news in hotels. The weathermen spoke of viewing areas whose borders I did not recognize and pointed at truncated maps I could not comprehend.

For a long time it seemed like there was only one enormous state between New Jersey and Missouri. Rural Pennsylvania blended into rural Illinois, creating a region with a way of life all its own. Whole towns often appeared to be asleep, or hiding—on weekday mornings or afternoons, on weekends, it didn't matter. Their houses and cars were there, but they themselves were invisible. I wondered why anyone lived here, or why they stayed. Then I wondered if they had in fact left long ago, but somehow arranged for their towns to be kept exactly the same, like Midwestern Pompeiis.

Between the grass and fields and forests, these towns would pop up at intervals. There were never a lot of houses in one place, but there were so many small concentrations of houses so far apart, that I wondered how there could still be unemployment anywhere—surely everyone in the nation could be put to work as mail carriers or census takers in rural Ohio and Indiana.

When I took the smaller roads I stayed in places that felt as if history had stopped just before the steamboat was abandoned in favor of the train. They felt not merely preserved but suspended, as if in amber. In Madison, Indiana, everything was pastel-colored. It seemed every business was an ice cream parlor, or a soda fountain, or a candy store. At a bright little coffee shop, you could have your coffee black, or you could add cream, as if the modern notion of milk in coffee had not yet arrived. From Main Street the side streets led down to the river or up to the highway. The town faded at its outskirts, its pastels turned to sepia, and then it simply stopped.

The Ohio River spawned other places like this, quiet and as sweet as if they were dusted with confectioner's sugar. The river was quiet too. It had none of the mythology, the romance and tragedy, of the Mississippi and the Missouri. But it had a sort of confidence, being the pathway to those other rivers, the first leg for every East Coast dreamer's journey. It flowed lazily; in places it hardly moved at all. It tolerated the pale blue bridges built across its width and the little boats, American flags flying, tied up along its docks.

From these fragments I created lasting associations, mostly to do with time. In my mind, it was always just before dawn in Ohio: either dark and cold and scraping snow from the windshield in motel parking lots, or waiting for the summer heat to come and burn away the fog. Ohio was sleeping trucks humming at rest stops, and sleeping towns.

Indiana was mist rising from fields and flocks of black birds taking off in formation and streaking across the newly sunny sky. It was a single pick-up truck racing along an access road, for the fun of it, not because there was anywhere to go. Indiana seemed to exist perpetually in intense daybreak; how could it ever be night or noon in towns named Aurora and Rising Sun?

Illinois was afternoon, bright and encouraging, because if I was in Illinois that meant I had just set out or was about to arrive. Since I was never tired in Illinois, I was always seeing things I might have overlooked when less alert, like vintage Americana arranged in the windows of antique stores, and post offices so tiny and bright white that they seemed capable of delivering only letters handwritten with a quill pen.

West Virginia was night coming on, which made the Alleghenies mysterious. I could never orient myself properly in West Virginia, because it had extra dimensions, not just forward and back but up and down. I admired the buildings planted tenaciously on the sides of mountains, the drivers who fearlessly navigated the roller-coaster roads, the hidden rivers with names I always forgot but which converged and flowed as proudly as if they were major thoroughfares. There was something a little dangerous, too, in the inscrutable mountains and the unexpected rivers. And then there were the back roads, roads that curved and dipped and sloped and bent, that kept your hands clasped on your steering wheel and your arm muscles tightened for hours at a time.

Pennsylvania was all about the weather. The skies there were like a time-lapse film of seasons changing. For years I never washed my car, I only drove every few months across Pennsylvania, and it was washed for me. In an instant the clouds would darken and the rain would pour down until the only sound I could hear was water splashing on the roof of the car and windshield wipers vainly fighting the deluge. Then the sun would come out and the landscape would feel altered, purified, blasted clean. In the fall the leaves changed in sections. On my left out the window, spectacular reds, yellows, and greens. On my right, soft russet and butter and pale pumpkin and sea foam, shimmering in the wind. It was in Pennsylvania that I rounded a corner and saw, for the first time, purple mountains. I thought, *Now I understand.*

Over time the patchwork quilt I had once seen only from airplane windows unfolded itself for me. I came to know this flyover country, not in the intimate way of locals, but in the fond, incomplete way that only outsiders can know places.

When I look back at the photographs I took along these drives, I see that they are all of the same things: rivers, boats on rivers, little multi-colored buildings in a row. I did not need to travel to take those pictures. I could have found those scenes in Missouri or New York. I realize now that they were not pictures of any specific place, really, but of a time. What drew me was that brief interlude of history when the roads were rivers, and rivers led to frontiers unknown and unimagined. And yet there is something settled about my pictures, too, something solid and domestic about those little buildings in a row. A stranger looking through my photos might conclude that I was looking for a home. I wasn't. But I found one, in a way, in the comfort of the road, the motion of leaving and arriving, the freedom of spending all day nowhere, everywhere, in between.

⭐ ⭐ ⭐

Johnna Kaplan is a freelance writer whose work has appeared in Newsweek, *the* Christian Science Monitor, *and various online travel magazines. She travels as much as she can, motivated mostly by a love of history and a congenital inability to stay in one place for more than about a month. She blogs about her conflicted relationship with Connecticut at www.thesizeofconnecticut. blogspot.com.*

❧ ❧ ❧

Educating the Body

Lessons learned from the tropics.

MY SKIN FAILED ME THAT FIRST SUMMER IN GUYANA. I tried pasty lotions and wide-brimmed hats, long sleeves in the midday heat. Still, I turned bright red: I shone like a cherry. *Miss, like ya get burn up?* my students said, pressing a finger onto the red glow of my shoulder. *Ya must careful! Sun hot!* But there was nothing I could do. Skin peeled from the part in my hair. Light streamed through my gauzy curtains, and when I left the house it burned through my clothes. It colored my days and savaged my pores until I was red and raw, until I could no longer remember what it was to be touched without wincing.

There are no vestigial British aristocrats in Guyana, none of the prim, post-colonial garden parties you might imagine in Barbados or Jamaica. The English lost sanity in the heat, counting mosquitoes by the thousands. Eventually they gave up and sent Scottish farmers, leaving behind generations of

McCurdy's and Douglases. I was one of only a few hundred white faces in the country, and the others were ravaged like mine. Guyanese call albinos "devil-whip." Blue-eyed and freckled, their skin is tawny and thick like a scar. The Guyanese with Portuguese ancestors have wrinkles that crumple their skin, starburst lines radiating out to their bleached hair. Every evening in my mirror I saw the day's burnings. In their faces, I saw a lifetime's.

Coastal life in Guyana is a temporary concession between two powerful neighbors: to the North, the Atlantic which mingles its muddy brown into the clear Caribbean Sea miles off the coast; to the South, the "Interior"—vast jungles, savannahs, riverways, and mountains, inhabited by some of the rarest flora and fauna in the world. The land is massive, thousands of tracts of virgin rainforest stretching across to Venezuela and Suriname, down to the Brazilian border. I lived, as the majority of the population does, in a narrow band of cultivation along a one-road highway, just miles from blackwater creeks that wind down to Kaieteur, one of the most powerful single-drop waterfalls in the world. Humans have created a viable habitat here, growing rice and sugar, irrigating fields, and building roads. These tasks are backbreaking and the results require constant diligence to maintain. When abandoned, the land quickly reverts to overgrowth. Life here is a constant campaign against an encroaching jungle.

There is lore that North Americans adjust over time, that their blood thins (or is it thickens?) in the constant heat. This did not happen for me. From the night of my arrival at Timehri airport, I sported small beads of moisture across my forehead and nose. My Guyanese friends laughed at my inability to "acclimatize," and took to pointing out how often I was sweating when they were not even hot. My constitutional deficit plagued me, and I wondered how others managed to rise to the demands of tropical living. Sun and insects were the grounding factors of my life, the burns and bites a constant reminder of where I was, and the physical battle I was always losing.

The sun was at the heart of it, impassive, granting its twelve hours of sunlight to all equally. Yet its constancy made it seem a foreign sun, very different from the one that had once merely tanned my skin and warmed my face. Because Guyana is just north of the Equator, daily, throughout every month of every year, the sun is at its strongest, rising at 6:00, setting at 6:00. It often seemed to pulse with white light, and it is this sensation that I remember most, a constant rippling that emanated from this blinding yellow ball in the sky.

From the sun came the heat, which bore down separately, an unwelcome layer resting on me, as willful as another being. It felt like many small children clinging to my body: one at my hip, two on my legs, another splayed across my chest and head. At first they are manageable, benign, but they soon begin to get heavy. You can't put them down, they are clutching at you. Other times it seemed a parasite. My body was inhabited. I became a complex system for the simple act of diffusing heat.

My burns always surprised me. They seemed to appear from the inside out, a new layer of skin forcing its way to the top, then peeling off in delicate ribbons. My fingertips, as they had applied the lotion, were often visible in the outline of crimson. In a vain attempt to stem the pattern, I once sat under an awning for hours at a school event. My colleagues laughed at me at the end of the day: *Miss Katrin, like ya still get red!* Every part that wasn't covered—my face, arms, and neck—was singed. I learned later that I had been burned from the reflection of the sun off the grass.

While the sun was of constant concern, it was flying insects that taught me the most about the life and death of the body. Sunlight and heat are general conditions, but the attentions of a fly or mosquito are a personal torment. They act as one unit, one encompassing blight: one fly is all flies, one mosquito all mosquitoes. It is rare to spend a moment in Guyana when something is not flying or landing near or on you. The air I breathed was often a swarm; I swallowed more than I care to remember.

Every time a fly walks on you it is a foreshadowing of your death. Tropical flies are persistent and, after awhile, there is no energy left to brush them off. They are satisfied to just watch and circle, like buzzards, exploring every crevice of your body to determine how useful you will be to them if you die. At first it is a ticklish feeling not entirely unpleasant, but each time you have to accommodate its legs, its disregarding death-filled eyes, you lose a little bit of your body. Flies leave you with no dignity. Their work is to scavenge you, even as you live.

Mosquitoes are a constant reminder that to live is to suffer. Malaria, passed by mosquitoes and endemic in Guyana, does not usually kill you. One type of the disease, *falciparum*, will make you very sick, with skyrocketing fever and jaundice. The other, *vivax*, quietly enters your liver, forever. Mosquitoes are a kind of religion in Guyana, demanding rituals for prevention and destruction. Weeks are spent clearing standing water, where they breed, patching holes in nets, burning toxic green coils inside and enormous pyres out. Regardless, the air is thick with them for months on end.

Regions of Guyana close their schools during mosquito season. A friend recounted being chased by swarms, carrying repellent with her as an urban woman carries mace. On a boat trip across the Berbice River, I once watched as the back of my companion's white shirt was spotted with twenty, then thirty, black dots. I brushed them off; twenty more appeared. They are most active after dusk, but at times I imagined that at every moment, a mosquito was on me, near me, or—paranoid from the incessant whining high in my ear—inside me. Exiting the mosquito net in the morning, the first bite is an outrage, the second an insult, the third an annoyance, the fourth, or millionth, a bitter defeat. Eventually, my skin stopped reacting to the mosquito saliva, did not swell, hardly itched. But the humiliation of the initial prick is eternal, the insertion of the microscopic proboscis a violation, a theft of blood to perpetuate a species that is a bane. Mosquitoes steal their lives from us.

The Guyanese word for the cumulative effect of tropical indignities is "stink." Stink is curdled sweat, sweat that has turned rancid. It is every drop of a day's working, sitting, breathing sweat, from the first beads as you walk out in the morning, to the most recent emission from your exhausted pores. Stink is about exposure: the battles with light and heat that demand carrying a handkerchief to mop your face and covering babies' heads with knit caps. It is the lost tranquility from tangles with flies, the lost sanity from encounters with mosquitoes. Stink is a wringing out of your body until the worst smells emerge, and, if not purged, the worst disease.

There is but one redemption. To reclaim the unscathed body that emerged into the world that morning, you must bathe. Bathing happens in small concrete rooms under an open pipe gushing only cold water. During blackouts, when water does not come to the pump, it is done from a bucket. It is a singular pleasure.

This is how the Guyanese taught me to do it: First, let the cold water run over you. Wash off the top layer of powder and perfume, blood, cow dung, mucus, tears, mango juice, and minibus exhaust. Heat draws down; blood recedes from the surface. Turn off the water and soap your skin to a thick lather. Do not overlook an inch or a crack because here is where the rash will begin. Scrub the dust from your hair. After you are thick with foam, munificent suds cresting, let the icy water run its numbing deluge. A simple alchemy— skin, water, soap—but it never fails to restore the memory of that first skin, before the burns and scars, before the day.

This cycle of daily physical corruption and ablution became a marker of my two years in Guyana, proof of the regularity of miracles. My mind was educated before I came to this country, but my body was not. I had never experienced such relentless exposure to the extremes of the natural world. Surviving the physical environment was not just a personal quest, it was part of my work. In the end, the lessons were simple: rest, bathe, heal. Take the world into your body, and then, as gently as you can, let it go.

≈ ≈ ≈

Katherine Jamieson is a graduate of the Iowa Nonfiction Writing Programs, where she was an Iowa Arts Fellow. Her work has appeared in The New York Times, Ms., The Writer's Chronicle, Meridian, *and* The Best Women's Travel Writing 2011. *"Educating the Body," is part of a longer manuscript about her experiences living in Guyana. Read more of her essays, articles, and stories at katherinejamieson.com.*

COLETTE O'CONNOR

❧ ❧ ❧

Sun Valley with Dad

She gets another lesson in how to be.

"IT'S LIKE I'M THE DOG," SAYS DAD IN THE BACK SEAT. "I never know what we're going to do until we do it." My sister is at the wheel and I'm riding shotgun as we pull off I-80 east outside Elko so the Flying J truck stop can refuel us with gas and also salty cashews. At age eighty-three Dad has lost his hearing to the extent, say the doctors, a 747 can rev for take-off next to him and one ear would not even know; the other might have a hint. So it's a surprise, our stop, since Dad missed the discussion leading up to it. But he is game for whatever adventure the Flying J flings at us.

"You girls get whatever you like," he says and rolls down the window to test the temperature of the Elko air. I flash on our childhood fox terrier, Molly, who on the road loved to sniff strange climes from the car. "This is *your* trip."

Our trip is a ski weekend in Sun Valley. It's a weekend worth the thirteen-hour drive to Reno and across the vast,

169

flat stretch of Nevada north to Twin Falls and north some
more into that part of Idaho where the Sawtooth Mountains
promise snow. Worth it for the ski fever burning me up
with yearning and the gotta-get-out-of-Dodge feeling seizing Camille. Dad is along, for there is no way in hell a car is
headed to Sun Valley without him in it, as the dog or not. A
lifelong skier, he has been making the trip at least once a year
since high school in '41, and the resort dubbed "an American
Shangri-La" after its discover by an Austrian count in 1935,
thrills him each and every time.

And, really, how could it not? With 2,054 skiable acres offering a descent of 3,400 vertical feet of fun, Sun Valley's Bald
Mountain—beloved as "Baldy"—has thirteen high-speed
lifts, sixty-five varied runs and a handful of on-mountain
ski lodges made warm and sumptuous by oriental carpets on
the floors, snazzy granite in the bathrooms and massive rock
hearths kept blazing all day. In a sport known for its cold and
discomfort and crowds and, yes, expense, Sun Valley's efforts
to eliminate all trace of…well, *suffering*, result in a rare ski
experience of remarkable beauty and comfort.

We feel completely Thelma and Louise, my sister and I.
The freedom of the road and the whizzing-by vistas empty
of all but the occasional grazing cows, wind-whipped tum-
bleweeds and lonely-looking homesteads with names like
Rancho Costa Plenty soothe our city-singed nerves. We talk
nonstop and laugh, and Dad in the back nods off often. On
the outskirts of Jackpot, Nevada's last stop for gamblers enamored of burgs built exclusively of neon, I twist in my seat
to see if he's breathing and regard the deep-blue shiner under
his left eye, the small scabby gash on his nose. Last month's
ski accident.

"Now, I don't want you girls to push me," he had said
at lunch hours earlier when we stopped at a casino café in
Winnemucca. Our perky server Angie, who was, she claimed,
age ninety-one and bent nearly double from osteoporosis,

scribbled his BLT order onto her pad with a gnarled-knuck-
led hand and zinged me a wicked wink. I swear that wink
said, *Go ahead. Push old Pops all you want—he can take it.*
We're tougher than you think.

"Don't worry, Dad," said Camille as slot machines pinged
and dinged in the background. "Everyone at their own
speed."

"I'm afraid I could be finished," he said, suddenly glum.
"My balance is shot and when the light gets flat I can't see
a goddamn thing. If I let myself get tired...." Well, it will
be a Dad on the ski slope crashed, we knew. Not once in at
least seventy years has the Ski Patrol had to haul Dad off the
mountain in an emergency sled, and to have that humiliation
visit him *now*, with us, simply was not the hope Camille and
I had for the weekend. We would not insist he ski with us.
As always.

So now as we zoom through Ketchum, the Idaho town
that's both home to Sun Valley and reknown for its famous
former resident, Ernest Hemingway—he now buried in its
cemetery—I worry, what if.... *Dad? Finished?*

All my life, never a ski season did pass that our dad of
derring-do didn't base his entire self-perception (it seemed)
on the state of his skiing. From "the steep" he reached via helicopter in the Canadian Bugaboos to "the deep" of the powder in Utah, from the Sierra's spring slush to the wide open
bowls of Colorado, no snow or slope was beyond his ability or
out of the bounds of his ardor. I cannot even imagine it, our
all-terrain Dad slow-poking down the bunny hill or, worse,
rotting in the day lodge where non-skiers and the injured sit
around waiting—and waiting—for their friends or family to
come in.

And yet: After a couple more miles we motor up to the
door of the Sun Valley Lodge and two young doormen in uniform unload our skis and bags, bags that in the swank of the
surroundings look especially old and sad and as down at the

heels as we now feel. Compared with the hunky, handsome doormen Dad appears particularly wobbly and gray—almost Angie-like in posture—but he strides into the lobby like he's Averell Harriman himself and charms the check-in girl with his signature suavity. Mr. Harriman, the Union Pacific Railroad chairman who in 1935 purchased the 4,300 acres of Sawtooth Mountain marvel that was to become the resort, at the time said "When you get to Sun Valley, your eyes should pop open." Mine certainly do at the lodge's enduring allure. No wonder Hollywood legends like Clark Gable and Errol Flynn made the place their winter favorite. No wonder alpine Olympians like Picabo Street and Cristin Cooper did, too. The lodge is so old-school beautiful with its glass-enclosed pool, ice-rink view and wood-beam, flower-frilled rooms that of course Hemingway in the fall of '39 chose to finish *For Whom the Bell Tolls* in suite 206. The place reeks of history, elegance, class. Never mind how hard times have rooms, *including lift ticket*, going for $100 a night per person; this means riff-raff now slump in the lobby in rude attitudes, their feet on the furniture, their cell phones in use. We are riff-raff, too, alas. But at least we have Dad, who knows well enough that when staying in the Sun Valley Lodge, one does not après-ski wander the halls on the way to the pool (heated to 103 degrees) without first donning the white spa robe and slippers supplied. This we do straightaway to revive from our drive. And as the cocktail server circles the pool in which hotel guests bob (or is it imbibe?) their way to a Sun Valley high, I notice Dad soaks with an air of tense apprehension.

"Are you O.K., Dad?" asks Camille. He paddles due north away from her voice, not hearing.

"Dad?" now louder. "DAD!"

He paddles back, not hearing.

"Listen," he says, "tomorrow I want you girls to leave me at the base of Warm Springs. I'm going to take it easy. I'm just not sure about my shoulder." He wings his right arm this way and that, testing, splashing. The same ski fall that blackened his eye and gouged his nose with his glasses also did a thing to his shoulder. And now the bitch of it will nix him from riding the gondola to Baldy's 9,150-foot elevation where the upper runs and chutes and bowls offer skiing supreme in a sprawl of challenging terrain that not *that* many years ago Dad would never have found beneath him.

When he rises from the pool, pale and dripping, Dad's spindly chicken legs look like they couldn't handle even the gentle, smooth slope of lower Warm Springs. And when he stumbles over a poolside chaise to retrieve his robe and nearly mows over a trio of spa-robed people dipping their toes in the pool, I wonder if he has any business on skis at all. My heart so sinks me in the water I hardly can rise myself, but still: There is something fierce in Dad's refusal to believe he's eighty-three, something hell-bent on sharing the Sun Valley experience with Camille and me like he's the same skier he was back in the day he'd hike a whole mountain, skis on his shoulder, because, really, what did it matter that they hardly had yet invented the chairlift?

What I mean is here he is next morning, knocking on the door of our room before breakfast, *before coffee*, and standing there in parka and pants and helmet with goggles, standing there *in ski boots*, if you can believe. We cannot.

"I'm ready," slurs a still-sleeping Camille from somewhere deep, deep within the strange luxury and unaccustomed comfort of the lodge's sheets, sheets whose thread count surely is in the tens of thousands. "I'll only be a sec."

"Don't hurry," says Dad and clomps awkwardly in. I hold the door open dressed in shower cap and towel. "When you're ready you girls can get the bus to River Run. I'll see you for lunch."

"Dad," I say, "the lifts don't open for a few hours. You've got your *boots* on?"

"I don't want to push it and try to keep up with you girls," he says. "I'm concerned…"

"About your shoulder?"

About his shoulder, his balance, his eyesight, his hearing, his strength, his speed and, not least, his very essence as a skier. Should bad falls or, worse, bad form on even Baldy's beginner runs cut into his confidence or take him off the hill for good, what then? For a brave millisecond I go there, to the fright-filled place I don't normally dare: *No Sun Valley with Dad? Ever again?*

No more lunches at Ketchum's Cristina's, where the home-made soups and thick Idaho fries are killer delicious? No more dinners of fresh-caught fish from famous Silver Creek River savored at the homey Ketchum Grill? And—too, too tragic!—no more après-ski evenings watching the people and loving the mood, the food and the music of the legendary local restaurant, The Pioneer? These are a few of Dad's Sun Valley favorites, pleasures he will share with my sister and me this weekend. So though he is in his element, and (honestly!) in his boots well before breakfast, eager and energetic, I ache to protect my dad from cruel reality, to blurt through tears I think he's the best skier in the world, the best Dad, and that every year, always, there will be for us, Sun Valley.

Instead I send him off with a scolding. "Dad," I say, my tone snippy, "Please don't run to try and get the bus, and please will you watch the ice on the stairs, and please *please* if you…"

"Now, I want you girls to dress extra warmly," he inter-rupts, entirely missing the gist of my admonishment. "It might be cold up there." He starts to clomp awkwardly out.

"Have a wonderful morning, Dad," I say and intercept him long enough to peck his cheek with a subzero kiss, icy with the worry we are sending him off to an uncertain fate at Warm Springs. "We'll ski together after lunch." He lurches a little after a few clompy steps down the hall, and coming upon the maids' cart catches the buckle of his stiff, bulky boot. It is a maneuver that nearly topples him. Suddenly, I feel

naked in my helplessness before time, horribly vulnerable to
what? I don't know.

Maybe it's the shower cap and towel.

"You girls be sure you have your mittens," he calls back
after righting himself and clomping on. My sister and I are in
our fifties and yet Dad still refers to our ski gloves as mittens,
same as when we were six and he sent us off to ski school so
he and Mom, giddy, could flee (fairly screaming) to the slopes
sans kids.

"It's O.K., Dad," calls Camille, now roused from her
swoon. "We've got our mittens."

From the top of Baldy the Pioneer Mountains to the east and
the Sawtooths to the north envelop us in peaks of thrilling
skiing promise. Snow! The gondola has dropped Camille and
me sky-high and below, the Seattle Ridge runs unfurl in a fun
I can't wait to have embrace us. Said by Sun Valley hype to
be greatest single ski mountain in the world for its absence
of wind, substantial vertical drop and abundance of varied
terrain, Baldy beckons and baby, ain't nobody going to take
exception to that. We're off. My sister and I? Well, we ski
and ski and ski still more until...well, until our legs can't take
it. Or maybe it's until one chair ride up the Blue Grouse run
Camille asks, "Do you think we should check on Dad?"

We race a winding way down to Warm Springs, unsure
of what we'll find and there he is, kicking back on the sun-
soaked terrace of the day lodge, his cup of tea hot, his mood,
inscrutable.

"How did it go, Dad?" I tense for his answer, for if he
says not bad or O.K. or pretty well, it means his skiing was
awful.

"How *is* it?" he says, leaping up in greeting and suddenly
as animated as Molly might have been to see us after a morning's separation. "Did you girls find Limelight? Was it great?

How is the snow?" We had, indeed, found his favorite black
diamond, hence most difficult run, and Dad's happy, eager
expression tells me he wants to hang on our every word—if
only he could. I hope our excitement alone tells well our
Limelight tale. Somehow.

"No, *you*," says Camille, exaggerating her mouth and
pointing at Dad. "How did it go for *you*?"

He looks off toward the band, now warming up to ser-
enade sunning skiers with peppy retro renditions of Loggins
and Messina.

"I'm giving it time to soften up," he says, sobering. He does
not meet our eyes. "Maybe after lunch."

Later in the gondola Camille and I go over how bad it is
that Dad is thinking he might be finished. And how we will
handle it if the afternoon goes like the morning and he sits it
out on the terrace, not even trying out his chicken legs, letting
his black eye and bum shoulder and balance on the skids hold
him back from being so much of who he is. A skier. What
will we do with him? What will he do with himself? What
if. What then.

After lunch, however, the Sun Valley slopes seduce us into
our own love affair with brilliant Idaho sun, fantastic, well-
groomed snow, and run after run—after run—of simply
sensational skiing. The afternoon passes in a bliss as big as
the burn in our thighs. Then, too soon, a few late afternoon
clouds gather to flatten the light and tell us it's time to go in.
It's our last run down when I develop a foreboding *ugh* in my
gut that when we catch up with Dad, it will be back at the
lodge. He'll be working the crossword between cat naps, his
shoulder on ice or his strained knee bandaged. Or worse.

Over. It will be over and the spell of Sun Valley with its
special tradition of showing Dad to his best advantage—he is,
after all, one of its longest-running and most ardent acts—will
be *poof!* broken. And the magic of this day, this place, will be

gone for Camille and me as skiers, daughters, who, because of Dad alone, in our lives always remember our mittens.

We schuss down Flying Squirrel, down and down. We arrive at the Warm Springs base and, as expected, don't see Dad.

"He probably got an early bus back to the lodge," says Camille.

"Or he could be still on the hill," I offer, hopeful. I imagine him on the hill, weighting and unweighting his skis with excellent technique; turning left, turning right with his athletic grace intact and his famous rhythm, undiminished. I imagine his thrill and his pride and his smile when he sums up his run for us later. "It was great!" he'll say, his passion for the umpteen millionth descent of his skiing career as fresh and fierce as it was for his first as a child in the '30s.

"Well, I don't know," says Camille.

We both without thinking look to the mountain, and not on lower but *upper* Warm Springs, steep and moguled, there is, by God, a dot of red on the move. Dad. It's not his ruby parka but rather his form that positively ID's him for us—that particular Dad stance and telling Dad-style Camille and I have known all our lives. The dot is moving—it's moving fast!—and as it descends something dying in me somersaults into joy. *Dad? Finished?* The dot grows larger, and as it comes closer and closer and Dad himself into focus, I can see that who he is in shoes, or even barefoot by the pool, is not at all who he is on skis. His stance solid, his posture tall, with turns that neither wobble nor fall, Dad skis his way to us free of any giveaway age and as strong and fluid as any Sun Valley punk parading his arrogant youth.

"Dad!" I fairly yelp when he swishes to a stop and flips up his goggles to greet us. "You look *great*! You were *amazing*! You're the best...the best...." My voice gets strangled by emotion.

"Are you proud of your old Dad?" His breath comes hard and his cheeks look rouged, but his smile, just as I imagined, is huge.

"YES," gush my sister and I together, in unison.

"You know, you just might be the best skier in the whole world!" I manage to squeak through my shyness; it's a mouse-peep I eke through my tears.

"Horseshit," says Dad, somehow having heard. He laughs. "I'm just the best skier in Sun Valley."

⮜ ⮜ ⮜

Colette O'Connor lives and works around the Monterey Bay area of California. Her lifestyle features and travel essays have appeared in many publications including the Los Angeles Times, France *magazine,* Travelers' Tales Paris, Sand in My Bra, Whose Panties Are These?, The Best Women's Travel Writing *(2005 and 2010) and* The Best Travel Writing 2010.

KATE CRAWFORD

❧ ❧ ❧

Alone in India—But Not for Long

The subcontinent is not for the claustrophobic.

THE NEW DELHI TRAIN STATION SEEMED LIKE A CROSS between a medieval army bivouac and a state park campground. It was after midnight. Family bands crouched around cooking fires or, curled in wool shawls, slept against mounds of luggage. People ate, bathed, brushed their teeth.

Traveling alone, I attracted a small band of followers as soon as I arrived at the station. The first enlistees, two red-smocked, officially badged suitcase wallahs, boarded my train before it stopped moving. Completely unbidden, one grabbed my suitcase, the other my tote. To carry the bags, they balanced them on their turban-wrapped heads like wacky hats.

The next enlistee, a slick dude, fell in with several young followers the minute I stepped from the train.

"Where to?" he asked in TV English.

My hotel had told me to meet its driver at the train station's restaurant. So, like a savvy sahib, I commanded, "To the restaurant."

"Wimpy's?" asked the dude.

Wimpy's didn't seem enough like a restaurant, so I suggested one where people sat down. Our band of six embarked on a ten-minute march through the station's cavernous overpasses and out-of-the-way corridors. I wasn't worried, because my attention was fixed on the rapid growth of my retinue. Next, four rogue taxi wallahs, to whom I explained I already had a ride, joined our ranks. Each was followed by more tagalong boys—a touts-in-training program, I guessed.

When the slick dude began to tell me how old my hotel was, I caught on. He was a go-to-another-hotel-where-he-collects-a-commission wallah.

My ride was not at the restaurant. Back we all trudged to our starting point. There a long wait at the booking service elicited only a "Sorry, Madame."

Call me crazy, but I was having a great time. I figured this was the closest I would ever come to having my own entourage. Seven days had passed of my three-week India trip, and so far, exemplary ground arrangements by my tour operator had deprived me of this quintessential Indian travel experience.

A handsome, turbaned Sikh had met me at the airport. We'd eased down New Delhi's wide avenues, enjoying the lemon trees and sweet peas flowering in the roundabouts. Then an uneventful van ride on a smooth toll road had led me to Jaipur, from where I'd just returned.

Very nice, but this was India, land of the epic journey. India, where a seventy-eight-part TV series enacting the Ramayan—which, along with the Mahabharat, is the Hindi Iliad and Odyssey—drew 40 million viewers in the late 1980s. The India of the Mughal sultan's mobile palaces: dozens of tents, with silk-embroidered walls and Persian rugs, powered by hundreds of men, elephants, and camels. And Mahatma Gandhi's epic political journey, in which he walked 240 miles to collect sea salt to avoid paying the British tax.

Now, at the train station, my journey was about to attain epic quality. I was no longer taking it; it was taking me. My people—I'd come to think of them that way—decided I must call my hotel. We deployed to the fire-engine-red booth staffed by people who make calls for you, the public call office (PCO). My suitcase wallahs, however, nixed the PCO in favor of a cheaper pay phone nearby. I did not have the correct change, so my people enlisted a tag-along boy who disappeared with my ten-rupee note. When he returned with the change, I realized I had lost my hotel's phone number.

So, we returned to the PCO, where I shouted my hotel's name at the official telephoner who could barely hear over the other shrieking telephone users. The telephoner put through a call and handed me the phone, but after a half-understood conversation, I gathered that I had not reached my hotel. I wrote out the hotel's name. The telephoner recognized it right off and gave me one of those pity-the-verbally-challenged looks.

I was having trouble with English. The elegant, lyrical English spoken by many Indians bears little resemblance to my Midwestern twang. My last name, Crawford, is quite common, but at each hotel, the desk clerk would look at his reservations book with puzzlement and say, "Sorry, Madame."

I'd point to my name and repeat, "Crawford."

"Ah, Crawford," they would say.

I started saying, "Crawford, as in Cindy, only shorter." In India, everyone knows Cindy Crawford.

Finally, I connected with my hotel. The driver, who had been waiting at Wimpy's, was coming back to the train station for me. PCO telephoner paid, suitcases aloft and ranks reduced by one hotel tout and his followers, we returned to where we had begun. More calls, waiting and trekking and still no hotel driver, so I decided to grab a cab. With hotel name written down, I headed for the prepaid taxi kiosk across from Wimpy's to purchase a set-fee voucher for a legal cab.

A feeding frenzy among the so-far-well-behaved rogue taxi wallahs began. They blocked my path, shouting, "I give you better price," "It's only for taxis to distant places like Agra," and the oh-so-Indian, "It's not working." Stunned, I froze. Then a man in a three-piece suit and matching turban broke through the swarm. He took my money, bought a taxi voucher, saw me into my cab and admonished me not to give the suitcase wallahs 200 rupees (about $4.50). He said fifty rupees was sufficient. I gave them 200 anyway; I'd promised it to them. Later, however, I realized that holding up two fingers meant they wanted to bum a cigarette, not negotiate a price.

Fearing I might not be ready for Delhi, I took inspiration from what I'd learned of India's women. They suffer everything from virtual slave labor to dowry deaths—the killing of a bride because her dowry was not large enough. But India also has a long tradition of powerful female figures—women endowed with Shakti, female power.

Mythically, the warrior goddess Durga embodied Shakti. Historically, Queen Lakshmibai, the Warrior Queen of Jhansi, who died in 1858 leading her troops against the British, had it. More recently, Indira Gandhi twice led India's unruly republic, and in 2004 her daughter-in-law, Sonia Gandhi, carried the National Congress Party back to power.

Earlier on my trip, I'd met some not-so-famous female powerhouses. They exuded grace, smarts, and serious authority. They wrapped their gorgeous power saris, hand-loomed cloth in muted colors, in the modern fashion. Unlike other women, they used few or no pins to keep the long swaths in place, thereby demonstrating their effortless mastery over every situation. Surely, I reasoned, emulating such women might help.

Lacking a power sari and the skills to wear it, I tried to dress for success in Delhi in an ankle-length khaki skirt, a long-sleeved blouse and a floral silk scarf swept over my shoulder. I used the woman-alone street smarts I'd been taught by an Indian woman: Walk quickly with firm purpose, look straight ahead, make no eye contact with touts or beggars and, most important, don't say anything. In India, even a firm "No!" is considered an encouraging word.

My next expedition, crossing Delhi's main Janpath Road, may not seem epic, but as I stood on its curb with traffic flowing in six lanes like the Ganges in flood, the other side seemed unreachable. Every lane had at least one bus, one truck or two cars. All the remaining square centimeters were filled with bikes, scooters, auto-rickshaws, and motorized carts. From the slowest bicycle with three passengers to the fastest Mercedes with just one, every vehicle moved as fast as it could whenever it could. Traffic slowed for cows, not people.

My plan was to cross from the luxe hotel where I'd lunched to the government-run crafts store. In hindsight, asking the hotel guard to point out the store was my first mistake. Whammo—bring on the touts. As drivers bid against each other, the price of a cycle rickshaw fell from fifty rupees to five—to be augmented by commissions from the stores where they would take me.

Then I made my second mistake. I said, "I'll walk." This elicited shouts: "There are better government stores," "It's a holiday—the store is closed," and, closest to the truth, "It's not safe." Striding to the nearest intersection, I lost all but one tout, who continued to yell that I'd die crossing the road.

I spotted a woman in a power sari on the curb and positioned myself next to her. When she stepped off the curb, I stepped off the curb. When she slowed, I slowed. When she sprinted, I sprinted. And when she made it across, so did I. Encountering more touts on the other side, I remained tight-lipped and plunged on—right into someone's private office.

It belonged to a kind gentleman who directed me to the store next door.

Two days later, at 5:00 A.M., I was back at the train station. Fewer people slept and more washed as commuter hordes stampeded for jammed trains. This time, I'd managed to hire just one suitcase wallah and felt confident that he would get me to the right track, on the right train, and into my assigned seat.

Imitating other women on the platform, I sat on my suitcase to wait. Even though I was covered like a nun, a dozen men stood around staring at me. This, I knew, would not be happening to a genuine powerhouse.

So, using a different approach, I pulled my scarf over my head and looked down at my right shoulder. The pose constricted my view, but I could still see the men's shoes turn and walk away. All except one. Curious about this persistent fellow, I inched up my head and recognized my loyal suitcase wallah.

Meek women might not inherit the earth, but I found out that if they play their scarves right, they can at least lay claim to a small portion of an Indian railway platform.

❧ ❧ ❧

Kate Crawford can cross the street all by herself in Sebastopol, California where she lives.

ERIN BYRNE

❦ ❦ ❦

Winged Victory

Stone animates the living.

IMAGINE BEING PLACED AT THE TOP OF THE MAIN STAIRCASE inside the most visited museum in the world. Daylight streams from above, bathing the arched walls in golden light, illuminating and exposing you. You're there for thousands to see, but have neither head nor arms.

Winged Victory stands boldly atop the sweeping Daru staircase inside Musée du Louvre in Paris. Her legs, caressed by wind-whipped fabric, are sturdy. Her chest is thrust forward, and her feathered wings fly out behind her. The loss of her head and arms is said to enhance her ethereal beauty, what she has more than makes up for what she lacks. She beams with boldness, for she is authentic.

Sometimes, if we are in the right place at the right time, a work of art can release a current of electric insight that challenges us to our very core. This is the story of how a trip to

185

Paris became a pilgrimage in which Winged Victory's spirit entered my bloodstream.

As I prepared to travel to Paris in January, I remembered a lecture by writer Phil Cousineau. He'd been speaking about his book, *The Art of Pilgrimage,* which puts forth a new model of mindful travel. Cousineau directs the traveler to weave his way through disappointments and follow the hunger for something deeper. As the traveler progresses through seven stages of pilgrimage—beginning with the longing to go, continuing all the way through to the arrival home and reflecting on the trip—the journey becomes transformative.

I remembered Cousineau's voice shaking with the excitement of reimagining the way we travel. "The truth of your life is as close to you as the vein pulsing in your neck," he'd said.

> *All of the answers are within us, but such is our tendency toward forgetting that we sometimes need to venture to a far away land to tap our own memory.*
>
> —Phil Cousineau, *The Art of Pilgrimage*

I was returning to the city I loved. I had been to Paris often—sipped wine and saturated my palate at tiny sidewalk cafés, dashed from the left bank literary haunts to the haute couture of the Avenue Montaigne, listened to violins inside candle-lit Sainte-Chapelle and wailing jazz inside crowded clubs.

On previous trips I had felt the city tug a string inside of me, threatening to unravel something tightly knit, though I knew not what. I had been certain Paris could melt me, thaw me out, and untangle me. The odd thing was that I didn't think I needed melting or untangling. I had known that this was a place I could be my true self. Each time I'd been there, awareness had crept in that this self was far, far away.

Indeed, my authentic self had disappeared sometime around 1963. The last time anyone saw her was in a black and white photograph of Miss Beckowitcz's preschool class. In the photo, a girl sits in the front row staring at the camera with quiet, solemn eyes. A million questions roll around inside her head. She is an observer, a thinker. She knows exactly who she is and is comfortable in her own skin. She is me.

By first grade, the unblinking little owl was usurped. In the first grade class photo, the girl tilts her head, shrugs her shoulders prettily, and wears an adorable smile. The same look appears repeatedly in the stack of photos that chronicle my life: the laughing teenager; the gregarious sorority girl; the effervescent wife and mother; the accomplished public speaker.

Was it perceived parental pressures or just America's expectations of little girls in the 1960s that made me decide at the age of four to act the role of the cute, center-of-attention-loving little red-haired girl? I'm not sure, but I remember making the conscious choice that it was easier to hide my brooding introspection than live with awkward reactions to it, so I cultivated perkiness instead. By the age of six, I played the part of the party girl to perfection. I had donned the extroverted persona that the world adored, and it didn't quite fit, but still clung to me forty-three years later as I prepared to travel to Paris.

One of the ancient functions of pilgrimage is to wake us from our slumber.

As drizzly night descended upon Charles de Gaulle airport, I climbed into a taxi. The cab glided into the city as streetlights gradually came on. Paris shimmered with light. The huge Corinthian columns of the church of La Madeleine held a white glow within, the opulence of The Opéra Garnier gleamed against the indigo sky. As we circled the Place de la Concord, its obelisk soared out of the mist and the gigantic medieval palace of the Louvre exuded a beckoning air of mystery that seemed directed at me. An awareness emerged out of the blueness of my brain that my soul was here.

My soul was *here?* It sounded melodramatic and new-agey—not at all like me. But in that taxi floating around the brilliantly lit city, I felt my soul stir, stretch and blink the sleep from its eyes.

Pay close attention to any dreams still frothing on the surface of your mind.

That night, as I floated in and out of sleep, I dreamed of The City of Light waiting outside my hotel room. The history of Paris is not for the faint-of-heart: the scarlet blood of its kings and queens has trickled along the cobblestones and mingled with sticky redness spilled out of the poorest street urchin. Every few feet one encounters statues of history's great thinkers. Hundreds of museums hold priceless artistic brilliance, thousands of bookstores cradle the questions of writers and philosophers. Cafés hum with contemplation.

There is nothing frivolous about Paris; it demands to be taken seriously.

The oldest practice is still the best. Take your soul for a stroll.

Every time I stepped out of my hotel, my feet took me to the streets where I greeted overcoated Parisians with a smile and a perky *Bonjour*. Tree branches were outlined stark against the sky, stone buildings frozen solid. Notre Dame's stained glass was colored ice, and the clanging of its bells cut through the frigid air.

I let the magnet inside me draw me to the Louvre, where I walked slowly up the staircase, never taking my eyes off Winged Victory. Nike symbolized victory to the ancient Greeks—in battle, athletics, love—in all areas of life. The

sculpture once stood in an open-air theatre on the Greek island of Samothrace sometime around 190 BC. She was nestled
in a niche carved out of a rock, the sky above her blending
with sea-blueness on the distant horizon.

Inside her home in Paris, I viewed her from all sides, from
afar, and from below among crowds gazing up worshipfully.
I knew she had a message for me. I wondered if her head and
arms had felt awkward and weighed her down like so much
ballast. She was proud without them, her wings spread out
behind her. What she had all seemed to fit. I felt suddenly
envious.

(Walking) allows time for your soul to catch up.

I winded through worlds of wrought iron, down tiny alleys
bordered by fragrant flower shops and miniature markets of
colorful fruit. I glided along the quays next to the steely Seine
where every so often a bridge would offer itself graciously to
be crossed. My eyes stung and my hands were numb, but my
core slowly began to thaw.

Repeatedly, an invisible thread pulled me to the Louvre,
to the bottom of the stairs where I'd stare up at the goddess
of Victory leaning forward on the prow of her ship, the wind
plastering her garments against her body. She presented her
self to the world so sincerely; I longed to emulate her.

The statue was unearthed in fragments and brought to
Paris in the 1860s. Reassembly continued over the next twenty
years. More recently, in 1950, her right hand and the tip of
her ring finger were discovered on Samothrace, and the rest
of this finger and a thumb were found forgotten in a dusty
drawer inside a museum in Vienna, Austria. These no-longer-missing pieces rest inside a glass case near her podium.

I walked. My breath, cloudy puffs in the icy air. In the
frosty Luxembourg Gardens, the statues of Balzac and
Delacroix were unflustered by the weather. The Panthéon

cradled in its chilling crypt the long dead heroes of La Belle France. Hurried footsteps slapped the sidewalks as the cold turned bitter.

Uncover what you long for and you will discover who you are.

I peered into a little café where glasses clinked and voices hummed. When the door opened, an aroma of exotic coffee and buttery croissants wafted into the street. I looked in at the people. Their faces…there was something in their faces that reminded me of Winged Victory. Something that challenged me.

A young student wearing round glasses, a scarf slung around his neck, puzzled over something his friend was saying. His forehead scrunched and his eyes darted as his brain twisted and turned. Here was a relentless thinker who didn't pretend to *know* but was comfortable just contemplating.

An old woman with white hair and coral lipstick sat alone and meticulously sipped from a tiny white cup; I could see her inner poise, elegance, and utter lack of pretention. She just sat there quietly, comfortable in her own skin. As I looked through the window I knew that the expression on each face revealed the true spirit inside with the same honesty I'd noticed in Winged Victory's pose.

My own face wore a smile that suddenly felt very heavy. It was not part of my essence, it was ballast. Slowly, I let go the mask. My brow straightened, my eyes relaxed, my face melted into the serious expression that reflected my own spirit. The muscles in my face felt reassembled into a no-longer-missing me.

We learn by going where we have to go; we arrive when we find ourselves on the road walking toward us.

❧ ❧ ❧

During the next ten days, the self of the preschool photo emerged right there on the streets of Paris. I welcomed her home bit by bit. I shed heavy layers of wide-toothed smiles and let the quiet observer emerge, watching, pondering, daydreaming. I mulled over questions rather than eagerly spilling forth answers. I let myself sit quietly, unsmiling, and sip a glass of scarlet Bordeaux. And for the first time that I could remember since the age of four, I was myself with the world. The truth of this was as close as the victorious vein pulsing in my neck.

In sacred travel, every experience is uncanny. No encounter is without meaning.

As my Parisian pilgrimage progressed, the people I encountered showed me exactly how I could *be*. In a tiny upstairs nook with books crammed in every crevice, a group of reflective young writers recited prose that revealed their cherished wishes and buried heartaches. Michèle, an artist who had carefully cultivated her observer's eye, shared her personal and creative secrets with me; we felt our spirits kindle. A shy Irish poet spoke his thoughts with a quiet confidence inside his lyrical accent. None wore a false mask of frivolity, and when I was with them I didn't either.

The challenge is to learn how to carry over the quality of the journey into your everyday life.

I am home from Paris and each day I'm faced with the challenge of my pilgrimage: to blend my inner and outer colors. Learning how to do this is an inner journey as meaningful as any trip across land or sea. It involves much excavation of traits I forgot I ever had: curiosity, contemplation, creativity, and seriousness. I am the girl in the preschool photo *and* the woman who walked the streets of Paris. I am charged with the current that flowed from the statue at the top of the stairs.

A worn postcard on my wall shows golden Winged Victory against a dark background. Inside the Louvre, day turns to night, the crowd empties out, the security systems are activated, and all is still. She stands there, Nike, the goddess who symbolizes the precise moment when victory was granted by the gods to the ancient Greeks…and to me.

❧ ❧ ❧

Erin Byrne writes articles and essays that dive deeper into travel, cultural, and political themes. Her essays have won numerous awards, including Gold Solas Awards and the Grand Prize at Book Passage Travel, Food and Photography Conference. Erin's work has appeared in Everywhere *magazine,* World Hum, The Literary Traveler, Brave New Traveler, *and a variety of other publications. She is currently working on a collection of essays about Paris. A complete list of awards and links to Erin's work can be found at www.e-byrne.com .*

❧ ❧ ❧

Protected

A dinner table conversation in Berlin reveals
more than the author expected.

IT WAS MY LAST NIGHT IN THE LAVISH VILLA ON THE LAKE in Berlin-Wannsee where I had holed up for the winter.[1] A noted Indian economist was scheduled to lecture on the underlying causes of the global financial crisis and its effects on the developing world. Call me an escapist, but I was not inclined to listen to the sad statistics. The world's affairs would muddle on without me, I thought, intending to grab a quick bite and slip off unnoticed to attend to my packing.

Such dinners were always a festive affair, the guest list sprinkled with Berlin society. My tablemate to the left, the wife of the German theologian seated beside the Indian

---

1. The author was the Holtzbrinck Fellow in Spring 2010 at the American Academy in Berlin. This account is excerpted from a book-length work-in-progress.

economist, was a tall, stately woman of late middle age with prominent cheekbones, Prussian blue eyes, and tightly braided, blond hair, who wore her years like a string of pearls. Straight-backed, head held high, as if she were not seated at table, but rather astride a saddle, ears pricked for the sound of a hunting horn, she had what in former times would have been called an aristocratic bearing.

Socially maladroit and constitutionally incapable of making small talk, a tendency further aggravated by chronic insomnia, I either clam up on such occasions or put my foot in my mouth.

Prodding myself to say something before taking up knife and fork to dispatch the appetizer, two luscious-looking, seared sea scallops on a bed of wilted seaweed, I wished her, "Bon appétit!"

"*Gesegnete Mahlzeit!* (Blessed meal)," she replied.

"Bless the chef!" I countered, immediately regretting the flippancy of my ill-considered response. "Please forgive me, but I'm not a believer."

She smiled to make clear that she took no offense. "Religion is a personal matter. My faith," she affirmed, "makes me feel *beschützt* (protected)."

A striking choice of words, I thought, while savoring the flavor and firmness of the first scallop. "I myself altogether lack the foundation of faith," I confessed. "Given my family history, feeling protected is simply not in the cards."

She seemed concerned, sympathetic, as though suddenly fathoming that I was missing a middle finger.

"I'm the child of refugees," I said to set the record straight.

"Oh?"

I might have changed the subject but I chose not to. With me it's a compulsion, a need to lay my cards on the table.

"My father's departure from his native Vienna was…" I searched for the appropriate adjective, "precipitous."

"Precipitous?"

"Involuntary," I clarified.

"I see."

Decorum should have compelled me to change the subject. But impatiently lapping up the second scallop whole, my tongue rattled on.

"Huddled, to hide his prominent nose, in the sidecar of a motorcycle with a swastika flapping in the wind, he was driven by an accommodating member of a motorcycle gang, who agreed, for a fee, to drop him off at sundown at a wooded stretch of the border with Czechoslovakia. And when, at the sound of what he took for a gunshot—but was, in fact, an engine backfire—they suddenly stopped, convinced his time was up, my father held his breath as the motorcyclist dismounted, only to return moments later with a bleeding hare he'd run over, knocked its head against the fender, and asked my father to be so kind as to hold it for him. Fresh meat being scarce, he meant to have it for his dinner."

The arrival of the entrée, one of the chef's signature dishes, rack of venison prepared "*von Himmel und Erde*" (heaven and earth) style, i.e. stuffed with a puree of mashed apples and potatoes, came as a welcome point of punctuation.

She eyed me in between bites with an intense, but not unfriendly, gaze, as if, I thought, considering a rare wild flower, which aggravated my malaise.

To smooth the way for my escape, I let slip that I was leaving early the next morning for a trip to Poznań, Poland, and so, unfortunately, would have to skip dessert and miss the lecture, to pack.

"To *Posen?!*" she burst out, employing the old German name of the region and city ceded to Prussia following the Congress of Vienna and reclaimed by the Polish in the wake of World War II; promptly correcting herself: "*Poznań!*" to make clear that she harbored no secret dream of reannexation.

I nodded to indicate that I understood.

"*Ich bin auch*...I too am"—she hesitated a moment—"*das Kind von Flüchtlinge*...the child of refugees."

It was the way she said *Kind...child* that made the years fall away from her face and gave her voice the candor of innocence.

"I come," she blinked, embarrassed and proud, "from a long line of Prussian aristocrats, the landed gentry of Poznań, Posen, as it was called back then.

"The War was practically over. The Russians were advancing from the East. It was a winter so bitter and cold the children broke the icicles from the windowsills and sucked them like candy. A decorated tank commander in the Wehrmacht who'd been away a long time, and whom the family thought dead, miraculously broke through enemy lines, and came rolling up in his Panzer in the dark of night to the family estate."

She described what followed in vivid detail, like an eyewitness, yet with a certain distance in the telling, like she couldn't decide whether to embrace it or hold it at arm's length.

"The officer leapt out in his neatly pressed uniform, in which the War hadn't made a wrinkle, tipped his cap, worn at a jaunty tilt, hugged his two sons and his trembling wife, who took him for a ghost."

She paused to mimic the hollow look in his eyes.

"That night the officer told his wife he wanted to make a blond-haired, blue-eyed daughter.

"'Are you mad?' his wife protested in a whisper, not wanting to wake the children. "The War is lost, we already have two sons to raise. Why bring another child into this world?"

"But the officer insisted, and his wife dared not refuse a decorated hero of the Reich."

Turning away, the theologian's wife bowed her head to mark a private moment, shut her eyes tight and seemed to be peering inwards, straining, as I suddenly fathomed, to remember the moment of her own conception.

"Bright and early the next day," she continued, her voice now taking on a strange solemnity, "Father put on his perfectly pressed uniform, set the cap on his head at just the right angle, pausing briefly in front of Mother's vanity mirror to approve his appearance, said he'd only be a minute, and as Mother watched from the bedroom window, he smiled, patted the protruding cannon, lifted the hatch, climbed in, set the great metal elephant in motion, and poking his head out, waving to her at the window one last time, leapt out and hurled himself under the rolling tread."

They cleared the table and brought in the dessert, a wild berry parfait that neither of us touched.

"Did she mourn for him?" I inquired.

"There was no time for mourning," my tablemate shook her head. "With the Russian artillery thundering ever closer all through the day and into the night, Mother pulled herself together, took a pick axe, buried Father's remains, and fled with the clothes on her back and a small bundle, with my brothers in toe, and the seed of a child planted in her womb, walking all the way to Berlin.

"Father posthumously had his wish, a blond-haired, blue-eyed daughter," she shrugged, with a look that wavered between disapproval and a proud affirmation of self. "The four of us lived together in a cramped attic room with a ceiling through which it rained and snowed. In that leaky attic I grew up with barely enough space to stretch my arms and legs, but there," she smiled, "I felt protected.

"When I grew up I met and married my husband"—she nodded at the theologian, who cast increasingly concerned looks to see his wife so stirred up with a stranger, to which she replied with reassuring nods. "I became a kindergarten teacher, had a long career, and just retired last year."

She was horrified, she said, at the number of broken families her pupils came from, one in three in Germany. She hoped to devote her "golden years"—the hackneyed expression took on a freshness framed by her radiant, tightly braided blond head—volunteering to help children in need.

I had stuck around too long to escape the economist's lecture, but I was preoccupied and don't remember a word of what he said about the present crisis or his prognosis for the future.

I kept glancing at the theologian's wife, now seated beside her husband, her hand in his. Born of conflicting legends, we were bound in braided tragedies. And though I still can't fathom what it means to feel protected, and doubt I ever will, as disparate as our destinies are, there is an undeniable parallel between the motorcycle that carried my father to one kind of freedom and the tank that took her father to another, on both of which history hitched a ride.

❧ ❧ ❧

Happiest when peripatetic, Peter Wortsman's restless musings have appeared in The New York Times, Los Angeles Times, *the* Boston Globe, *the* Washington Post, *the German newspapers* The Atlantic Times, Die Welt, *and* Die Zeit, *and the popular website* World Hum, *among other print and electronic outlets, and in the last three volumes of Travelers' Tales* The Best Travel Writing. *"Protected" first appeared in* Habitus, A Diaspora Journal, *in an issue devoted to Berlin. The text is excerpted from a work in progress in search of a publisher, working title "Ghost Dance in Berlin," inspired by the six months Wortsman spent as a Holtzbrinck Fellow at the American Academy in Berlin in 2010. He is also the author of a book of short fiction,* A Modern Way to Die, *two plays,* The Tattooed Man Tells All *and* Burning Words, *and an artists' book,* it-t=i, *produced in collaboration with his brother, artist Harold Wortsman. His numerous translations from the German (a verbal form of border crossing) include the German travel classic* Travel Pictures, *by Heinrich Heine, and most recently,* Selected Prose of Heinrich von Kleist. *His column "Rx for Travel" runs in* P&S, *the journal of The Columbia University College of Physicians and Surgeons.*

❧ ❧ ❧

The Chilean Cliff Carver

When the heart calls, do you answer?

WE MET IN A BULLRING UNDER THE VELVET CLOAK OF night. An evening lit by a pale pearl, bruised full moon. This was where I first encountered the pitch-black-haired Chilean who sported a smirk on his perfectly chiseled face. He stared at me while I was lifted to the heavens yet again. Not a human sacrifice but a contact dance performance I was hired to do at a private party on the island of Ibiza in Spain.

The Chilean and I skirted each other on the dance floor. Like matador and bull. I find attractive men dangerous and try to avoid eye contact with them. They terrify me.

Just as I did allow myself to look into his relentlessly piercing eyes, he swiveled and turned his attentions onto another woman. A real beauty. Slowly, they danced close together. Barely perceptible tendrils of steam were rising from their entwined bodies. He then danced with a man. He danced with the woman again. He danced again with the man. Then he danced with both of them at once. They were svelte and sensual, and wielded sly, flirty smiles. In my direction! Provocative. Especially in the flickering torchlight.

He came close again and grazed my bare arm. Red alerts were going off in my left brain. He looked like a heart landmine. Step toward him and my heart would surely be torn to bits.

This inner torment spiced up my dance routine with Oscar, my California dance partner, who seemed to be getting a little jealous that the Chilean was moving into his territory. Party guests were now standing in a circle around him and me, hemming us in as we increased the acrobatic lifts and spins. This hyper performance, fueled by alpha male competition and magnetic physical attraction, went on until the moon, exhausted, fell into the sea that caressed this limestone island in the Mediterranean. Wiping away the fine grit from the bullring that powdered my arms and face, I did not see the Chilean depart. He had vanished on the arm of another woman. Perhaps another man, too. For the best—I was not there to have a fling. I was there to perform.

My dance troupe did do more than dance on Ibiza. Several days after my encounter with the Chilean, in glaring sunlight, we went in search of the sunken civilization of Atlantis. Local lore had it located off the tip of Es Vedra, an island floating offshore Cala d'Hort's bay.

The scorching heat of the sun beating on the steep trail that led down to the bay released intoxicating herbaceous oils of wild rosemary, lavender and thyme that clung to the cliff side. When we reached the sea's edge, salt bream filled our nostrils. It was enlivening to be awake and outside during the daylight after so many all-night dance extravaganzas in Ibiza's uber-clubs and mega mansions.

As we leaned against the smooth, sun-bleached limestone boulders in this quarry on the sea's lapping edge, Sana handed each of us a ritualistic tab of ecstasy. Sana was our group leader and instigator of all things outrageous. As the zing zip of the drug effervesced in my bloodstream and my defenses dissolved, stifled emotions welled up. The secret burden of my life surfaced.

I had *so* wanted a little girl child. My son was adorable, but I wanted more kids. The abortion I'd had several years before due to my ex-husband's wishes was a sore, a gash still bleeding into my veins daily. As the heat emanating from the rocks penetrated my tense body, the iceberg-shard tips of that anguish melted and rivulets of sorrow slid down my cheeks pooling, in the hollow of my collarbone.

My maudlin grieving was interrupted by a shuffling sound. My teary eyes snapped open and there stood a young girl with long dark hair. Not a hallucination. Her jade green eyes stared directly into my sea blue eyes. By God, my wish was being granted. Who had waved the wand? Drugs are amazing. I'd always wanted another child, a girl to take to Paris. And here she was!

This little girl even spoke French. Her name was Marie-Claire. We bonded immediately. She grabbed my hand and pulled me up. She wasn't put off at all by the tears streaming down my face or my herky-jerky French. She wanted to play and to show me the crab.

Still holding hands, we walked past my bemused friends who could not figure out how I had suddenly conjured up a child, and waded into a tepid tide pool. She dove down, pale shiny child butt sticking up in the air. She popped up breathlessly and said I *must* do the same thing to see "him." Sure enough, once I did as she commanded, the crab was waggling his antennae eyes at me from under the rock through the murky water. Our upside down antics had stirred up the sand.

She then took me up a trail and around a ledge and we both peed on the dirt. Both of us were fascinated by the yellow streams gushing out from between our legs. Suddenly, hearty laughter startled us. On the boulders above us stood a man who was pointing and laughing. "Papa," she yelled, wagging her finger at him.

The Chilean! The dark handsome dancer from the bullring full-moon party.

For some reason, I wasn't self-conscious about having him see me peeing with his daughter, both of us totally naked. She explained to me that they had a camp beyond the rocks where he was standing.

Marie-Claire grabbed my hand again and ran down to the sea where the gurgling ocean waves sucked in and out over rocks covered in yellow-green algae. She beckoned me to sit on the green seaweed carpet and slide down into the water. A wave caught us and pushed us upward. We slid back and forth with the tide, laughing until tears ran down our sun burnt cheeks.

I'd completely forgotten my sorrows and desires. This happy child had invited me into her world, an enchanted playground of quirky sea creatures and hidden caves.

Then she slipped into the malachite green waters and disappeared. Her silhouette moved below the water's surface. She looked like a mermaid. Then, there was another larger shadow with her. I worried that it was a predator and dove in swimming to her depth. The shadow was her father. They didn't seem to need to come up for air. They showed me how to swim deep with the colder currents. These people were fantastical and mythical, dancing through their watery world like manatees or dolphins or selkies.

Marie-Claire was hungry after all her romping in the water and on land. We followed a narrow path that wound between the skyscraper-size Mesozoic boulders to where they were camping. He had created an other-worldly living space veiled in cream-colored canvas roofs, with thin slabs of pink slate as tabletops, white smoothed boulders for chairs, and Persian carpets that lay over the taupe sand.

The only way to get to their Bedouin-style encampment was by foot down the steep trail, or by Zodiac. As he prepared lunch, he told me he came here from Belgium every year and brought his boat and his daughter. They held court in this old-world quarry for the entire summer.

We grazed on large green olives, Manchego cheese, tomatoes, and fresh sardines. He had a soft yet radiant smile and told me his name was Patrice. He was from Dalcahue in Chiloé.

My mouth dropped open like an attic trapdoor. I was sitting in a dream setting of opaque rock and turquoise sea, without clothes, completely at home with a man who had terrified me several nights before. He was also blessed with a fairy princess daughter who was affectionate, intelligent and gifted.

Yet, this wasn't the reason my mouth was gaping open. It was because Patrice was from my favorite place in all of South America—perhaps the entire world. An island floating off the southern toe of Chile, only accessible by boat or seaplane, and only for six months a year when the savage winter storms subside. A place where the fishermen's wives knit bulky wool sweaters dyed in natural hues from the blood of walnut husks, moss, berries, seaweed, and mushrooms.

I knew Dalcahue well, as I went there many times in the 1970s to import those handspun sweaters. It took several days on planes, trains, ferries and small fishing boats to get there from Santiago, the capital of Chile. Nobody outside of Chiloé is from Chiloé.

His voice pulled me back to this island in the warmer climes of the Mediterranean. As he sliced ripe tomatoes on a stone slab, he shared that he was a ballet dancer and lived in a church in Brussels that he'd converted into an art and dance studio.

Damn!

Why couldn't he be pompous or stupid? Or from Milwaukee? This was all too delicious and tempting (and I'm not talking about the sardines!).

He flipped through a photo album and showed me pictures of his sculptural work. Full-size men and women engraved in the sand on the beaches of Normandy. Tides in the area shift, as described by Victor Hugo, "*à la vitesse d'un cheval au gallop*"—as swiftly as a galloping horse. The tide comes in at one meter per second. When the long tides were pulled in, Patrice filmed the encroaching foamy salt water eroding the Rodin-quality sculptures he had carved over many days. He chronicled the licking away at their curves, the dissolving of their shapes.

As he ran his fingers over the seashell-gray-toned photographs, describing the feel of the sand as he shaped these voluptuous bodies, his voice soft and faraway, I found him, his lifestyle, his family, all excruciatingly captivating.

A spell had been cast and I completely forgot about my friends back on the rocks.

In the late afternoon sun, after more explorations and a nap in their kasbah, Marie-Claire and I wound around the stones littering the hollow quarry pit they called home. There in the amber afternoon light, Patrice was squatting in front of a carving on the limestone face. It was a man and a woman embracing under water as they swam together. Botticelli delightful, da Vinci beautiful. Classic perfection.

As his golden arms and long-fingered hands chiseled these people into the rock, Patrice told me he was involved with the couple I saw him dancing with at the bullring. The sculpture depicted them. "It is complicated," he said. I don't know why he shared this with me but it made me feel very two-dimensional, simple, and boring. And American.

Suddenly, he looked at me mischievously out of the corner of his twinkling eyes and asked, "Would you like to spend the night? My daughter needs feminine company."

Maybe I wasn't so boring after all....

"What about my friends?" I asked in an embarrassing squeak. My vocal chords weren't cooperating. I was scared and looking for the exit. The intensity of the connection wiped me clean of sensibility and instead of feeling a resounding thunderclap *Yes!*, I practically tripped over him as I ran away. I didn't even say goodbye to Marie-Claire.

As I speed-walked past my astonished friends, who were halfway up the trail, one-way conversations bounced around inside my skull. *You would abandon your young son for a life with a bisexual, polyamorous man in cold, gray Belgium?* My mind spun out dramas as fast as it could to distract me from my attraction to this gorgeous man who had just invited me to spend the night with him. I mean, his daughter.

After I plowed over my friends to get in the car, they asked, "He invited you to spend the night? What are you doing here?"

I muttered something about them worrying about me if I didn't come back with them.

In unison, they all chanted, "Stupid! Isn't that what you wanted?"

On my last night in Ibiza, Sana choreographed yet another party. This one took place in an abandoned military fort. She turned each cold cement room into a vibrant temple celebrating various goddesses from Isis to Aphrodite.

Looking up from the flames licking the sky around the perennial bonfire ring, I saw his eyes across the fire's golden flicker. Panther eyes.

The Chilean and I skirted each other through the evening's mayhem of rituals and exhaustive dance-a-thons. I ended up collapsed in a sweaty pile next to him on one of Sana's makeshift temple floors. He draped a pashmina shawl over me as I pretended to sleep. No kisses. No hugs. No sex. No goodbye.

I arose at dawn and Oscar drove me to the airport for my long journey back to California.

⚜ ⚜ ⚜

I can still see the jaggy edge trim of his thick pitch-black hair framing his face. I can still feel the tidal pull of ultimate attraction. I'm still in love with that artist. Or at least the concept and packaging.

What if I had spent the night in that stone pink-tented wonderland he created? I muse about this every few years. What if I let the artist from my favorite remote island in the world woo me?

At first, I always repeat the same old litany, "No, no! I had to go home to work and take care of my son." But the blanket of reason that vigilantly guards the door to my heart falls off, and the truth speaks in a timid yet convincing voice, "I don't want to be swept away by the murderous riptides of love. No heart landmines for me (even if they are just in my imagination)…"

⚜ ⚜ ⚜

Lisa Alpine is the author of Exotic Life: Laughing Rivers, Dancing Drums and Tangled Hearts *and co-author of* the Self-Publishing Boot Camp Workbook. *She is the founding publisher of Dancing Words Press and the Global Getaways columnist for* Examiner.com. *She is also an acclaimed teacher and leads workshops on travel writing and dance as a healing art form.*

Lisa is a member of the Wild Writing Women, California Writers Club and Bay Area Travel Writers. When not wrestling with words, exploring the ecstatic realms of dance, swimming with sea creatures, or waiting for a flight, Lisa is planting fruit trees in her garden in Mill Valley, California, or orchids in her jungle hideaway on the Big Island. Her gardens of vivid flowers and abundant fruit remind her that the future is always ripe with possibilities. You can find out more about her at www.lisaalpine.com

꙳ ꙳ ꙳

Alone, Illegal, and Broke Down

In the late '90s, she rode northern China solo.

I T IS MY FIRST DAY ALONE ON THE ROAD AND I AM LOST. The mountains of northern China beyond Beijing are vast and enormous. There are no road signs, only larger roads and smaller roads, paved roads and dirt roads. When I stop to ask directions the peasants simply stare because I am the first foreigner they have ever seen, and a woman. Putting myself in their place I can sympathize. I ride up on a big black Chinese sidecar motorcycle, the most expensive motorcycle in China. Then I remove my helmet. A blond braid tumbles down the shoulder of my black leather jacket and I mutter something incomprehensible and then look at them with slightly crazed green eyes.

"*W mílù le*," I say. "I'm lost."

But most villagers have never traveled farther than their network of about a dozen villages all of their lives. And there are no taxi drivers or buses or truckers to ask.

Nearly out of gasoline, I am sure that Lijang, the town I had targeted for my first night on the road, will not appear anytime soon. The going is slow not only because of the dark but because of the potholes and badly banked curves and the asphalt that ends without warning.

Where might I be? I might have looped back to where I began. I could be far, far away. I remember how the land looked in daylight: the jumble of pyramid-shaped mountains covered in soft green foliage jutting through the landscape, the crumbling hillsides, the plunging cliffs.

Another tiny village passes; windows covered in thick, oiled paper glow with the flickering light of cooking fires. Exhausted, I consider stopping but would they be friendly? How could I tell them what I want? If I stop here it might cause an uproar. Do they have food to spare? A bed? Certainly not. My thoughts loop on the problem of where to sleep that night and on the problems that hadn't yet come. In the background the unfamiliar engine rumbles. I am still working out its idiosyncrasies. I don't yet know this machine well enough to take comfort in its working noises, its hard clunk down from third gear, its slight pull to the left.

Shadow trees fly by and another village appears. I shift down, slowing in anticipation of the many potholes a village brings, and a small animal suddenly bursts into the road. A rush of adrenaline prepares me for hard braking, for swerving or impact.

I hold my ground, trusting my instincts. I can't tell if the side of the road dives off into a five-foot ditch or heads straight into a two-foot wall. The animal races alongside and, improbably, others join in. Finally I realize they are piglets. We travel together down the road for several long moments of dark indecision. I hold my breath while they grunt and squeal hysterically, invisibly.

Several times it seems that they will move off the road and out of my way, and several times it seems that they will run under my tires. Finally, I gently let pressure off the throttle, decelerating very slowly. The engine noise deepens and, in response, one piglet lets out a sudden, long, high-pitched squeal. The others squeal in response and follow it off the road into darkness.

Heart racing, I am alone again. Dirt road. Dark night. Miles later I notice that my fingers are still stiffly poised above the brake lever. The icy night air leaks up the sleeves of my jacket and between my collar and helmet. My joints ache from working the clutch and the gears of this heavy beast of a motorcycle, bumping along a barely paved road in the pitch black backwoods of China.

That afternoon my friends back in Beijing, the four Chinese bikers who formed my send-off party, led me through Beijing in a complicated route into these mountains. They turned back at the Beijing-Heibi province border with regret in their eyes and I rode on. They were tied, without specific government permission to travel, to the province where they lived. Before I visited China I'd had no idea that people living in one province were forbidden to travel in other provinces without special permissions and special license plates. Their plates were the blue provincial plates, mine was the special black plate that allowed me to cross borders. We said goodbye and I traveled on, alone.

I had spent the previous week in Beijing trying to get my papers in order. Permissions. Signatures. Chops. Both the American embassy and the Chinese government proved useless in helping with permits. I was required to obtain a Chinese driver's license to ride outside Beijing province, but that required residency, a driving test, lots of paperwork. First of all, I had no residency. It seemed that, though the Chinese government was newly eager to welcome independent travelers, they didn't know how to accommodate them.

My expat friends, people I'd met through the embassy, explained that since the tourist policy was in a transition period, the lawmakers wouldn't know what the rules were. It would probably be safe to go, even without papers, they said. "They won't put you in jail for more than a day if you get caught," one explained. "And you probably won't get caught...at least not for a while."

It had been a hot, humid Saturday, a particularly auspicious day for weddings, it turned out. Brides in layers of white silk and chiffon perspired in the back seats of economy cars trailing red and white streamers, their drivers honking incessantly in celebration.

My new friends rode Chang Jiang sidecar motorcycles that belonged to two Chinese members of the international CJ motorcycle club in Beijing. We crawled along Beijing's third ring road until, right in front of us, a truck plowed into a taxi and slid out of the intersection. For a moment, all was still. Then, suddenly, traffic on all four sides lunged toward the center. Within seconds every car was touching the bumper or door of another car, resulting in a tightly woven fabric of glittering metal.

We escaped by riding into a shallow ditch and onto a railroad track that our sidecar bikes easily managed, for they were designed for use by messengers through the rough terrain where World War II was fought. They are essentially carbon copies of the 1938 BMW motorcycles, built hastily with inferior materials, yet still robust.

I was sweating in the deep heat of polluted urban Beijing, though I'd stripped to my tank top. Our leader, Jiangshan, had to be steaming in his Harley Davidson jacket, but he kept it zipped up. His girlfriend, Yang Xiao, sat slightly away

from the leather back of the sidecar chair, one hand grip-
ping the edge of the car and the other held up to her aviator
glasses. Every so often she'd turn around to smile and give
me a thumbs up. Her glossy black hair tangled in the fringe
of the brown suede sleeves of her American-Indian-styled
motorcycle jacket. People driving, riding bicycles, waiting
to cross the road, stared. Beautiful, wide-eyed Yang Xiao.
She always had a slightly haunted look, except when she was
riding, and then her black eyes sparkled, and her movements
were almost careless. Jiangshan, an unusually tall, dignified
man of around fifty, also brightened when he rode. His movements became larger, his voice louder. On the motorcycle,
they seemed almost American.

Lee and Liu followed on another Chang Jiang through
the ruthlessly dense Beijing traffic until we rose above the
city into the relief of a beautifully paved single-lane mountain byway. The air cooled as we passed farming villages, a
lifestyle in harmony with nature. I glimpsed grain drying in
courtyards behind village walls made from mud and straw.
The traditional curlicue roofs seemed carefully maintained
in the old style, with protective demons painted on doorways.
Here, I forgot about the problems of urban life, enjoyed the
scenery and dodged donkey carts full of twigs, maneuvered
around diesel tractors pulling into the road from the fields, a
dusty wind in my face.

Country roads, sunshine, and the camaraderie of fellow
riders should have made for a perfect Saturday, but the realization that in a few hours I would be riding alone for as long
as six months through this strange country sent bolts of fear
shooting through my heart and stomach. The Heibi Province
border appeared.

Our moment of separation was inevitable. My borrowed
bike, with its expensive black license plates, was authorized
for operation in any province, though its rider wasn't. These
black plates, an indication of importance, of *guanxi*—their

term for power, freedom, prestige—would keep me from being harassed by the police—or so I hoped.

Jiangshan gave me some extra wheel spokes and told me I would be lucky. Yang Xiao game me a hug, and Lee and Liu shook my hand.

I rode alone with a knot in my stomach trying to enjoy the first few hours of my solo journey but I was completely cowed by the wildness of Northern Heibi province. I still had the vague impression from childhood that all of China was densely populated. But this lonely country backwater was riddled with potholed roads among jagged mountains covered in soft brushy bushes and trees. The air was fresh and cool in the late afternoon, and the green mountains gave the atmosphere a healthy glow. I never imagined that China had such wide-open spaces, and then the road forked into three with no signs to mark the way. I switched the engine off and, for the first time since I arrived in the country, experienced absolute silence.

After a while, I pulled the map from the sidecar to consider it seriously now for the first time and to search, unsuccessfully, for my three-pronged crossroads, when a peasant wearing ragged cotton pants and a peaked cap appeared. He pushed a jumble of tree branches in a wooden handcart, his arms and shoulders straining against the slight decline of the road.

"N h o," I said to him, expecting him to return my hello. He stopped and I shoved up the visor of my helmet, to be better understood. "N h o," I repeated carefully, intoning as properly as I could in my basic Mandarin. "W mílù le," I said, slowly. "I'm lost."

He stared, as if he understood, so I continued, asking the way to Liajang. "Z nme qù Liajang?"

The man was tiny, and looked eighty but was probably only sixty, badly bent from work and probably mineral deficiencies. His face was tan and flat, lightly wrinkled, and his eyes, though bright, were sunken deeply. I saw that he was a little startled when he stepped nearer to me to peer up into my helmet.

"*Liajang?*" I repeated, rattling my map and punching the name of the town with my finger. Its name was clearly written in Pinyin, the Roman characters that appeared under the Chinese pictograms, but I really couldn't tell how to pronounce it correctly and it's possible the man couldn't read. The paper rustled, ignored in the gentle breeze as the man continued to stare at my face with the bald curiosity of a child.

I'd been stared at in Beijing but this was absurd. The man acted as if I was a statue in a wax museum. He studied my jacket, then bent down to study my jeans and my boots, and rose again to take a look at my helmet and gloves before walking all around the motorcycle.

At least it gave me time to stare back. So this would be the peasant so reviled and absolutely dismissed, usually with a disgusted sneer, by the Chinese middle class. In his peaked cap with his wrinkled old face he was a museum piece himself, a caricature of the Chinese peasant in his blue Mao clothes, with his stringy gray hair, pushing his battered wheelbarrow. I asked one more time the way to Liajang, but he continued to stare, slack jawed and glassy-eyed.

Starting off again I chose the middle of the three equally unlikely looking roads. The middle way seemed appropriate as a spiritual path, at least. Not that I was practicing moderation just then, but it wasn't a heads or tails situation.

The middle way twisted around and down and up and around again and I no longer had any idea of the direction it would lead. It didn't really matter, I told myself. I wasn't on any particular deadline and I needed only to head roughly west, toward Tibet and the setting sun. With that thought I settled into a not unpleasant resignation. The scenery was wild and serene and the tension knotting in my stomach dissipated. I had chosen Liajang because it was a fairly large town with a few hotel choices, according to my Lonely Planet guide, but surely another town would appear. Or so I thought.

The joy of exploration waned with the fading daylight, the absence of a road sign, a gas station, or a town. I continued to choose my way randomly at forks in the road and, like the first road, they followed the contours of the mountains to take me on a tour of all the directions of the compass. By the time darkness fell I had passed only the tiniest of villages. The peasants performed their end-of-day tasks. They were poor, desperately poor. Their windows were covered in oiled paper. Their water was fetched from who knows where in buckets hung from sticks carried on their shoulders, and their grain was sorted and ground by hand and their small gardens protected from the animals by fences of bricks made of mud and it seemed impossible that anything would change for them tonight, or tomorrow, or in the years after.

Ten kilometers of empty road passes between the village where the piglets had run beside me and here, where the road narrows and deteriorates into dirt and gravel. The dark shapes of trees hover above on either side. Long ago Kublai Khan had traveled through China and was dismayed at the unbroken monotony of the roadways. He ordered trees planted on every roadside to give solace to travelers.

The trees do not give me solace as my headlight shines on one after another after another white painted tree trunk giving me the impression that it is they which move past me, and that I am sitting still like an actor on a movie set, the wind machine blowing in my face.

What does give me solace is the sudden appearance of two gas pumps under a brightly-lit shelter. Beyond it stands a building strung with white lights that I hope is a hotel. I pull up to the pumps and after a moment a woman peeks out of the doorway of the attached shack. She hushes the two small children peeking out behind her to walk toward me. Her outfit is garishly illuminated under the fluorescent lights. She sports a shapeless lime green dress sprinkled with large white polka dots and opaque knee-highs that have left a sharp dent halfway up her short fat calves, and bright pink rubber pool sandals.

She decodes my rough Mandarin as she pumps gas into the tank. Yes, she nods, smiling. The lit building is indeed a hotel—her *luguan*. I can stay there, and it will cost twenty yuan.

Equipped with a full tank of gas and this happy information I follow the road she traced with her finger. I would otherwise have never found the entrance, a steep dirt and gravel driveway that passes over a shaky wooden bridge built over what seems to be a very deep ravine. The sound of water running far below me quickens my heart. It will be interesting to see in the morning what death-defying feat I am performing by crossing over these rickety beams.

I pass underneath a concrete archway and through a pair of open wooden gates into the compound where a low, cheaply built stucco building stands. It is L-shaped and there is a glassed-in hallway with motel-style doors in regular intervals, each painted bright red and illuminated with a bare bulb.

I pull up to a partially open doorway that I figure is the manager's office and switch off the engine. It is difficult to unfasten my helmet strap with cold, stiff fingers. My back aches and my left ankle throbs from the constant shifting through gears. I toss my helmet, gloves, and scarf into the sidecar and dismount, only vaguely aware of the rush of people emerging from the door in front of me. I step away from the bike, allowing several people to push it closer to the building. My forehead itches, my hair is stuck to the skin.

Despite my aches, I feel a profound gratitude for having found this place, for the reward of having pressed on without panicking. It is dark and cold, but I'd soon be safe and warm. Finally my eyes adjust to the dim light and looking up, I meet the gaze of a dozen young ladies dressed in pajamas. When I smile they burst into giggles, covering their mouths with their hands.

So many maids! Why would there be so many maids for such a small country motel? I look at them more closely. Their black eyes flash. So much makeup! They giggle some more, then, suddenly shy, lower their eyes heavy with liner and false lashes. Their lips glow with thick red lipstick and their lurid peach-colored polyester uniforms shine. They aren't maids at all, I finally realize. I'll be spending the night in a brothel.

A man pushes his way through the girls and speaks in sharp tones that makes them stop giggling and stand aside. He is very young and so thin that his brown wool pinstriped suit hangs on him in folds as though on a coat hanger. His hair is carefully clipped and gelled into a stiff American fifties-style flat-top, with one lock left long to hang rakishly in his face. He tosses his head back to fling the lock out of his eye, and says something that makes the girls laugh nervously and flutter a little farther away.

I greet him with a Chinese hello and a look him straight in the eye, and the girls giggle again, their hands flying up to cover their mouths. Sighing, he beckons me to his office, a lit doorway just in front of us, and takes me by the arm to guide me inside. Surprisingly, he is a few inches taller than I, perhaps 5 feet 10 inches tall.

The girls follow us in but after few sharp words from the boss they recede into the darkness and we are left alone in the office: a square concrete box with a steel desk and a ratty Naugahyde couch bursting at the seams. I fish through the pockets of my black leather motorcycle jacket and hand him twenty yuan, the amount the woman at the gas station had quoted. He laughs and pushes it back to me. I am too tired to go through an extended haggling process, and too tired to remember that I am desperate for sleep. After riding all day in the heat, after the stress of being lost, the uncertainty of the motorcycle, finding gasoline, night falling unmercifully black and those tiny villages with fires and stray pigs and white-trunked trees, I am exhausted, and I could strangle him for what he is doing, opening drawers to find a pencil so that he can write the digits 200 on a piece of paper, ten times the price the woman at the gas station had quoted.

I hold the paper and we stand silently together on the stained burgundy carpet. It is as thin as denim, and glued badly onto the concrete floor. The walls are covered in crackling stucco, and the sagging ceiling is stained with water. The black and white television set is turned on full volume, the sound horribly distorted. Two attractive anchorpeople, a man and a woman, report the news. Their announcements are a combination of guttural and singsong nasal whining. Footage of a public execution flits across the screen: two kneeling men, blindfolded with hands bound behind their backs, a mass of enraged or excited people. Would they be shot or beheaded or hanged? Then they show blond Russian children digging through a vast garbage dump for scraps of food, followed by stills of President Clinton who is due to visit in a few months. I'd seen the same footage in Beijing, over and over and over again. It is 1998, the year that China would remove borders and other barriers to sharing in first world wealth.

I study the piece of paper. I could counter with thirty, and he would insist upon 100, and I would write down thirty-five, and he would then write fifty, and then I would hand him forty. He would take it, and I really should do all that except that the woman at the gas station already gave me the price of twenty yuan and in my exhausted state I'm not thinking about all the trouble I will cause here with paperwork and lack of language and writing skills and my need for hot water. I shove the paper back at him and explain in succinct English that the owner told me it was twenty yuan and twenty yuan was all I was damn well going to pay and hadn't he heard that the days of Foreigner price were over. I wave the twenty toward the gas station and tell him that if he thinks I'm going to pay two hundred for a dump like this he is crazy and I push it into his hand. He takes it with a little shrug and a smile that means, "Well, I had to try," and I stomp back to the motor-cycle but it's not there anymore. Stunned, I look around and see, with no little relief, that it has only been pushed away into the crook of the L-shaped compound near the wooden gates. I feel the manager watching me as I stomp across to it. I jerk my suitcase out of the sidecar, unlock and open the trunk to get my computer case and camera, and two of the girls sud-denly appear to escort me to my room.

The hallway is glassed in, and we step up two shallow stairs onto the same thin, wrinkled burgundy carpet that was in the manager's office, and even more blotched. Standing by each door is a little yellow pot decorated delicately with pink fleur-de-lis, a quarter full of water. As I puzzle over the purpose of these, moths bash themselves to death on the bare light bulbs in front of each door, falling in the collected heap in front of each threshold. Every tiny impact creates a tinging sound that is just audible over the sound of a river.

The room is a concrete box. One of the girls pushes by me to rush in and turn on the television at full volume. The other girl walks in behind me bearing a thermos of hot water and a small, thin towel. I walk into the bathroom—it was built into the corner of the room like an afterthought, with walls that fall short of the ceiling by a foot. The hot water tap runs cold, as does the cold water tap. I request more thermoses of hot water, and she returns shortly with three more.

I put my suitcase on the double bed and the girls come closer as I unzip it. I had packed very little but carefully; a Gortex rain suit, a fine-gauge, bicycle-weight wool sweater, long silk underwear, thick hiking socks and boots, sports-bras and tights, quick-dry shirts and a toiletries kit with neat little bottles of shampoo and conditioner, moisturizer and sunscreen and a clear plastic bag full of bottles of medicines I might need.

I wonder how to get the girls out of my room so I can have some privacy, and then the manager strides in, barking at the girls, who wander out reluctantly. Alone again, he looks at me and sighs, then hands me a form, knowing that this is going to be an ordeal for it's in Chinese and I'm illiterate. We settle ourselves down at the fake walnut desk at the foot of the bed and study the form and my passport, attempting to figure out which information goes in which box. After studying each other's documents, we look up at each other, shrug, and begin.

I ought to have asked a clerk in a Beijing tourist hotel to give me a form that was printed in both English and Chinese, as a reference, but I didn't, and so with a combination of my phrasebook, sign-language, grimaces and some laughter, we manage to fill out about a third of the boxes when he abruptly pulls the paper away. Either that's all that's required or he's fed up. I expect the latter.

Now that we're done I realize how much trouble I am, and sympathize. He really is just a very young man and I create a lot of hassle because of the form and demands for many thermoses of hot water and the motorcycle parking and the uproar.

I put my passport away and we walk outside together. He returns to the office and I walk over to where they've moved the motorcycle. Suddenly, a large blue truck roars in at an alarming speed to screech to a stop exactly in the place I'd parked the bike. No wonder they'd moved it. Two girls in peach polyester pajamas run to the door as the truck door opens. One literally catches the driver as he falls from the cab. The moonlight illuminates the empty liquor bottle in his right hand. Even though it's empty he struggles to keep it upright during his fall. The other girl knocks it to the ground where it lies, empty and unbroken in the dusty light, as they escort him, stumbling, to the room next to the manager's office.

I'd been warned that these big blue trucks were piloted by drivers fuelled by amphetamines and alcohol. They'd be my most frequent companions on the road, but that's changing, fast. Though private cars have been allowed for many years, most Chinese haven't been able to afford them, and so trucks and official vehicles make up ninety percent of the traffic out here in the country.

The excitement over, I finish locking the bike up, covering it to keep the dust out and to hide the attention-getting black Beijing plates. Back in my room I notice that the door doesn't have a lock. But I'd brought a solution for that—an alarm that slides into the doorjamb. It works on a circuit breaker—if the door opens the device also springs open, activating a piercing alarm.

I pour the hot water from the thermoses into a red plastic basin on the bathroom floor and take a sponge bath. Brushing my teeth, I peer out from between the tattered curtains to catch the action in the compound. Apparently I have arrived just ahead of rush hour. Blue truck after blue truck roars in, their drivers and passengers falling out of their cabs, spilling empty bottles of high-octane liquor. I am forgotten.

This is my first night on the road, and my mind busies itself on the problems of my trip. I am traveling without a license, nor permissions of any sort from the Chinese or American government, and risk arrest at any moment. Just a few hours into my trip I discovered that I couldn't rely on road signs or local people to tell me the way. Since I just generally want to head west, that doesn't matter so much. I have no particular place to be at any certain time. But it is also now obvious that hotels are difficult to find. Is this at all dangerous, or simply inconvenient? Since I feel perfectly safe—even in this brothel—I don't feel it's too risky. But tomorrow would be the time to turn back if I'm going to, only one day's ride from Beijing.

I miss Beijing. In Beijing people interacted with me. Foreigners are not rare, and they laugh good-naturedly when I practice my Mandarin. They willingly look at maps and point me in the right direction. I miss hanging out with Teresa, the agricultural attaché at the U.S. Embassy. We rode together through the countryside once before I left, and the farmers were astonished at us, the motorcycles, and at her fluent Mandarin. She talked endlessly with them about the state of the crops, the weather, and whether the government had paid them in cash or pink IOU slips. Tonight, at the brothel, I long for Beijing.

In the morning it is eerily quiet, which makes me nervous until I remember that, of course, a brothel operates at night.

In the bright morning light I see that the short red carpet is a puzzle of dark splotchy stains. The walls are stained with moisture and the bathroom tiles are caked with mold. The tiles themselves have been shattered with a hammer to let the plumbing in. Caulking does not seem to be a talent the local handymen possess. Neither do they seem to have a grasp of the force of gravity—the bathroom drain is located at the highest end of the room so that a puddle of stagnant water sits in a corner with drowned bugs floating at the edges.

I half-fill the red basin with cold water from the dripping sink faucet, and uncork one of the green plastic thermoses of hot water they gave me the previous night. Amazingly, it is still piping hot, hot enough for a cup of instant coffee. I check my skin for bedbugs. None. I hope that this will be the rattiest place I ever have to stay in.

Seeing my face in the mirror, I'm shocked at my puffy eyes and pallid skin. Riding a motorcycle for so many hours at one stretch is never healthy, and I am still also recovering from the effects of Beijing pollution.

In Beijing my expat friends were still sleeping in their luxurious, American-style homes and apartments with filtered water and filtered air before a day of work in offices with filtered water and filtered air. Maybe they will think of me this weekend when they ride out to the Ming Tombs on one of their forays into the countryside. Last week the little trips seemed the height of adventure.

I take my cup of coffee outside, passing the other rooms where pairs of male shoes sit neatly outside each door. These black shoes made of leather and so carefully polished cannot be truckers shoes. The little yellow pots of water had been moved to the other side of the hallway. I peer in cautiously. They don't look like chamber pots but there is something in them. What can it be? I look closer to see globs floating on top of the water. Gross. They are spittoons.

Suppressing a gag, I hurry outside. The courtyard is empty except for a small Chinese motorcycle leaning on its side against the opposite wall: there are no trucks in sight. I surmise that the drivers pumped themselves back up with amphetamines and continued on their route.

Now to see where I am. I hear the river and try to find a way out of the compound to take a look at it. Tiptoeing down the hallways I find an unlocked door that leads outside onto a natural terrace overlooking a beautiful river cutting deeply into a stone canyon with a deeply striated stone cliff rising to the mountain behind.

All this hidden behind a crappy stucco compound, valueless in contrast to the income-generating brothel. In the West this place would have been the site of a luxurious resort with a terrace overlooking the river where one could sip coffee in the morning and beer in the evening, enjoying the spectacle of nature. It would have at least been a campground. But who wants to visit such a place here, in Northern China? Heibi Province is the poorest of the northern provinces, the mountains offer no weird and spectacular rock formations like those in Gualin and Yunnan, so tourists don't come. This is merely a relaxing, beautiful, natural place, only a day's journey from a major city. But in the United States it would be swarming with backpackers, kayakers, and mountain climbers.

Back in Beijing, an American friend, Rick, had told me a story about camping that illustrated the Chinese attitude toward nature. Jiangshan, the leader of my send-off party and the owner of a camping supply shop, had led the group on an overnight outing. Jiangshan had described beautiful mountains and clean air and a perfect riverside campsite. The group had been thrilled with the ride but the "perfect place to camp" was an asphalt parking lot with bright streetlights standing sentry all around. Rick had difficulty explaining diplomatically why their faces had all fallen flat. Jiangshan was quite taxed to understand why they'd rather pitch their tents on uneven ground in the messy, dark woods.

Jiangshan's adventure shop is stocked with a few tents and sleeping bags but only Western visitors buy these things—the students, teachers, and expats who discover that China has amazing and beautiful countryside. They camp, and inevitably a group of locals comes and stares at them as they cook their meals and fish and put up the tents and bed down. It is a concept absolutely and completely foreign to Chinese villagers, and when I look at their lives I see why. Most of them are already camping, with their coal stoves and hand-carried water. They see the forest as a source for wood to burn and food to forage. It's easy to understand how they would wonder why wealthy people would make themselves so deliberately uncomfortable.

Back in Beijing most of Jiangshan's customers are nouveaux riche who buy Patagonia jackets and Swiss army watches as status symbols to wear on the streets of Beijing, or on touring vacations to Guilin or Yunnan where they tiptoe along the trails in designer shoes.

After the stress of the past twenty-four hours I welcome the surprise of vast nature. There are probably some pretty little villages in the hills here. What if I left the motorcycle behind for a few days, put on my hiking boots and tried to find them?

Not on my first day out.

Or can I?

I'm lost already, much too early in the trip. And my plans are vague. The general idea to cross China from east to west, heading south through Sichuan and Yunnan is just a sketch. I now realize the roads are not as mapped, and that I have some hardcore dirt riding ahead of me. If the bike holds up, and I can get to the south, how will I get back? That's the part I can never figure out when I look at the maps. The coasts are too crowded and the interior impossibly mountainous.

Sitting by the rushing river against the high coppery cliffs provides an anchor. There will always be the force of nature. If the human face of China is impermeable, threatening, nature renews and relaxes. Confronting foreign nature has always been more comfortable to me than confronting foreign cities, and today's ride promises spectacular scenery.

Suddenly I can't wait to get back on the road. Who cares which road? I need only head generally west. And when I hit a barrier, south, then when I reach my destination, north.

But first is a ritual that will be repeated each morning.

Back in the parking lot I unlock the motorcycle cover and fold it up into a big red duffel bag. Nothing had been touched. I'd been told that the Chinese are scrupulously honest. The more generous claimed it was an innate trait; the less generous claim it's because there are so many tattletales around and the penalties are so harsh.

I try to open the trunk with as little noise as possible but every creak and bang echoes from the walls of the enclosed compound. I stand still in the stark yellow sunlight on the stark yellow dirt, and listen, but no one stirs.

First, the spokes. Sure enough, a lot are already broken from the deep potholes I'd hit the night before. The asphalt had ended abruptly several times and I'd ridden miles of

dirt before the road was paved again. No road hazards were
marked so I'd gone careening off the edges a few times.

I squat in the dirt and begin work as the sun's rays rise over
the mountain.

With a pair of needle-nosed piers, I pull the broken spokes
from their seats in the wheel. Seven of the long ones are broken but all of the short ones are intact. I stop in astonishment.
The day before, when we'd finished replacing three spokes
that had broken on my bike, Jiangshan handed me all of the
extras in his toolkit as a parting gift. His spokes were made
of steel and not the cheap aluminum that I had packed in my
kit. Lee translated his message, eloquently presented with a
small bow: "Seven is an auspicious number, and I predict you
will break no more than seven during your trip."

With seven of them broken on the first day out, it would
be a miracle.

I take each end of a spoke and bend it slightly, maneuver
it around a cross-spoke, then bend it back straight, pressing
both ends into the threaded nipples sunk into the wheel.
The nipples depress slightly into the wheels for this purpose.
They're threaded, and when I twist the spoke it catches the
thread. It takes some work with a pair of pliers to thread each
spoke in all the way, until the nipple pops back out again
when it's seated. Now it's only a matter of banging the spoke
straight. Easy enough, if you aren't too attached to the defini-
tion of "straight."

The sun beats down hard on the compound. It is difficult
working bent over so low to the ground, forcing the spoke
rods into the nipples with the tip of the needle-nose pliers. I sit
back on my heels and spot one of the girls walking across the
compound. Her hair is a rats-nest of black tangles falling out
from the pins that had probably, the night before, formed an
elegant coif. She glances furtively at me as she passes, holding
her thin blue robe closed with tight fists. Her eyes are rac-
coon-black from smeared mascara and a red streak of lipstick

stains her chin. She disappears into a darkened hallway and I hear the sound of water running.

Checking the oil is next. It needs about a quarter of the quart bottle I'd packed in my trunk. That isn't bad, really, for the distance I traveled yesterday.

Then I touch all the nuts and bolts—some are loose and, not surprisingly, so is the electrical connection to a turn signal.

Back in the room I take a quick sponge bath with the remaining thermos of hot water and scrub the grease and dirt as best I can from my fingers. It would be interesting to find out a little more about the brothel, I'll have to ask Teresa when I get back. I already know that, like most places, China has interesting and conflicting views on sexuality. For one thing, the government insists that homosexuality doesn't exist, and even claims that HIV isn't a problem. Condoms are not routinely used, and the condoms manufactured in China are of the poorest quality. Abortion is the most common method of birth control and is provided at no cost by the state, which supplies traveling doctors in medically-equipped vans for this purpose. As for the brothel, I surmise it is state-run, like everything else in the country, but still I'm uncomfortable with the thought of cops dropping by, just in case it's run like the ones at home—an illegal activity sporadically enforced and profitable for corrupt officials.

I haul my suitcase, a soft-sided convertible backpack, from the room, and slide it into the toe of the sidecar. The motorcycle cover goes into a duffel bag with the tire repair kit and pump, which rests in the seat. I shove my maps (with town names printed in both Roman and Chinese characters) between the duffel and the seat back of the sidecar for easy access, and there is also room in the duffel for food. A trunk located behind the seat back is lockable and holds my valuables in its two-by-two foot compartment.

First into the trunk is the video camera, which lies on top of miscellaneous spare parts like an extra headlamp, signal

bulbs, oil filter, voltage regulator, cables, and spark plugs.
My laptop computer in its padded case slides upright against
the back wall of the trunk and the toolkit against the opposite wall. This leaves just enough room in the middle for
two cameras—one film, one digital—in their padded cases.
A quart or two of oil can easily be wedged in the odd small
spaces and a couple of rags keep the leakage from spilling
onto everything else.

In the pockets of my motorcycle jacket is a small packet
of tissue, small amounts of money for purchasing food, my
passport and a phone number to call in case of emergency, the
trunk key, and a phrasebook.

One final ritual look around the motel room for forgotten
items and I am ready to go. However, the big wooden gates
to the compound are still closed and locked. Just as I consider
knocking on the office door, the compound gates are pushed
open toward me as if I'd said "open sesame." An adolescent
boy walks through, key in hand, and stops, startled, when he
sees me.

"N h o," I say, casually, and push the bike through the
gates. I quickly put on my helmet and start the engine. The
cacophony of the engine warming up rattles through the
canyon and echoes from the cliff walls. Without waiting for
it to warm up I take off over the wooden bridge, peering carefully over the side. Shuddering, I can't believe that a constant
stream of heavy blue supply trucks roar over it. It is even
more rickety than I had imagined the night before. If it collapsed, I'd be immediately swept away in the whitewater that
rushes through the rocky canyon two hundred feet below.

Without thinking about my doubts of the previous night
I turn west, away from Beijing. From a height I can see the
brothel in its U-shaped configuration and some other buildings, also sloppily made from concrete blocks and plaster,
scattered on a very flat area of dry dirt between the river and

the road. It would have been a perfect escape, the setting for a fishing lodge or a campground and a base camp for hiking trips. But the only travelers in China are truckers.

Suddenly, I can't stop laughing. If I had wanted to alter my reality, achieve a true escape from my life in San Francisco, I had certainly succeeded. It's so far away I can barely imagine it—my apartment on Nob Hill on the cable car line, my boyfriend Michael making coffee after an all-night party in some Multimedia Gulch warehouse with electronic music and designer drugs, not to mention the everyday realities of refrigeration and indoor plumbing. And for fun, an afternoon at Baker Beach under the Golden Gate bridge, a motorcycle ride to wine country, or a weekend at Harbin Hot Springs for baths and massages.

I rumble past the now-lifeless gas station and head into the green mountains, passing a village with houses made from mud and straw. It's a tight jumble of rectangles standing on a natural shelf between the road and the river with smoke rising lazily from metal pipes sticking sloppily out at angles from red-tiled roofs.

The sun is bright and hot but the air is still cool. The only other person on the road this morning is a man in blue Mao pants, jacket, and cap pulling a cart of twigs toward the village. He must have been up to gather them before dark.

Centuries ago the peasants lived the same way, in mud and straw houses with wood-fuelled cooking fires. I catch a whiff of smoke and then it's all wilderness again, only mountains and trees as I make my way up a series of switchbacks.

❧ ❧ ❧

Carla King is an adventure travel author who specializes in riding unreliable motorcycles around the world. Her Motorcycle Misadventures dispatches have been published on the Internet since 1995, in realtime from trips around America, China, India, Europe, and Africa. She is a member of the Wild Writing Women and co-founder of Self-Publishing Boot Camp. You can track her down at carlaking.com. The story "Alone, Illegal, and Broke Down" is excerpted from her upcoming book, The China Road Motorcycle Diaries.

≫≈ ≫≈ ≫≈

Wilding Horses

In wildness is the preservation of the world.
—Henry David Thoreau

NOT FAR FROM MY HOUSE IN THE HIGH DESERTS OF northern New Mexico is a large tract of land held by the Bureau of Land Management. It's wide-open land on top of a plateau above the Galisteo River dam. Some years ago two horses were dumped there and left to fend for themselves. Nobody looks after them, but they seem to do pretty well. They have the Galisteo for water, a few cottonwoods for shade and several hundred acres of scrubby grass for grazing. Now unapproachable, the horses are not wild by birth, but made so by circumstance.

One January morning I was walking my dogs across the BLM tract, following a rutted path that snakes across the vast treeless plateau. As my two dogs and I came over a small rise, we found ourselves less than hundred yards away from the wild horses. We were downwind and both grazers startled when they saw us. I had seen the chestnut and palomino before off in the distance, but never so close. Now I could see the scruff of their red and cream winter coats and the snarls of tumbleweed in their tails.

My older dog and I stopped and stared at the horses, but they ignored us and focused on my puppy Dio, who had been racing on ahead. He was much closer to the horses, curious and oblivious to any danger. Worried, I whistled for him and at the sound, the horses charged.

In my experience most horses will run down a dog if they have a chance. My own childhood pony loved to harass any strange dog, cat or small child that dared enter her pasture. Some horses chase dogs just for fun and some will kill a dog if they catch it. These shared their land with a pack of coyotes and while no coyote could take down a healthy horse, these two evidently had a strong distaste for anything resembling a four-legged predator.

Little Dio took one look at the onrushing horses, turned and ran for me full tilt. My other dog, having learned his loose horse lesson before, bunched close beside me. The horses galloped towards us, ears back, teeth bared, intent on running Dio down, but I could see he would make it before the horses caught him. I stooped low and clapped, keeping Dio's attention, encouraging him to run fast and not look back. The panicked puppy reached us when the horses were about ten yards away and once he joined us, I stood up straight, raised my hands to the horses, palms forward, fingers tense like claws and yelled "Hey!"

The charging animals stopped short as if I'd reached out and held them back. They didn't stay still for long, snorting and tossing their heads, looking for weakness. I held my ground and kept my hands up. Staying close together, the horses began circling the dogs and I tightly, in hurried canters, eyes rolling, ears pinned back against their heads. I turned with them, hands still raised and talked to them softly.

After a few passes, their ears relaxed and I felt their tension ease. I lowered my hands and the two of them came to a stop a short distance away and faced me. The whole dance had probably lasted no more than a minute or two.

I stood still for a minute, catching my breath, watching the horses. They were unkempt but beautiful, as wild horses always are. The chestnut took a step towards me and I raised my hands again, stopping him. I wanted to touch him, to run my fingers over his rough coat, but even more so, I wanted him to stay wild. Stepping forward I said loudly but evenly, "You two are lovely, but you'd better give us some space." The horses took a few steps back together, side-by-side, in pace with my advance. I stopped and so did they, their eyes softer now, ears forward, watching and listening to me, more curious than aggressive or afraid.

Then one of the dogs whined, reminding me both were still crowded around my feet. I waved them on ahead, keeping myself between the dogs and the horses. I faced the horses another moment to make sure they were going to let the dogs go, but they ignored them and kept watching me. I studied their blazed faces and long whiskers and watched recognition come into their eyes. I wondered if they were remembering a person they trusted long ago, before their wilding. Slowly, I lowered my hands, turned my back to them and walked away, continuing down the path towards home. As we headed across the open field, every few steps I glanced back, and each time the horses were still standing where I left them, still watching, still wild, letting us walk away.

Communicating with unruly horses is an artform that I began studying at an early age. I grew up in Strasburg, Pennsylvania in the heart of Pennsylvania Dutch country. When I was twelve, I bought a pony, complete with cart and harness, at auction. An Amishman I knew gave me a quick driving lesson on the spot, told me to stick to back roads, and sent me home at the reins. My parents were shocked, of course. But I had taken riding lessons for years and knew how to handle a horse. I named the little red mare Saturday, put her up in a big stall in our big red barn and grazed her in circles in the backyard on a dog tie.

My pony, cart and I fit right in on Strasburg's already rutted country roads and in time, Saturday and I drove up and down all of them. Once, in town, Saturday untied herself from a hitching post and set off on her own for home. An Amishman who recognized my rig and managed to catch her said she'd been following the rules of the road "like a proper pulling horse."

At home, however, Saturday was not at all proper. Somebody in her past had been cruel to her and she had gone past the point of cowering and had learned to fight back. The first time I entered her roomy stall, she pinned her ears and charged. I spent weeks earning her trust, feeding her carrots and apples and her favorite treat: hard candy. I soon discovered that while Saturday feared space between us, she loved to be touched. I learned how to sidle up next to her shoulder, where she felt unbalanced between using her feet and her teeth, and to put my soft hands on her. After a few gentle touches, she'd follow me around the barn like a lamb.

For Christmas that year, my parents promised Saturday and I a fence and the following spring, I helped dig postholes all around our half-acre. Once she was loose, Saturday reverted back to her wild ways. Every time I left the house she'd whinny a greeting but as soon as I neared the fence she'd start pacing nervously and those ears would go stiff. Out in the field there was too much room for her to maneuver her feet and teeth so I couldn't use my stall tricks to get near her. So instead, I plied her into coming to me. I would jump the fence far away from her and without looking her way begin walking slowly around the field.

I always brought a pocketful of hard candy—butterscotch, peppermint, fruity—any kind worked as long as it had a noisy wrapper. I'd walk around, ignoring my nervous pony and crinkle the candy wrappers. After a few minutes, enticed by the sound of the wrappers, Saturday would slowly sneak up behind me. If I ignored her for another minute or two, she nudge her nose against my back, begging for attention. Only then would I turn, sidle up to her neutral shoulder and say "Well hello, girl," and give her a piece of candy.

By the following summer, Saturday had learned to play tag. I could jump the fence, go right up to her, slap her playfully on the rump and run away. Saturday would run after me, beside me, ahead of me, delighted, as all horses are, to have somebody to run with. Then she'd bump me with her nose, whirl and take off, prancing showing off her high-kneed hackney gait. My neighbors found our games highly entertaining, so much so that one of the neighbor boys hopped the fence one day, hoping to play. Saturday nearly trampled him.

Saturday did mellow with age, but not before I got years of practice saving unsuspecting children and small animals from her hooves. By watching her ears and body language, I could read her moods and with small gestures and changes in my body positioning, I could control her. Nobody was ever seriously hurt—though she did leave a tiny hoof print in deep purple on my thigh once—and I treasured her wild side.

My next encounter with the wild horses came months later, in late fall, as the first licks of winter wind swept across the high desert. After spending the summer in Montana, I was back for another winter and my return to New Mexico had felt like coming home. My footpaths still lay waiting, radiating from my home across the desert and the wind still blew from the West every afternoon, carrying the familiar scent of dry air and junipers.

But not everything was the same. Over the summer somebody had abandoned a dozen or more horses on the BLM tract, and what was two strays had become a herd. None of my neighbors knew who had dumped the horses; nobody had seen a trailer come and go. But in a few short weeks the desert began to wear under all those hooves and most of the already struggling grass was cropped close. One night the herd broke through the BLM fence and pillaged my neighbor's barn for hay and grain. Once they were loose, the horses began roaming, creating well worn paths up and down the mesas, plundering the prairie for grass and drinking stock ponds dry.

Calls to animal control were futile. With unemployment rates in New Mexico at an all time high the agency was already overrun with unwanted horses. Even if the herd could be caught, no small task in such open, rugged country, they would almost certainly be euthanized. My neighbors who'd lost hay, grain and precious water to the marauders were told to put up fences around their own properties. This land is zoned as rangeland and the old Wild West laws still apply: roaming animals must be fenced out; they are not required to be fenced in.

New Mexico is not the only place overrun with wild horses. Parts of California and Nevada are so beset, the federal government has taken to rounding them up with helicopters. The animals are run for miles—they have to be exhausted before they'll go quietly—and led into chutes and onto trailers by tame Judas horses. Hundreds of horses die in the roundups each year. Many suffer horrible injuries. Young horses are often run off their feet, their delicate ankles reduced to shreds by their panicked poundings. The injured are shot and dragged onto slaughter trailers, in haste, before animal rights advocates with long lenses can get a shot of their ignoble deaths in the dust.

Those that survive are hardly the lucky ones. The majority are shipped to Kansas and Oklahoma, where more than 30,000 wild horses and burros languish on private ranches, awaiting rare adoption or common death. Having known no barriers but the sky their whole lives, the animals are reduced to milling in endless circles, enclosed by metal pipes. Family groups, with their carefully sorted hierarchies and politics are separated and remixed. Crowded into the corrals, they fight and panic and call for one another, for the range, for their freedom. They will never gallop to the horizons again. They are the symbols of the once wild American West, reduced to flightless birds in corralled cages.

Upon my return to the high desert, I heard all about the horses. At first my neighbors' frustrated stories amused me. Oh, to live in a place where the biggest problem is a herd of wild horses! But then I saw what all those hooves were doing to the land and the desert, which had seemed so infinite, suddenly became much smaller. I had wanted to believe there was enough room out here for all of us, horses and dogs and coyotes and hares and people, but the chopped ground and suffering grass seemed to prove me wrong.

One day, out walking the dogs, I was traveling a hoof-chopped path up the mesa south of my house, when I had my first encounter with the herd. I came around a juniper tree and saw the horses ahead on the trail, strung out behind a familiar palomino. They were only a stone's throw away, alert and agitated. The palomino, their leader, remained steady, searching the air for my scent, watching me intently as the others shifted nervously behind him, ready to bolt. My dogs were fanned out on either side of me, but they remained calm and quiet, waiting to follow my lead. I took one long look at the palomino, raised both hands to him said, "Stay," and then swiftly cut off the path to the left, heading towards a neighbor's house not far away.

I knew the Dunns weren't home yet and that their one-room adobe was still boarded up, awaiting their return from a summer on the east coast, but I was hoping the skittish herd wouldn't follow me there. I didn't run, but I hurried, keeping both dogs just ahead of me. As I approached the house, I stole a look back and my heart skipped. The palomino was following me, with the herd close behind. The dogs and I backed up onto the Dunn's porch, protected by a few square feet of uneven wooden planks and a knee-high adobe wall. There we faced the herd, gathering ten yards away.

As the horses lined up facing me on either side of their leader I counted seventeen. They were noticeably colorful—paints and reds and appaloosas—showy, once valuable horses dumped out in the desert. Their coats were roughening, their ribs just barely showing, beginning to show signs of stress, of winter wear. We all stood and watched each other, the dogs the horses and I and in those moments we were the only creatures on Earth. In that remarkable calm, my nervousness gave way to clarity. I had wanted the horses to belong here. I had wanted them to be wild but seeing them all up close, I had to admit they weren't. Like the dogs, these animals just wanted somebody to follow, a kind person to lead to them to food, to water, to safety. It broke my heart that I couldn't help them.

I told the dogs to stay put and walked out slowly towards the herd, talking softly to the horses, holding my hands in front of me, at waist level, palms up, fingers curled slightly to show I had no weapons. A few of them wavered, and began backing away, but the palomino and two others, a paint and a chestnut, took a few curious steps in my direction. I stopped, dropped my eyes and my hands, turned my body slightly sideways and let them come forward. The three approached cautiously, blowing their worries out through their nostrils, ready to bolt should I make a fast move. I breathed evenly and spoke softly and slightly beckoned with my fingers. As they approached, I held out my hand for the brave paint to sniff. Stretching out his thin neck, he tested my skin and then softly lipped my fingers, looking for a handout. I stroked the soft skin of his nose and at my touch he lowered his head and blew a satisfied snort, telling the others I was okay.

One by one, I went around to the rest of the herd, stroking the tamer ones, giving the skittish ones a kind word from a few feet away. A couple followed me closely, pestering me for more attention, while others backed away nervously, preferring to remain untouched. I remembered my camera and snapped a few portraits. One chestnut, whom I now recognized as part of the pair from last winter, was curious about the camera and seemed to like the snap and whir of the shutter. I don't know how long I spent with the horses, but by the end of our visit, they were searching for grass and milling about, calm and unconcerned to have me in their midst.

Back on the porch, the dogs lay quietly. I rejoined them, sat on the low porch wall, praised their calm cooperation and watched the horses. The camera curious chestnut started to approach again, but I held up one hand, palm out and stopped him. After a few minutes, the herd began wandering away, heads low, searching out the few blades of dry grass. As they left I got up quietly, jumped off the edge of the porch and retreated behind the house, out of sight. Before they could notice, the dogs and I reached the edge of the mesa and descended a steep, rocky path, one the horses would be reluctant to follow.

By December, the desert outside was cold and gray. The herd was still out there, somewhere, but I saw them rarely. A neighbor a few miles down the road was able to get reimbursed for buying a truckload of hay to feed the strays and I had heard they'd been hanging out over there, amassed together on the leeward side of a few sheets of plywood, bunched against the wind.

Nobody has any easy solutions for what to do with the horses come spring. Every now and then, especially on nice days, I catch myself daydreaming about keeping one or two for myself, taming them to carry me bitless and bareback, but I know that plan is best left a fantasy. For the winter they'll be warmer as a herd and come spring, I'll be leaving New Mexico and I can't take them with me.

More than anything, I want the horses to stay on the land. Out here, the desert stretches to the horizons, unbroken by fences. If feral horses don't belong here, in all this space, they don't belong anywhere and I don't want to live in an America without wild horses. Some people say there are no such things as wild horses in this country. That even those born free are mere descendents of ranch stock, pioneer horses or Spanish cavalry. Those people have never watched horses run through open space or faced down oncoming hooves while out on a hike. These horses, born captive and set free, may not be truly wild, but this desert is a wilder place with them in it.

≈ ≈ ≈

Mary Caperton Morton is a freelance science and travel writer, photographer, and professional housesitter. In the past five years she has lived in nine states—PA, OR, MD, VA, NM, MT, MI, WV, and ME—and hiked in forty-nine out of fifty. Everything she owns, including her two border collie mixes Bowie and D.O.G., fits in a little Volkswagen, and everything she really needs fits in a backpack. Follow her travels at www.marycapertonmorton.com.

❧ ❧ ❧

In the Fields of My Lai

"Maybe we can start again.... We'll start over. But you can't start. Only a baby can start. You and me— why, we're all that's been. The anger of a moment, the thousand pictures, that's us. This land, this red land, is us; and the flood years and the dust years, and the droughts are us. We can't start again."
– John Steinbeck, *The Grapes of Wrath*

MS. QUY, HER FACE WRINKLED AND EYES TIRED, sat five feet away. She held her hat in one hand and ran her fingers over the chin strap with the other, fidgeting with it in a way that suggested a mind throwing up memories that needed an outlet. I had never looked into eyes like hers and I had never felt so compelled to say "I'm sorry" for something I didn't do. But each time our eyes met they became a mirror, and I saw my nationality sitting squarely on my shoulders.

Just a minute before we shook hands, Ms. Quy had been gathering food for her pigs. Seeing me, a lone visitor across the small stretch of grass, she walked over to take a break from the sun. We were now on the steps of a tiny museum of photographs, but these grounds used to be the hamlet she called home until it was destroyed and her neighbors murdered on the morning of March 16, 1968. I looked toward a ditch less than a hundred meters away and then back at her. I knew that she had once been in that ditch for hours, covered by the corpses of her friends and neighbors, and was one of the very few to survive. Hesitant to ask the question now on my mind, fearing what raw emotions it could stir and how it would affect the seventy-eight-year-old woman hunched over before me, I asked anyway: "How do you feel about Americans today, Ms. Quy?"

The reflection in her worn-out eyes showed the faces of my countrymen who had once been here, most just a couple years out of high school. They wore uniforms, and they brandished guns and grenades that left scars still visible today on the trunks of palms and in the eyes of Ms. Quy. Most of these former soldiers—about one hundred fifty were involved in the operation—are now in their early sixties and have jobs and families in towns across America. Yet their shadowy forms still linger in the soul of Ms. Quy. At the nearby ditch 170 men, women, and children were cut down, according to the museum, and their blood and last gasps surrounded Ms. Quy as she lay with them, waiting for the Americans to leave before she dared crawl out. Somehow she survived. She was forty-two years old.

Having cast her stare into the grass, Ms. Quy answered: "I am still very angry. Very angry." Shifting her stare to the bare wall next to us, she continued softly: "I feel angry, but I don't know what to do with it."

My Lai (pronounced "Me Lie") is in the history books now, something American students may read about for a few minutes as they rush through their studies. For these distant readers, My Lai is an insignificant and perhaps irrelevant fact of history. It was an event long ago, far away, and having nothing to do with them. For Ms. Quy, however, My Lai was two children, her mother, her neighbors, her home. It was her innocence—or whatever she had left of it after living so long in a land convulsed by war. Like the Oklahoma characters in John Steinbeck's novel, forced by brutal reality to say goodbye to the only life they knew, Ms. Quy was deeply scarred by her world's collapse. There is no fresh start when you are forty-two years old and your neighbors and relatives are murdered around you. No wonder she stared at the wall.

At ten o'clock the previous night a bus had dropped me off in a dark dirt lot on the northern edge of the provincial capital Quang Ngai. A motorcycle taxi then brought me to the center of town, where I checked into a dank hotel room and settled in for a night's sleep.

I had come to this part of Vietnam for one reason: to visit My Lai, thirteen kilometers away. I wanted to do this alone and on a motorbike; this way I would be free to explore the countryside at my own pace, wander down dirt paths to meet locals, and have ample time with my thoughts.

At 9:30 A.M.—after a long search for a place that would rent a motorbike—I pulled out of town. The road was paved and one stretch passed through the shade of pine and eucalyptus trees. Rice paddies and palms, homes and businesses lined it elsewhere. I passed bicycles and exchanged many smiles with the folks on them.

After half an hour I slowed and turned into a grassy yard, parking the bike in the shade of a tree. I cut the engine and gazed around. *So this is the place*, I thought. The grounds brought to mind a botanical garden. I thought of other places of slaughter that I had visited and how they have been pre-served: Auschwitz, where Germans murdered Jews, has kept its buildings, railroad bed, and fence to remind the world "Never Again." Deir Yassin, the Palestinian village on the edge of Jerusalem where Jewish forces murdered over one hundred people in April 1948, is not so well remembered and today, rather than being a memorial, is home to a mental hospital and fuel storage depot. I've seen other places as well, but I cannot recall ever being in one that both "remembered" and took pains to make the area beautiful. It was a wonderful combination.

I was alone for only a few moments when a bus of fifteen German tourists arrived. I sat near a coconut palm, waiting for the Germans to leave, and watched them blitz through the museum in an astonishing twenty minutes. Germans, with their own dark history, shook their heads at the photos of Americans making their dark history, and were being led by a Vietnamese guide who certainly wasn't going to share any of the communists' dark history. A part of me wished that the museum had devoted a section to remember Vietnam's own war crimes. But I knew full well that this was, after all, My Lai. It was appropriate to remember the story of the people who lived and died here, and it was the American side that committed the atrocity. I would spend three and a half hours here, and once the Germans were gone I would remain the only visitor.

Most of the memorial is outdoors, but a small building displays photographs and artifacts. Photo captions read like this:

> "US soldiers looking for air raid shelter of villagers to murder them."

> "The US soldiers reaching up every house of the villagers to murder."

> "US soldiers shooting farmers on the way from the village to the rice field."

"American People holding demonstration to protest against Johnson's government for the latter's directing the aggressive war against Vietnam."

I doubted the accuracy of some of the descriptions. The caption stating that Americans were protesting Johnson, for example, was beneath a picture of Americans calling on Nixon to stop bombing Cambodia. Most Americans would expect these captions to describe the military of an authoritarian regime, not their own army, but despite the inaccuracies and occasional overstatement, the photos described a true story. The Vietnamese say that 504 villagers, ranging in age from one to eighty-two, were killed here; some U.S. sources put the figure lower, but not by much. Whatever the number, the photos of the dead are sometimes incredibly graphic. You can imagine what a high velocity bullet does to a woman's head at close range, or what bodies look like after they have been burned. Perhaps even more difficult is to see a picture of terrified women and children moments before their executions. The last faces they saw were not those of some vague "evildoers;" they were the faces of American men, many of whom probably loved their country, ate apple pie and steak, and watched the NFL. The faces they saw teach Americans that barbarism, far from being something found only in the dungeons of Baghdad or in the mountains near Kandahar, can come from Anytown, USA, too. Ask Ms. Quy and she'll tell you.

Driving home the tragedy of My Lai even further were several photos of individual American soldiers who participated in the killing, taken after they returned to civilian life. The museum included a photo of the only American casualty at My Lai, a private by the name of Herb Carter, who suffered what is believed to have been a self-inflicted gunshot wound to the foot. The final photographs drew attention to two Americans who saved lives in My Lai—Hugh Thompson, a twenty-five-year-old helicopter pilot, and Lawrence Colburn, a nineteen-year-old helicopter gunner. They are respected, honored names in the museum.

I sat on the floor beside the photos of Thompson and Colburn and took some notes. As I wrote, a young boy, barefoot and wearing well-worn shorts and a t-shirt, squatted quietly beside me. I, too, was silent, taking just a moment to smile and nod at him before turning my attention back to my notepad. The boy stared back and forth between the words I was hurriedly scribbling and the photos of Thompson and Colburn. I was struck by his quietness, and pleased to share the muggy building with someone like him. At some point he reached over and ran one finger up and down the outside of my busy hand, feeling the veins. He then felt the hairs on my arm and tapped on my kneecaps. Still in silence, he walked behind me to feel the padding of my backpack and continued his circle to feel the bracelet on my wrist. The silence only broke when, my notes complete, I turned to ask his name. "Linh," he replied in a whisper, as if he knew it would be in poor taste to speak loudly among the horrible photographs watching us.

While Linh had been warming me with his gentle touch and silence, I had copied the following words that describe the moments immediately after Thompson put down his chopper between several fleeing civilians and the soldiers pursuing them:

> If the Americans began shooting villagers, Thompson said, Colburn should turn his machine gun on the Americans. "Open up on 'em—blow 'em away," Thompson urged him. Colburn turned his gun around to face the GIs, though he was unsure whether he'd be able to open fire [on fellow Americans]. Concerned for their own safety, Colburn wasn't sure it was a good idea to land in the middle of a combat zone. The pilot confronted the lieutenant in charge [Calley]. He said he wanted to help get the peasants out of the bunker.

[Calley] told him the only way to do this was with hand grenades. Thompson shouted that he personally would get them out and told the lieutenant to stay put. With that he went across to the bunker and gingerly coaxed the civilians out.

Thompson later flew over the ditch where more than a hundred lay dead. He saw a young boy moving among the bodies and sat the chopper down to pick him up, and then flew him to the hospital in Quang Ngai. Ms. Quy would have been somewhere down in that pile as well, scared and wise enough to remain quiet and still.

My friend Linh vanished as quietly as he had appeared, and I walked outside to the steps alone and leaned on a wall. While watching the old woman I would soon come to know as Ms. Quy, a voice as soft as Linh's caused me to turn around. Chung, a twenty-five-year-old museum guide wearing a conical hat, a gentle expression, and speaking the English she learned so well in university, wanted to know if she could help with anything. I told her I was fine, just spending some time with my thoughts. She stood quietly for a minute, observing me watch the woman across the way. "That is Ms. Quy," she eventually said, "one of the survivors." Suddenly looking upon the old woman with new eyes and interest, I asked Chung some questions about her. When later Ms. Quy walked over to visit and rest, Chung would serve as our translator. Linh would also join us, popping up from behind a bush, and Chung would stun me by saying, "This is Ms. Quy's grandson." That simple sentence would affect me more than anything else all day, because this child who had kept me company came so close to never existing. But he exists, and I can still feel his touch on my hand.

Chung walked with me to the ditch and then to the foundations of several destroyed homes. She said the museum receives an average of thirty visitors a day. I would meet some of them through the visitor book in the reception room as I came to the end of my visit. I took special interest in the words left by Americans, folks like Jennifer Adams of New London, Connecticut, who visited a week before me:

> I can honestly say that I am 100% ashamed to be an American. It is beyond my comprehension how my country could partake in the massacre and not punish any of the men who took part in this. I still keep hope, however, that America will learn from its mistakes & instead of killing will work to help the world and bring peace. Thank you for making this site; I will use my tears to educate those @ home.

My guess is that Jennifer is in her early twenties, idealistic, and never had much exposure to those dark areas of U.S. history that school textbooks don't deal with very well. She is open to new information and has good intentions, and she was shocked by what she saw here. But I hope she isn't really 100 percent ashamed to be an American since the United States is more than the My Lai massacre. But even if she were, I think to be around her would be easier than to be with Dottie Payne, who had visited a couple weeks before Jennifer:

> I am an American and I remember March 16th well. I fought hard against the Imperialist war my government waged against the heroic Vietnamese people. I pray I will be able to always.
> Do not forgive them Lord, for they know what they do. They know.

Dottie and I would agree that U.S. policy has sometimes been poorly, even immorally, made and carried out, contributing to the deaths of millions around the world. But while she felt the liberty to borrow the words of Jesus and alter them, I would not. I imagine that those who killed Jesus were quite aware that they were killing him—they too knew what they were doing. On another level, though, did they? Did they truly know what evil they were committing? Did they ever glimpse enough truth and light to realize just how dark their actions were? Perhaps in one sense they didn't have a clue what they were doing, and this is why Jesus asked that his killers be forgiven. I will never be an apologist for the crimes committed by U.S. soldiers in My Lai and in other, less famous hamlets around Vietnam, but I cringed at Dottie's approach for it assumes that there is a great gulf between those who murdered in My Lai and those of us who did not and think we never would. Oppose wrongdoing, yes. Understand the difficulty someone may have in forgiving another, certainly. Ask God himself to deny forgiveness to another, never.

Chung came into the room to refill my cup, and also to play a thirty-minute video about My Lai that included footage of Thompson and Colburn's return in 1998. They had a chance to meet some of the women they saved, and it was only as I watched Colburn begin to cry as the women grabbed his arms that tears welled up in me as well. And how could they not? I was now sipping tea served by Chung, holding the cup with a hand caressed by the grandson of a survivor; my elbow sat on the guest book, filled with so many entries that expressed arrogant anger and no humility; and on the table behind me were two other papers, certificates belatedly presented by the U.S. military to Thompson and Colburn for heroism in 1996. They left them behind on their 1998 visit to My Lai.

Here I sat, an American in the fields of My Lai, moved by both the past and present, and reminded for the thousandth time that this is a broken world. But I was also moved because the world is home to such beauty, unexpected gifts of grace, and opportunity after opportunity after opportunity to save, to do good, to love, to reach out.

I do not usually leave messages in museum guest books, but now I felt it would be wrong not to. And so I wrote:

There are no clear words. But there is loss, sadness, anger, evil, and pain in this beautiful place. At the same time, today there is peace and hope…and such wonderful people in the towns and villages of this province, as I'm sure there were also in 1968. Thank you for preserving this ground and the memory of those who were murdered. And thank you for your kindness toward me, an American who is in love with Vietnam. Peace to us all, and may we indeed not just have nice sentiments about peace but have the creativity and courage to concretely contribute to right relationships and to justice—to peace. Joel Carillet, Washington D.C., January 18, 2004

I climbed back on my motorbike, ready to explore more of this stunning land.

≈≈ ≈≈ ≈≈

Joel Carillet, a Tennessee-based writer and photographer, is the author of 30 Reasons to Travel: Photographs and Reflections from Southeast Asia. *His work has appeared in numerous publications, including the* Christian Science Monitor, World Hum, *and* The Best Travel Writing 2008. *For more of his writing and photography visit www.joelcarillet.com or www. istockphoto.com/jcarillet.*

DEBORAH TAFFA

❧ ❧ ❧

The Year We Bought
Our Hitchhiker

They left the reservations in which they were born,
and made everywhere their home.

ONCE SIMONE DEVELOPS AN OBSESSION, THERE IS NO
hope that he will change his mind. Looking back, I
believe his obsession with living on the road is directly linked
to one of the first family vacations he took as a child. In 1974,
when he was a six-year-old, his parents took him on a month-
long road trip all the way from their summer home in Como
to the toe of Calabria. They towed a tiny 3.2-meter camping
trailer, about the length of a VW bug, behind their family car.
They called their rolling home the "Roller," pronounced in a
stiff north Italian accent. His father says it was the perfect way
to see Italy in the '70s; it freed them up to explore remote areas
that had no hotels. The tortuous Mediterranean Coast thrilled
Simone and they stopped in village after isolated village,

swimming, camping on beaches, and exploring the shoreline. It was a major adventure, unforgettable despite his age due to the natural beauty but also because they had to stop every ninety kilometers for his little brother Matteo to be carsick.

The Nuway Hitchhiker we purchased outstretched the "Roller" his family took to Calabria by thirty feet. It was an American behemoth, a super-size version of his childhood trailer, with white siding, red stripes, and pink frilly curtains. There were two entrances to the trailer. One door opened out from the living room, the other the kitchen, where we squeezed past each other to cook and prepare meals. It was like living in a long hallway and we spent every bit of warm weather outdoors, underneath an expandable shade-awning that could be opened and shut (and eventually ripped when it filled like a sail on a blustery day). The Hitchhiker featured a pull-out sofa and a wooden cabinet for our small black-and-white TV, a table that folded down into a bed, a bathroom with a step-flush system, and an accordion-door-closing bath-shower, but my favorite part was the "upstairs" bedroom.

To imagine us in our first family home, it is important to understand that our Hitchhiker had a unique design, re-ferred to by industry insiders as "a fifth-wheel." A fifth-wheel is towed behind a truck like a trailer, but it doesn't connect to the bumper, it sits in the middle of the truck bed on a hitch. The portion of the trailer that sits above the truck is usually the bedroom. It bends like a zigzag, an upper-branch sprout-ing off the main trailer. Thus a fifth-wheel is not the average rectangular trailer, though the lower portion is stable on four wheels like a trailer. Neither is it a motor home with an en-gine, a converted bus, or a collapsible pop-up.

A fifth-wheel has steps inside, leading from the normal "trailer" portion of the home, in which a person can stand up, into the upstairs-bedroom portion that rests over the truck bed when the trailer is being towed. Once you climb the four steps from the main level bathroom into the upstairs bedroom it is impossible to stand up straight without bumping your head. This design lends a comfy feeling to the bedroom. It's like a camping loft and makes the bedroom feel like a small hideout or cave. When there's a storm outside a fifth-wheel, the raindrops on the aluminum roof sound like a thousand tiny feet dancing. The organic rhythm of raindrop music is especially peaceful at night. It makes you feel cozy and safe. This feeling of safety is important because when you are moving to a new state every three to four weeks, awakening in the morning sometimes means a moment of confusion before you remember where you're parked.

It seems to me that one need only compile a list of Recreational Vehicle names through the decades—the Road Yacht, the Nomad House Car, the Palace Expando, the Aerocar, the Jungle Yacht, the Redman Trailer Coach, and the Rolohome—to see that the desire for road travel is closely tied to the imagination as well as a craving for mobility and freedom. The Palace Expando, for example, sounds like a magician's trick: "Ladies and gentlemen, watch me as I place this tiny 3.2-meter Roller in my top-hat and slowly pull out a Long, Long Trailer." The marketers of the Nomad House Car might have easily called it the Gypsy Caravan with the added slogan, "There is no such thing as home."

Even prior to the official Recreational Vehicles industry, in the early decades of the automobile, people in America used their creativity to independently fuse their living quarters and their transportation. The earliest versions of Recreational Vehicles were do-it-yourself systems. I've seen several RV Hall of Fame photos circa 1920 that were fascinating: one do-it-yourself weighed eight tons, stretched two-stories high, and was modeled on an English manor. Another do-it-yourself model used the body of a hollowed-out tree trunk. The stump in the picture is enormous. It was easily as big as the car that towed it. The inside of the stump-home was obviously round, with sloped inner walls. I imagine one had to stoop to get inside.

Our Hitchhiker years took off quickly. The impetus for the purchase was our first pregnancy, a wonderful gift as it turned out, but unexpected at the time. Simone and I had planned to be rounding the corner of West Africa, specifically the Ivory Coast, and instead we were on a plane back to the United States, where we would head to my parents and break the news of our recent addition.

My parents were anxious to see us. It was 1990 and they had been (in our minds) foolishly worried about us traveling during the first Iraq War, especially in Muslim countries. We didn't think they had guessed why we were returning early because they were distracted by the fact that I had been hospitalized with malaria in Italy. Simone had had to change our return flight plans twice while I convalesced near his parents' home and though his parents knew about the pregnancy, they couldn't speak English, didn't know my parents, and therefore could not have informed them of our situation.

Simone was twenty-one-years old. I was twenty. We were married, but without degrees or careers. We were unprepared for parenthood. We had eloped a mere nine months prior, the summer of 1989 when we were roaming in our own do-it-yourself system, indulging Simone's (then) obsession with lakes and the great American West. My father teased, "You're the only guy I know who has his house in a trunk." The joke was a gentle prod to settle down.

The summer of our wedding, we were on the road in my old college automobile, an Isuzu I-Mark. Our living quarters were, of course, in the trunk. When it rained we leaned back the driver and passenger seats and slept in the car. We prowled dirt roads in New Mexico, Colorado, Utah, Wyoming, Montana, California, Oregon, and Washington. We slept off the highway, in rural places, while we drove. We were always looking for free places to pitch the tent. Simone's tourist visa expired. He was an illegal alien in the United States and so we stopped in downtown Winnemucca to be married.

We pulled into town and went to the best-looking of the three wedding chapels. They said we had to have a witness and wanted us to pay extra for one. Not knowing anyone in Nevada, and not wanting to waste ten bucks, we invited a man off the street to attend the ceremony. His name was Todd W. Bell. Mr. Bell must have been in his thirties. He wore a leather jacket and grumbled when he realized he had to sign paperwork. When his signature was done he gave us both hugs, went out the door, and disappeared down the street in his beat-up sneakers. To celebrate, we went to eat Mexican food then we jumped in the car and headed to Lake Tahoe where it rained and we slept in the car.

The woman who married us used road-trip lingo during the vows, "You've made a special promise to travel down the road of life together, etc." We guessed by her condescending attitude that she didn't bet on the probability of our staying together—it didn't matter—we told ourselves a wedding's size was no indicator of future happiness. We had chosen a private ceremony on purpose; standing in front of a room full of loved one would have felt too mawkish, besides which we didn't have time to stop and plan. Yet here we were, cut off after only a month and a half in West Africa, standing in my father's living room, expecting a baby. We had no idea what to do next. My father said he could offer Simone a temporary position on a welding crew at the Four Corners Power Plant if Simone could learn how to pipe weld well enough to pass the X-ray test. (High-pressure pipes are dangerous if air bubbles are left in the metal.) After nine months of stuffy and stagnant apartment living in Phoenix, Arizona, Simone had a pipe welding certificate and we had added a baby daughter to our team.

Simone passed the pipe X-ray test at the Four Corners Power Plant and was hired for the temporary chromaly position. A temporary welder is hired for industry "outages," maintenance moments when electricity production stops for repairs to be made. He was paid twenty-five dollars an hour. It was now 1991 and we were both twenty-one-years old. We told ourselves it was fine, welding was a temporary situation, something to hold us over until our genius struck. What was really important was building capital for a future business investment and what we referred to as our ultimate goal: the financial freedom to travel to places off-the-beaten track. Four weeks later Simone was laid off.

We knew this would happen, my father had warned us that "turnarounds," or "outages," as they are called, are simply temporary shut-down periods for annual maintenance. Not knowing where to go next, Simone made friends with a few Navajo welders (the Four Corners Power Plant is on the Navajo reservation) and they told him where the next outage was: Yuma, Arizona. I say "next" because a welder can keep busy year-round if he is willing to relocate every month. Of course, most migrant welders leave their families at home while they travel, so their kids can attend school, play in Little League, and take part in religious and community activities. Migrant welders sleep in hotels and mail their checks home. They support their families from afar.

We refused to be separated. Simone became fixated on building a do-it-yourself style RV. He walked us through junkyards and used car lots looking for the perfect shell, an old school bus that could be rebuilt and painted over with soulful expressiveness. Though we talked about it constantly, nothing ever came of his dream to build a do-it-yourself RV because the right vehicle and engine never appeared. We packed up our bags, buckled our new baby daughter Miquela into her seat, and went to the Yucca Power Plant in Yuma by car, for the outage the Navajo welders had told him about.

There was another X-ray test, as there would be prior to each new outage we went to, but at least in Yuma we didn't worry where we would stay. Despite having spent the bulk of my childhood in the Four Corners region, Yuma was my birthplace and I had relatives living there: both in town and on the Fort Yuma Indian Reservation.

Yuma also happened to be the RV Capital of the World. In 2009, a family willing to shell out fifty thousand dollars for a 400-square-foot "apartment" minus real estate and with a motor on wheels, is a family longing, perhaps ironically, for a return to simple living. They are often Americans seeking a set of old-fashioned values that include independence from society. They are sometimes on a quest for Nature. I say this because I believe that the average Recreational Vehicle consumer wants, at least in the beginning, to drive away in their purchase, rather than park it on a slab of concrete with full hook-ups, water, sewer, electric, and cable. They want to abandon, at least for a time, the urban lifestyle, the mundane and repetitive day-to-day tasks, their immersion in work, their child's immersion in commercials—"I want to buy that!" They dream of exiting society, taking the off-ramp away from the interstate. They dream of embarking on small, country roads, and parking their rolling "home-sweet-home" in a National Park.

The enduring trend of RV ownership in America, the sight of those behemoths rolling down the highways, is evidence of the imagination modern families still have for freedom and wilderness. Perhaps this is the reason many people refer to Recreational Vehicles as "Winnebagos," even when the make and model of their purchase is not from Winnebago Industries. The etymology of the world is rooted in the Sioux language and refers to the indigenous people of eastern Wisconsin. The word translates as "people of the murky water who eat fish," an allusion to Fox River below Lake Winnebago. It did not appear as a term for Recreational

Vehicles until 1966. It seems fitting—what could be more suggestive of wildness and freedom then living in a vehicle named after a tribe of American Indians?

After arriving in Yuma for our second outage, this time at the Yucca Power Plant, we headed down to the RV Peddler, a dealer on the frontage road along Interstate 8. We were living at my aunt's house and hoping to buy some privacy. I was worried about the price tag, but Simone was very persuasive. He noted that the trailer-style RV's without motors were much less expensive than the Winnebago, or motor homes. He ignored my obvious concern: we did not own a truck to tow a trailer and wanted to look at every used fifth-wheel on the lot. He asked question after question until the baby cried, my feet hurt, and I was desperate to go back to my aunt's house. "You mean the refrigerator can work on propane or electric?" "How much extra for one of those swiveling hitches?"

We were exceedingly proud to pay nine thousand dollars—cash—for our Nuway Hitchhiker. We had saved for it and our new home was a jewel, pre-owned but clean. It had no smoker's smell like some of the other used models we'd seen on the lot. The dealer at RV Peddler delivered it to the small thirty-space, horseshoe-shaped trailer park we'd picked out at the edge of town, and near the border with Mexico. The only existing Yoga Ashram in Yuma County sat next door. Their peacocks, considered sacred by Hindus, strutted over to our trailer park often and paraded through the court with their tail fans spread.

Living in this trailer park, we were close enough to the Yucca Plant that Simone could bike to work. I'd hang laundry on the community clothesline with the baby in a sling and watch Simone as he faded into the distance in his welder's cap, a baseball-hat-spun-around-backwards-on-the-head look. He shrank into the distance on that no-gear two-wheeler, into cantaloupe fields that wafted a heady perfume on warm days. One advantage to working outages was that the plant's smoke stacks were asleep for the duration of the repairs. He worked long hours, six day weeks, twelve hour days, which paid good overtime but made us lonely for more time together.

My aunt said Simone reminded her of the witch in the Wizard of Oz when she visited and spotted him pedaling through the cantaloupe fields, coming home from work. It was the bike, I think, an old-fashioned version with a basket in front. We had borrowed the bike from an elderly neighbor: most of our RV neighbor's were elderly. Retirees are the demographic group that purchase and drive RV's most. They are often known as snowbirds in the vernacular of the southern towns they descend on in winter. Not only for their snowy hair, but because they drive down from colder climates in the northern U.S. states and Canada. As they age, many of them start to fly down rather than drive back and forth, choosing to leave their RV parked in a snowbird trailer park at their permanent winter home.

As a child, I grew up seeing these snowbirds in Yuma, at least for the first six years of my life. They ballooned the town, crowded the stores and restaurants. They always seemed to move in pairs, like swans that mate for life. Never did I dream I'd be living among them. Those years living in our Hitchhiker I noticed that they were always outside, watering plants or strolling around the snowbird courts. Recreation Vehicles are too small to stay inside, cooped-up all day, so one tends to see more of their neighbors than in normal neighborhoods. Our elderly neighbors had odd hobbies, enjoyed playing bingo and bocce, and loved to tell stories, mostly about the wars. One old guy told us, "Sometimes a man needs a story more than food to get by." They loved our babies, as we added them through the years, and loved to hear the story of how Simone and I met. We had a string of grandparents waiting to greet us no matter where we moved.

The overhaul at the Yucca Power Plant lasted just under a month, and then we were off with our traveling group of

Navajo welders to Rock Springs, Wyoming. The day before leaving, a WWII veteran called us out to watch a desert succulent bloom, a once annual event. It was evening. The bud opened in response to the sunset. We stood and watched. He said it was a Reina de la Noche and that in twelve hours—just after sunrise the following morning—daylight would wither the flower and it would be dead. I stared at his cactus bed in order to avoid his eyes, I think because his voice trembled notably as he spoke.

Several American films have made a splash with the RV as a centerpiece. The earliest being Lucille Ball and Desi Arnaz in *The Long, Long Trailer*, about a couple and their screwball antics on the road. In one scene, Lucy tries to cook as Desi drives. She is jostled around in their kitchen in a bit of terrific slapstick humor. Likewise, the movie *Lost in America* is a 1985 comedy about some wealthy yuppies who decide they are fed up with their bosses and their materialistic lifestyle. They buy a Winnebago and escape with their nest egg only to have the nutty wife gamble it all away in Vegas and foil their plans.

About Schmidt stars Jack Nicholson as a widower, depressed and emasculated by his discovery that his wife had a lifelong affair with his friend. He sets off in a Winnebago to visit his daughter and convince her not to marry. He returns home a renewed man. Something about the RV, about getting on the road and experiencing a physical change of landscape, reminds us that life is and should remain an adventure.

Simone's grandfather, Nonno Marcello, the wealthy patriarch of his small family, sent us five million lira in those pre euro days (about four thousand dollars) so we could purchase a truck to pull our Hitchhiker out of that horse-shoe shaped snowbird park in Yuma, Arizona. We added another four thousand to this and bought a sand-colored, 6.2-liter diesel (a piece of shit, Simone tells me to write) from Vicker's Used Cars in my parents' hometown of Farmington, New Mexico.

It took us a few years to figure out that the truck was a lemon. It was personally disappointing as the Vicker kids were my friends during high school. In Farmington, the kids with parents who had been in the Peace Corps, worked at Indian Health Services in Shiprock, practiced Asian martial arts, or were seen eating any ethnic food other than Mexican were considered strange. Everyone admired the Vickers because they came from Texas and their dad owned the used car lot. They drove classic convertibles off their father's lot. The girls won homecoming queen titles. They were gracious and polite. Our town chose two separate homecoming queens per year, one from the Indian population, another from members of the mainstream population.

Vickers Used Cars was in Farmington in the Four Corners region, and after purchasing our truck, Simone had to drive back to Yuma to retrieve our Hitchhiker. I stayed with the baby and my parents, while he embarked on the job: a ten hour drive, followed by work. He had to mount the hitch with the help of his friend Miguel. They fabricated brackets out of angle iron to connect to the chassis of the truck. The bolts that came down through the hitch to the truck bed had to fasten to the frame of the truck otherwise the hitch would rip right off the metal. He had to purchase and install a plug, wire the blinkers and the brakes. The first time our Hitchhiker took to the Interstate it was with Simone alone.

It's important to note that Simone didn't ask Nonno Marcello for money, it came as a surprise when he offered. We could have made payments. On average, it cost us ninety dollars a month to rent a space for our Hitchhiker. We were making between four and five thousand dollars a month and our bank account seemed to be piling up fast. We took gaps of time between outages to do fun things: go to Yellowstone or the Grand Tetons, stop in Laughlin, Nevada to stay at a hotel and swim, or head to SeaWorld in San Diego.

I remember our Hitchhiker now—can see it clearly in my mind—especially the way it looked while it was hooked up and towed like an obedient, oversize pet. Especially since much of my time was spent following Simone in the Isuzu I-mark my father bought me for my first year away at college. I remember its giant body sliding back and forth on icy mountain passes, perilous as a scene from *The Long, Long Trailer*, Simone as Desi Arnaz. I waved and directed Simone back into tight spaces when we visited majestic forests and beaches. It had a wood window one winter; we wanted to order a new one but were moving from outage to outage so often that there was never a stable address for the Nuway factory to ship the part. There was a sun roof in the bathroom where I looked up at night when I stepped out of the shower and saw stars.

I bent a gas pump over (they are surprisingly flexible) one time in the middle of the night at a Giant station in Bernallilo County, coming off of Insterstate 17 south of Santa Fe, across the street from a Lotta Burger. Simone was asleep in the upstairs bedroom when he heard the screech of metal. We had been driving all night from New Orleans and he was tired. I turned too sharply as I entered the gas station and the Hitchhiker rubbed up against the pump. The truck and the Hitchhiker sat jack-knifed together at a severe angle and I could see Simone clearly from the driver's seat of the truck, since the cab and the rear were bent close. He pulled back the bedroom curtain, his eyes humongous and staring as he saw what I had done. Nothing exploded. He simply came to me, slipped behind the driver's seat, pushed me out of the way, and backed us up. The gas pump returned to its normal position.

Simone says Nonno simply offered the eight million lira because he wanted to help us out, to reach out and be kind— remarkable since the lifestyle Simone was living was completely out of order with his wishes for us and his sensibilities in general. It hurt him that Simone had rejected the grand houses, the fur-coated women, the Mercedes Benz lifestyle, in order to wander around with me, our expanding family, and a gang of migrant Navajo welders. It hurt him that English was dominating Simone's life. Simone was in fact learning English well, with a beautiful Milanese accent, though every once in a while, on certain words, I heard a slight hint of Navajo accent slip in.

Not everyone associates Recreational Vehicles with nature, an experience of freedom, or a way to break away from stiff societal standards. Take my friend, Jonathan, for example, when I asked him what he associated Recreational Vehicle's with he said, "Meth labs."

"You're joking."

"No. In the Midwest they're used as meth labs, I saw an article in the *River Front Times*."

"How odd. I guess it makes sense. What else?"

"FEMA trailers for Hurricane relief..."

"That's right...how depressing."

"Oh, and Warren Oates, the B movie actor..."

Peter Fonda, Warren Oates, and Loretta Swit—the actress who played Hot Lips in the television series M*A*S*H— starred in *Race with the Devil*, a 1975 horror flick with humorous elements. They play a group of friends headed for a ski trip in Aspen in their Winnebago. While camping in Texas they accidentally witness a crime, a killing, a human sacrifice by cult members. For the rest of the film they are chased. The sheriff they approach for help, as well as the Texas community whose help they try to enlist, seem to be in cahoots with the psycho cult members. Little by little their Winnebago falls apart, as they are attacked in chase scene after chase scene, and the movie ends with the evil cult members trapping the innocents inside the Winnebago in a circle of fire. As far as horror movies goes, it's half creepy and half goofy. Simone and I joke that of all the Recreational Vehicle

movies to come out of Hollywood, *Race with the Devil* may be
the most apt comparison to what we thought we were doing
in our Hitchhiker all those years ago.

We were young and romantic and needed a place of our own
where our parents, friends and family couldn't meddle. The
Hitchhiker we lived in was an egg, a protective environment
to live in, and argue out our goals, plans, and lifestyle. We
were in a complicated mating ritual, trying to figure out
which traditions and values to choose from his side of the
family, and which to choose from my side of the family. He
talked about running from the devil of materialism, excess
consumerism, and status concerns of northern Italy, and what
he considered close-minded provincial thought. He had read
the *Bhagavad Gita*, and wanted to believe that life is, at the
core, a spiritual adventure.

For my part, I was running from the pressure of traditions,
fatalism, and the dysfunction often seen in post-Indian board-
ing school families. I was enthralled by Thoreau's *Walden*,
and the Hitchhiker presented opportunities to both live in
nature and hike every chance I got. Migrant work made life
simple, the small space we called home made it impossible to
buy junk, and there was an independent quality to it that I
enjoyed very much. We relied on pay phones to call our parents collect and traveled so frequently that it was impossible
to forge lasting friendships. Occasionally a Navajo welder
would come to our fifth-wheel for a home cooked meal. His
worldview was as separate and marginalized as our own. We
liked it that way. We had seen in our respective hometowns,
a limiting vision of freedom and life, and though we knew
we couldn't escape it forever, we knew that we were buying
time. The longer we stayed in hibernation, the longer we delayed our indoctrination into society, and pressure from our
families to conform to some dead-end office job. The longer
we lived in the Hitchhiker, the longer we could retain a sense

of our childhood, and believe whatever our imagination led us to explore.

I admit that much of our speculation was simply the romanticism of youth, but in retrospect I see how, in many ways, our life in the Hitchhiker had an impact on our lives that can still be pointed to today. We are still not big shoppers. We still remain independent, and more immune to peer pressure than average, or the idea that we have to keep up with the Joneses. We only recently had cable TV installed and still have only a vague idea about what is going on in pop culture.

Simone worked. Every town we moved to I had to locate four things: the grocery store, the library, the park, and the post office. These were the essentials of life and they point to how I spent my time, reading to myself and the kids, walking at trails in parks, and cooking homemade meals that we drove out to Simone on his lunch break. I didn't bother signing my oldest daughter up for school, even when she hit Kindergarten, I just schooled her at home though we both knew, as the kids grew older, that it would soon be necessary for our years in the fifth wheel to come to an end.

I would have never expected to own or live in a fifth-wheel for as long as we did, a total of five years, not including the three months every summer when we parked our beloved Hitchhiker at a storage facility and took a flight to Simone's parents in northern Italy. I think our summer abroad each year made it possible to maintain our migrant-welder adventures because it helped Simone avoid burnout. I am certain that going home to relax gave him strength to return to the long hours and grueling work when we got back to the States. For my part, I saved every penny he earned, even baking our bread from scratch. After five years of Hitchhiking adventures, we had earned and saved enough money to start our own business, which put an end to this phase of our life.

Looking back I remember the many trips, the travelers, the snowbirds we met, and the woods, beaches, and deserts where we set up home. The cyclical pattern we moved in, the same seven states, the same seven or so power plants, reminds me now of the ancient hunter gathering societies. We met plenty of homeless people, hoboes catching trains, refugees camped out in America's wealthy backyards. During those years we couldn't help observing as if from the outside, looking in. All those people who think of themselves as tethered, who cling to the idea of society and place, people who live with an illusion of permanence and safety, people we have joined. Simone and I are stable now, middle-class with five kids, we only go away for Christmas break and summers. However, we still do not have that luxury of centering and place, because our family roots and individual cultures are important to us and they stretch to two different continents. When one of us arrives home, the other is necessarily traveling.

We went back to my birthplace on the Fort Yuma Indian Reservation to sell our Hitchhiker in the end. We put an ad in the *Thrifty Nickel*, a classified section that contained RV's for sale and that features the Buffalo head nickel on the cover.

A lady with frizzy split-ends and a harried expression answered our advertisement. No, she did not have the total amount we were asking. No, she did not have a truck to pick the Hitchhiker up. She planned on parking it in a permanent location for herself and her adult son. Between the two of their jobs they'd be able to make a second balloon payment. She could give us one thousand today and another thousand-five-hundred in a month.

We hooked up the fifth-wheel and drove it out to her. It had its scrapes and bruises. Our oldest kids got teary-eyed watching it go. When we arrived at the designated meeting point we discovered that the woman was a squatter on a section of land between Yuma and the reservation known as No-Man's-Land. The shoreline of the Colorado River has changed occasionally through the years, mostly due to earthquakes. Since the Colorado River creates the boundary of ownership between the city of Yuma and the Yuma Indian Nation, this creates disputes: in the late '40s a man looked to increase his real estate and farm land by using dynamite blow a new bend in the river's shoreline. The resulting section of land, No-Man's-Land, is still disputed today.

We dropped our Hitchhiker off at the squatter's park on No-Man's-Land and collected the money the woman had on hand. As we drove back down the dirt road, I looked back in the rearview mirror, at the white paint, the red stripes, the frilly pink curtains of our first home together in America. I suspected we would never receive the balloon payment, though I didn't mention it to Simone who tends to be gullible about the goodness in people. Ten years later, it doesn't matter. It is a consolation that the Hitchhiker sits steady in a place that belongs legally to no one.

~❧ ~❧ ~❧

Deborah Taffa was born for the Keepers of the Water clan on the Fort Yuma Indian Reservation. A writer of mixed Yuma/Laguna/ Latina ancestry, she has backpacked in rural Africa, Asia, Europe, and the Americas. Her work reflects both her roots and wings. She is currently an M.F.A. candidate in the CNF program at the University of Iowa.

❧ ❧ ❧

Death Road

If you have a death wish, this is a ride for you.

I LEANED CAUTIOUSLY TOWARDS THE ROAD'S EDGE, WHICH gave way to a sheer cliff, a gashed rock-face stretching towards the distant earth. At the bottom, a mere speck of yellow on the floor of rocks, lay the tiny carcass of a yellow bus—tiny from here, at least. Squinting, I could see spray-painted designs covering the bright yellow shell like psyche-delic graffiti. If I didn't know any better, I'd think some 70s hippie collective had taken an ill-fated road trip out here to the Bolivian cordillera. But I recognized it as one of the *micro* buses, the kind that rushed haphazard through the city of Cochabamba, tiny indigenous women crammed against their dusty windows. They lurched around corners in a blur of color, pedestrians leaping from their path, occupants swaying like the bobble-head Homer Simpsons and Catholic crosses strung from the rear-view mirrors. This *micro* had lurched too far. It looked like a toy, a little plastic truck thrown carelessly aside by a bored toddler. But another squint revealed rusted edges and missing doors, missing windows, the glass blown out and scattered among the rocks. These rocks, boulders I should say, were nearly the size of the bus itself, stark and bare in the dry of the Andes. Lying among them, the bus looked like a colorful fossil.

A sharp cliff and a crushed vehicle are not the sort of things one wants to see at the beginning of a mountain-biking trip. They are especially not the sort of things one wants to see before biking down this *particular* mountain. The road doesn't seem all that dangerous, its medley of names sweet and inviting: North Yungas Road, Grove's Road, Coroico Road, *Camino de las Yungas*. These are the sorts of names which conjure up images of meandering paths into chirping tropical woodlands. You feel like you could saunter along these trails with binoculars in hand and a Nutri-Grain in your pocket, stopping occasionally to snap photos for your *I've been to the Andes!* slideshow. You are deceived. The truth is that this is a boulder-strewn chute plummeting 11,800 feet in half a day's bike ride. The lucky ones start in the bone-chilling cold of the Andes, shivering through their ten sweaters and five pairs of mis-matched socks. Their fear is magnified by the adjacent precipice, which, unlike their fellow travelers, stays by their side the whole way down. For several hours they descend at a near-vertical angle, passing bus memorials such as this, imagining their parents' faces when the consulate calls to inform them that their child hurtled over the edge of one of the highest mountain ranges in the world, until they find themselves at the bottom, where they swelter in their shorts in the middle of the rainforest, thanking God to be alive.

Then there are the unlucky ones. Hundreds of people die on this road. People die when a pebble sends them sliding off a vertical cliff on the left, or smashing into a solid rock wall on the right. People die when slick water dislodges their bike wheels and sends them skipping off into the mist. People die because a dense and blinding fog unexpectedly descends upon them—or because, suddenly confronted by a mass of sharp rocks, they are audacious enough to hit the brakes (which we all know, *of course*, reduces wheel traction). People die taking photos, stopping to reach into their backpacks for a Cliff bar, or taking their eyes off the road to glance at the passing scenery. They meet their ends by looking over the edge after a friend has fallen, perhaps down one of the road's 1500-foot cliffs (the antenna of the Empire State Building doesn't reach that high). Mostly, people die in car crashes. They'll smash into buses careening around blind corners and plummet off the edge in a screaming heap of limbs and metal. Once, a single crash sent a hundred people flying off into the abyss. That's right: a *hundred*.

All this excitement has inspired many other names for the road. Most include the word "death." If you're an English speaker, you might call this the Highway of Death; if you're a Spanish speaker, perhaps, *El Camino de la Muerte*. Or you can stick with the classic: Death Road. One of its most famous names comes from the Inter-American Development Bank. Back in 1995, having been informed of the road's legendary perils, some sub-sub-committee of statisticians thought it would be useful to find out how many poor saps met their end on this sad mountain pass. Having discovered a new record (congratulations!), they swiftly christened it The World's Most Dangerous Road. The name stuck. And not only did it stick, but it encouraged a whole host of macho thrill-seekers to come bike down it. Your basic granola-crunching, twenty-something, adventure-seekers unaware of their own mortality. Dopes. Like me.

So back to the crushed bus. Back to me, standing near the first of many cliffs, clutching the handles of my mountain bike and peering over the edge in an extraordinarily inadequate pretense of detached interest and composure. I had, entirely of my own free will, taken time off of my unpaid job and spent the Bolivian equivalent of two months' salary to book this trip with a group called Gravity Assisted Mountain Biking. And, knowing full well that gravity wouldn't assist me as much as drag me forcibly down steep mountains, I woke up at 6:30 A.M. to sign my life away on liability forms ("I will not sue Gravity Assisted Mountain Biking in the likely event that I die"). And I arrived. Here, where I would catapult myself down a wobbling path of dust and ruin on a spindly scrap of shaking metal. Here to babble to myself in terror, passing over razor sharp rocks and under pelting waterfalls, on a two-way road no wider than a hatchback. And I'd be 5,000 miles away from my doctor, hoping to make it from the continent's highest peaks to its sweltering jungle on a road named after *death*.

Yes, it was a fantastic idea.

Like all regrettable undertakings, this one was conceived impulsively in a bar.

The place was called *Casa Blanca*, and it was one of those hole-in-the-walls that was frequented by anyone with a semblance of a social life. We all had our own reasons for discovering it, but I'll tell you why we all came back: of all the cafés and eateries in the Bolivian city of Cochabamba (a city known for its good eating) it had—by far—the best pizza.

The four-cheese was Dave's favorite. (I have to agree). Dave, or *David*, as his Latin name is pronounced, became a good friend of mine while I was working in Bolivia. Reserved yet easy-going, lanky yet muscular, and a fantastically awkward dancer, Dave was a 6 foot 4 inch eyesore from Colorado who worked with a local organization giving loans to small Bolivian businesses. Though quiet, Dave led a spontaneous life. From bumming around as a surfer in Costa Rica ("All I could afford to eat were rice and beans!") to bartending in Alaska ("Have I seen bar fights? You're kidding, right?") to ranching in Colorado ("Ranching is really just building fences and watching cows..."), Dave had seen much in his twenty-five years. The two of us liked to make lists of the crazy adventures we wanted to thrill our lives, trying to avoid ones more likely to end them altogether. (It's harder than it seems.) This particular evening we were talking about my upcoming travels.

"You should take a few days in La Paz," Dave said, biting into a particularly thick slice. "Hmmm," he said through the pizza, "you know what you should do: Death Road."

As if this is something one does. *Oh, wait. He's serious.*

"It's one of the best things I've done. Hands down, you should do it."

I eyed Dave, who was balancing his slice, the cheese draping elegantly from the sides. I couldn't help but indulge him: "What, do you hike it or something?"

"No. No, no, no. Mountain biking."

"Dave, I'm not a mountain biker." *Although*, I thought with a flash of confidence, *I do bike around campus.*

"It's all downhill," he said matter-of-factly.

"It's not hard? Besides, I only have one day."

"It only takes one day."

Hmmm. Death Road. What's with these tourist attractions and their dramatic names?

"Go with Gravity Assisted Mountain Biking. They're the best."

I get easily inspired by adventurous people. Unfortunately, there's a mercilessly thin line between the thrill-loving soul with a sparkle in his eye and the hairy guy in the trailer park who's building a paraglider out of cardboard. My mother, bless her, has always attempted to dissuade me from emulating foolish people. "If *everybody* were jumping off the Mill Valley overpass, would you do that too?" Ok, Mom, let's ponder this image: I'm standing at that overpass, a bulky slab of highway concrete connecting my picturesque hometown with another California suburb, and looking over the Western wetlands of San Francisco Bay with one of my best friends. Let's say she hops over the side, vanishing faster than I do when your friends ask if I'm applying to grad school, and I'm left gazing over the edge in a full-blown panic attack. If, minutes later, she appears next to me, smelling like a sea lion, strands of slimy brown kelp decorating her shoulders like oversized necklaces, and she says something along the lines of "Dude. That was *awesome*. You've *got* to try it!"

Guess what? I would.

"Hi Mom."

"Hi honey! We're so glad you called—we've been thinking all about you. Sending positive vibes your way," she cooed from the other end of the scratchy connection. Scrunched into a tiny telephone booth at an international call center on calle Santa Cruz, I didn't forget for a moment that we were speaking from opposite edges of the earth.

"We sent you a card! Did you get it?" came an enthusiastic query.

"Um, no." It took me a second to get used to thinking in English again, "When'd you send it?"

"Must've been three weeks ago."

I pictured the abandoned army bunker the city calls a post office. I thought about the two employees working there: one who sat at the counter stacking envelopes into elaborate structures while avoiding eye contact with anyone resembling a customer, the other marching in and out of the *solo empleados* door as if the back room would disappear if left unattended for two minutes. I imagined the mail of a million city residents filling that room with giant paper mountains that the staff would swim in on slow days. "Yeah, Mom, I'd give the post office another couple weeks."

There was a long pause. I struggled between a million stories, tried to grasp something that she could picture: toothless street vendors selling buckets of oranges, mountains of flowers and home-baked cookies at the plaza festivals, boys kicking old soccer balls in abandoned basketball courts at the foot of mountains. I twisted the ivory phone cord around my finger in contemplative silence, listening to the static on the line.

"Are you traveling again?" she asked.

"Yeah, I am. I'm meeting up with Carolyn at Lake Titicaca. We're going to see some ruins." *God, I sound like a tourist.*

"That's wonderful!" she sounded positively delighted, "How are you getting up there?"

"Um, I'm going to bus into La Paz." *Hmm, hope there aren't blockades. Or riots.*

"Are you going to explore the city?"

"No. Actually…" *I shouldn't tell her.*

"Actually?"

Don't tell her.

"I'm going mountain biking."

Idiot.

"Mountain biking? Really? You're not much of a mountain biker."

"Yeah. Well, this is a guided trail."

"Oh, what's the trail?"

"Um, it's just a trail. It goes to this little town…*Coroico,*" I muffled.

"What was that sweetie? Wait, let me get my pen…"

"Actually, Mom, don't worry about it."

"No, I want to know."

"It's O.K. I've actually got to go. I'll talk to you later …"

Click. *Idiot!*

At the trail-head, our bikes were lined carefully on their sides in the dirt, each rider positioned at a pair of wheels. In the silence, we fidgeted nervously with our black racing gloves. One of our guides, a peppy English-speaking Canadian with red-flamed bike shorts and blonde hair wedged back as if in a wind tunnel, paced ominously before us. It was time for our pep-talk.

"There's a reason we've stopped here," he said, pausing in his paces, "and it's because this is the last chance you have to turn back." He took his shades off to illustrate the ceremonious profundity of the occasion. "There is no shame in getting back on that bus."

I glanced at the others: they gave him a tense but attentive silence.

"In that case, I want each of you to listen to every word I say. Your lives depend upon it.

You'll see other tours where people bike along untroubled by the constant threat of death and danger. Groups where people make stupid mistakes because they don't understand the magnitude of their peril. *We* don't do that. I'm serious," he took on a genuinely grave face, "this is serious, what we do."

Fortified by our rapt expressions, he continued, "There are rules. First rule: always bike on the cliff side."

The group burst out in murmurs: *What?!? On the cliff side??*

"If you want, you can bike close to the rock-wall, but when a bus comes screaming around the corner you have less than a second to react. You're going to be squashed like a little bug. Either that or you skid out of the way and break every bone in your body on the rock face. We had a guy break both wrists, several ribs, a collarbone and lose all his front teeth that way. Had a gorgeous scar across his face," he drew his finger above his jaw-line, "skin ripped clean off. If you want several seconds to see the bus and react, bike on the cliff side."

Duly noted.

"Second rule: always get off on the *right* side of your bike. We each go at our own pace, so to let the people in the back keep up, those in the front will be stopping from time to time. Couple years ago, there was a French woman, real nice lady, got off on the left side of her bike. Most right-handed people

tend to do that. How many of you are right-handed?" He
paused to survey the group. Every single person raised their
hand. "O.K., listen up then. This woman gets off her bike on
the left side. Now, what's on the left side? That's right: the
cliff. So her friend takes out a camera, tells her to take a step
back, and—fft! She's gone. Blank picture."

I sat riveted. *Bike on the cliff side. Get off on the right side.
Bike on the cliff side, get off on the—*

"Third rule: you lose traction, especially on curves, last
thing you wanna do is brake. That causes you to skid, and
you'll skid off the cliff. So whatever you do, DON'T BRAKE
ON TURNS. Ride out the bumps. Keep your gears low to
angle yourself and keep your inside knee high—that's very
important. Stay to the outside of the hairpins, on the left
of the track since cars are coming on the right. Go straight
through water, always look forward, don't look down. Ignore
what your body tells you. You have to override those signals
if you don't want to end up off the cliff. You have to listen to
every single one of these rules, because you can't trust yourself. You trust the rules. If you don't, you're fucked.

Any questions?"

We stared at him dumbfounded.

"Great!" he grinned fiendishly, "Let's get going then."

O.K.. Totally doable, right? I peered down into the shifting
mist, catching glances of the sharp ridge that marked the
cliff-side. I just needed to bike there, along the gravelly brink,
and make sure not to brake, especially if I skid...towards the
ravine where they would never find my broken body and I
would die among thousands of rotting corpses! No, alright,
calm down. Just remember the rules. Bike on the cliff side.
Don't brake on turns. What was the second rule again?

"You're over-thinking it, Bergmann," said one of the other
bikers, a tanned Aussie in his mid-thirties sporting a dime-
shaped goatee.

Over-thinking! I wanted to shout at him, *I'm supposed to be following the rules!* I gave him a look of indignation, which may or may not have disintegrated into a petrified plea for help.

"You'll be *fine*," he said, the last word pronounced *foyin*.

I nodded at him, still unconvinced, and he joined the end of the line of bikers. Those in front of me had already taken off, their tiny figures bouncing over the rocks, each one looking like a discombobulated Raggedy-Ann on ineffective seizure medication. Pebbles flew from their tires. When they came to the first bend, they skidded around the corner and plunged out of sight. When it was my turn, I took a deep breath and stepped on the pedal. I lurched forward, and I felt like Icarus must have felt when he realized the wax was melting from his wings.

My first instinct was to go as slow as humanly possible. I clutched onto the brakes as if I could fuse them to my hands, which didn't slow me down as much as create a lot of turbulence. To say that I was biking would be inaccurate. Bumpy would really be an understatement. Picture a chubby, mischievous six-year-old aggressively shaking a cola bottle to make it explode with foam. I was the cola bottle.

Then there was the first corner. I realized right away that the guide was right: I couldn't trust my own body. As the corner approached, my gut told me to brake. My rational brain stepped aside a second, took a good look at my gut and said, *Look, pal, we can't brake on this corner, because we'll lose traction.* At which point my gut looked from the brakes to the cliff, then back at my brain, and erupted in a laugh of incredulous betrayal. This complicated things. As we (my brain and gut and everything else attached to them) approached the first curve, I started to chant aloud, so that all my organs were clear about what we needed to do:

"Don't brake, don't brake, don't brake…"

My fingers released their Tonga death grip and my tires flattened into the dirt, the jolts replaced by quick (but relatively smooth) undulations. Immediately I picked up speed, and as I began to fly towards the corner, my chant rose in pitch:

"Don't brake! Don't brake! Don't brake!"

In a moment of curious insanity I felt the urge to close my eyes. I battled this unexpected compulsion by willing myself towards an invisible point on the other side of the turn, which I approached like a shrieking banshee:

"DON'TBRAKEDON'TBRAKEDON'TBRAKE DON'TBRAKE!"

And I didn't.

A middle-aged Bolivian man was driving up to La Paz on El Camino de las Yungas, minutes from the end of a long journey. He'd passed dozens of cars and bikers without scratching a smidge of paint off his car, quite an accomplishment. He daydreamed of a cold beer and wondered if the watchmen at the drug check-points were on strike today. He approached the last turn, and that's when he heard it: a crazed scream in some unidentifiable language. Before he could wonder at its cause, a tall blonde woman in racing gear hurtled around the corner in a jumble of screeching metal and exclamations. She flew past his car, skirting the edge of the cliff, her face a mess of emotional fireworks. As he craned around to gaze at her shrinking figure, he shook his head in weary puzzlement. *It's been a long day*.

We stopped at a crescent-shaped lip of gravel, waiting for Cesar, the last of the guides, to bring up the end of the line. I rested my right foot on the gloriously solid ground, and peeled my reluctant fingers from their desperate handlebar clench. My eyes wandered off the jutted edge, and a wave of beauty pummeled my unprepared eyes. We stood at the edge of a ring of mountains, circling the valley like giant green countesses sitting for tea. They were blanketed with lush forests of a dozen green hues, lined with ridges sculpted into deep gullies. I peered up at the crown of my mountain, where rocks the color of rain-clouds drizzled my eyes with mist, and I saw that from the billowing mists rose a spectacular peak, a pinnacle of bare rock piercing the cloudless sky. When I lowered my eyes, I was met by the cavernous expanse of open air which sat eerily before us, curved in the belly of the circlet of mountains. It was a crystal ball of cloudless nothing, world-sized and distant. We peered into its center, mere dots along the mountain's cracked roots of rock, like ants standing at the shoelaces of a giant. Aware of my swift breathing, of my timidly positioned feet, of every standing hair on my arms, which flexed as I grasped my bike handles again, I took one last look at the towering mountains and then took off down the road.

It became easier to breathe as we met invigoratingly warm air from the canyons below. At the next stop I shed my jacket and welcomed the rush of sultry air, warm blood and coursing adrenaline. My arms flushed red, my goggles fogged with patchy breaths, and my skin buzzed with shivering excitement. Again I greeted the road, sinking into the bike frame and trusting my tires, which hadn't yet spun me into the abyss. I carved myself into the side of the mountain at each curve, then soared out of hairpins like a pinball released from a spring. At each moment I felt like I was both flying and grounded, relieved and expectant. *This isn't so bad*, I thought.

First I heard it: a deafening *crack!* and metal grinding rock.

Then I felt it: the twisting bike frame violently wrenched away.

And then...freefall.

At least I was still breathing. I lay supine, staring at the unblemished sky like a kid lying in a field of grass. I didn't feel like I was hurt. But then again, I didn't really feel much of anything.

After an indefinite number of seconds, I gingerly unbuckled my helmet. I lifted my head, which felt heavier than a cannonball, and *then* I felt everything: stinging cuts all along my limbs, head pounding furious discomfort. I winced away the pain and dragged myself up into a sitting position, so as to assess my final resting place.

I was still on the road, only about twenty yards from where it happened, whatever "it" was. My bike had also managed to stay on the road. Barely. It was poised at the outer edge, teasing the cliff. The back tire looked like a pack of starving lions had attacked it in a Discovery channel featurette. As I pondered the tire, I heard the skid of another, behind me, and then the crunch of feet on gravel. I craned around to see who it was, ignoring my protesting muscles.

It was Cesar.

"*¿Que pasó?*" he shouted as he tossed his bike aside: *What happened?*

Still trying to ascertain that myself, I gave him a blank stare, which he took to mean that I didn't speak Spanish. At this he sighed, pulled down his shades to look at my shocked expression, and then silently walked over to assess the damage—on the bike, that is. I continued to sit in the dirt while he clicked his tongue at the back wheel, as if the bike were a teenager that had taken the keys to the family car without asking. While he looked at the rubber, I looked down at my limbs, which I gratefully determined weren't disfigured.

"You need a new tire," he said with a thick accent.

After giving him the same blank stare, I started to laugh. "*Obviamente.*"

This was the only time I ever saw Cesar surprised—his dark brown eyes narrowed a second—and then his face transformed. The edges of his spiky black mustache turned upwards, and though a black kerchief covered his mouth, I could tell he was smiling. He walked over and extended his hand. Grasping my pale hand in his, he pulled me up.

"I'll just get you a new one," he continued happily in Spanish. "The bus will bring one."

We sat by the side of the road, waiting for the tour bus to amble down the curves behind us. I told him I didn't particularly want a new tire, that I'd rather walk than get acquainted with the ground like that again, thank you very much. He nodded his head appreciatively, but noted that walking would take much longer than necessary. When he switched the tire, it was with an ease that revealed years of expertise. I bet he could do it blindfolded and upside-down. Perhaps I could ride on his shoulders...

As he handed me the fixed bike, I hesitated. "I'll be right behind you," he reassured me.

"I'm not worried about in front and behind, Cesar. It's the up and down I'm worried about."

He laughed jubilantly and extended the bike again. I grabbed the handle and turned back to face the road. It stretched before me in false innocence, a relatively wide stretch. I realized with a sinking feeling that had I fallen on a slimmer section, I would be permanently married to the valley floor right now. I was very lucky. I probably wouldn't be that lucky again.

By the end I wasn't faring well. My back was aching from leaning over my handle-bars and my fingers could barely grasp the brakes anymore, their muscles shaking from fatigue. I had a cramp in my left calf. And my right one. Clumps of hard dirt leapt from my tires as I sped down, gashing my shins; my elbows were assaulted by the sting of liberated dust and stones. This road was beating the shit out of me, but I didn't care. I just wanted to get to the end of it. I had reached that critical point where terror surrenders to exhaustion.

I'd learn later that this section of road is one of the most perilous for bikers—despite being one of the widest and flattest sections. Many who make it this far succumb to either growing fatigue or overblown cockiness, which tend to cause trouble whenever a biker is "tested" by the road. Messing up at this stage must be very disappointing. Think of all the valiant (though admittedly masochistic) road-bike warriors who have battled the steepest, rockiest, most perilous passages of the World's Most Dangerous Road only to crash on leveling slopes mere minutes from their destination. That's what we in California call a Major Bummer. And all it takes is one small problem: a misjudged corner, an unseen water slick, or gradually drifting towards the center of the road.

That last mistake can bring a biker forehead to bumper with an oncoming driver. This isn't the best of situations, as Bolivian drivers can't always be inconvenienced by silly rules such as Don't Drink and Drive or Keep You Eyes on the Road. They'd much rather multi-task, be it by napping or sipping rum. Seriously. I once had a fascinating conversation with a Bolivian about the dangers of strapping extra tanks of gas to the hoods of cars. While he admitted that it makes minor collisions rival dynamite-embellished blockbuster crashes, he also noted that it's helpful if one can't find a gas station. Needless to say, I now have a near-religious awe of the ability of Bolivian drivers to be blasé. And to make things a little more interesting, drivers on the World's Most Dangerous Road drive on the opposite side from any other road in Bolivia. At least, they're supposed to. Apparently not everyone got that memo.

Rocketing down the road, I was struggling to gain my focus back when a massive truck swung around a corner ahead. For the record, he hadn't got the memo. I skidded to a halt by the road's edge, hands cramping from braking. I paused in my panicked pile of dust as the vehicle continued to bumble along, taking the entirety of the road. The driver looked a deep shade of bored. I scooted as close to the cliff as I could muster, the truck's hood passing within inches of me. I gave an incredulous, *how-rude-of-you-to-nearly-cost-me-my-*

life look to the driver, which he returned with an *I-might-as-well-be-comatose* zombie stare. The massive truck bed went past, contents strapped precariously together with ropes and blue tarp. I continued to watch agape, even after the truck passed us. As it turned the next corner, one of the wheels bumped off the edge for a moment or two, before finding its place on the brink again.

"Traffic picks up on the flats!" Cesar informed me. "Bigger cars!" I half expected him to wink at me. Oh, to hell with fatigue. I fixed a newly determined glance ahead, hoping that my concentration would last longer this time, since I seemed to be the only one who had any. But there'd be no need: I could already see our destination.

I stood, stooped under the shower head, warm water running down my back (I didn't even know Bolivia *had* heated showers!), the smell of roasting meat buoyed towards me with the happy chatter of survivors. We had made it. From mists and rivulets through the waterfalls, all the way to our last river crossing and now, to warm showers. As soon as we were dressed again, we did what any group of people who have skirted death would: we feasted.

We ate platefuls of buffet food: bread, pasta, chorizo, juice. And we lounged in hammocks, listening to the chirping of the rainforest, gorged on sausage grease and relief. Afterwards, we piled back on the bus and headed to a shack down the road to buy rum and coke, which to our giddy delight came premixed in liter-sized bottles. I headed to the back of the bus with my loot: a liter of the rum-coke mixture in each arm, a giant bag of chips sitting at the crease of my right elbow. Cesar came and sat across the aisle from me, watched me uncap the first bottle. I took a lengthy swig and then passed it to him, and as he took it a knowing smirk tilted his mustache. Before the liquor even set in, I was drunk. Drunk on oxygen and carbonated soda. As the bus rolled forward, my

abs tightened and my breath quickened with the realization
that we were finally heading home.

I barely registered that the driver had made the U-turn, I
was so engrossed in recounting the tire incident to the back
three rows. When the laughter subsided, I gazed out the front
window, and heads began to turn. We were now facing the
World's Most Dangerous Road from the other direction. Our
giggles gave way to a somber reverence, spreading through
the bus like darkness encroaching on a twilight sky. And
then, much to our collective dismay, the bus set off into the
maturing dusk and began the long drive *up* Death Road.

We wound our way up the mountain in lingering twilight,
exhausted heads leaning on windowsills, watching the blur
of green foliage play along the right-side windows. I tried to
guess how far up we had gone by inspecting the vegetation,
which thinned as we climbed. I was sitting on the mountainside of the bus, next to a young woman who sat meditatively
at our window, which was filled with the gray of passing
rock. It was hard to tell if she was lost in thought or actually unconscious. I was drunk and exhausted, but couldn't
conceive of sleeping, and so I turned back to the cliff-side
windows and watched Cesar watch the road.

He couldn't have been older than thirty. I wondered if
he had a wife and kids. How much did they worry when
he went to work? The thought of these hypothetical family
members made me anxious with worry and exasperation.
Cesar, you idiot! I wanted to shout, *Do you know how lucky
you are to still be alive, after all the times you've come down this
mountain?!*

He must have sensed my silent tantrum because he turned
around to look at me. I searched his eyes for any indication
of fear, of pain, of guilt. I only saw a kind confusion, which
turned my exasperation to compassion. And so I asked him.

"Oh sure, it's dangerous," he said matter-of-factly.

No duh, I thought. "What I mean, Cesar, is...have you seen anyone, you know..." my voice trailed off lamely as I gazed back out at the cliff.

"Oh. Yeah, it happens," he whispered secretively, though he knew I was the only one fluent enough to understand him. After a beat, he seemed to deem me trustworthy and continued: "The worst was a couple of years ago. It was the Sixth of August, but so many people wanted to do the ride that we said, 'O.K., we'll work the holiday.'" A flash of regret passed his eyes, and he furrowed those characteristically sharp Bolivian brows.

This didn't seem like such a big deal to me. For *our* independence day, we keep a lot of businesses running. If we didn't, where on earth would we get all our last-minute BBQ supplies and frustratingly small fire crackers? But then again, Bolivians tend to take their holidays very seriously. (I remembered election day, when motorized transport was illegal, and you weren't allowed to walk in groups of more than two people.)

"It was somewhat risky," Cesar continued, "you know, because everyone takes the holiday and so there wouldn't be a rescue team ready were something to happen to—"

"Wait a minute," I interrupted. "Rescue teams don't work on holidays?"

"Well, for this road, it doesn't really matter. It wouldn't—"

"*Rescue teams don't work on holidays?!*" I interrupted again. A couple of weary heads turned, but none registered comprehension.

"It's not like the States, where you can have a helicopter come air-lift you out. You fall, it's the end." I gave him a defeated look. "Let me explain," he said, "there are two types of cliff here. There's the kind where you die quickly after you fall..."

I had a flash-back to those skyscraper-high precipices. My voice cracked like a fourteen-year-old boy's when I asked about the second kind.

"Those are the ones where you die slowly." He nodded with finality.

I would never let Dave talk me into doing anything again. Ever.

"So we took a group down. They were really excited. Everyone always is. I was guiding the back of the group—I'm always in the back with the slower ones." He smiled at me, which probably meant I was one of the 'slower ones.' "There were two women at the tail end, friends, I think. We were really far behind. The others must have been down the road, waiting for us." He sighed. "I was right behind them when it happened. They went to turn a corner, too close to each other—less than the bus length we tell you to leave between bikes—so when the *micro* came around the corner..." His eyes were unfocused, and I realized that he was picturing what happened: "From where I was, I could see the driver was asleep. Maybe he was drunk, or maybe he closed his eyes for a second, I don't know. Then—" He raised his left hand in a fist, and struck it with his right palm, "the bus hit, one woman, then the other. They crumpled onto the front of the bus, which woke up the driver. He slammed on the brakes while still on the turn and the back tires skidded, swung the back of the bus over the edge...then the cabin pitched sideways and they all went over...then down...hitting trees as they went..." His eyes widened.

Oh God. "Cesar," I said as calmly as I could. His eyes came into focus and he looked up.

"You know how I said there were two kinds of cliff?" He whispered grimly.

I nodded reluctantly.

"This was the second kind."

I closed my eyes. I opened them when I felt Cesar's patient

gaze. He continued the story: "I got the others. We could hear survivors, but there were so many trees, we didn't know if we could get down in time. We took machetes from the bus and started to cut towards the voices, but it took a long time. When we got there, most had gone quiet. Many were crushed underneath the bus, which we couldn't lift, but the two women were still alive. We had to carry them up, and they were in bad condition, one had her feet ripped off at the ankles—"

He saw my hands fly to my face in horror and stopped immediately, meeting my terrified expression with a worried one. "Oh no, Sabine, I'm sorry…"

Oh my God.

"I'm sorry."

"Jesus Christ, Cesar!"

It came out in English, and suddenly I felt the entire bus looking at me, choking the atmosphere with attention. As I tore my gaze away from Cesar to face the inquisitive expressions, I let the horror slide off my face like silk.

"He says he can do a double back-flip on a mountain-bike," I huffed, raising my eyebrows skeptically.

The words settled on their drunken audience, and then the emotional charge of the moment evaporated. Within moments, everyone was involved in a fervent discussion of the physics of mountain-bike tricks. Dozing passengers woke up, and bottles were passed once again. By the time I looked back at Cesar, he was staring out the window again.

Things had started to get out of control. For one thing, the door of the bus was open, and people were leaning out of it, laughing maniacally as the gravel whooshed underneath. The bus' drunken occupants were bouncing around the cabin with their cameras out, making faces by the windows. I felt a potent mixture of intoxication, exhilaration and concern, at least until the whole circus finally came to a halt.

We were looking across an expansive ravine at a section of road dubbed Postcard Corner: a sharp turn rimmed by a perfectly vertical drop, straight as if drawn with a ruler from its cusp, which kissed the air with tantalizing innocence.

"Get out! We're documenting this for posterity!" yelled our Canadian drill sergeant.

One by one, people started to hop off the bus. I watched my fellow riders march out to the edge, posing for their camera shot.

"Do you want me to take your picture?" Cesar asked me, the first words he'd spoken since my lie twenty minutes earlier. *Bloody hell,* I thought, *I've come this far.* I handed him my camera wordlessly.

I walked out with a young woman from our group whom I had befriended with nervous chatter at 7:30 that morning. She had been with me for more emotional turmoil in the last eight hours than some of my friends of eight years. We walked out to the corner, arms clasped around each other, until we were only a couple feet from the edge. My stomach tightened as the security of the ground seemed to shrink away. I did not look down. We held our free arms out in triumph. I grinned stupidly, and the moment was gone. We were standing there for perhaps three seconds.

Gratefully, we scuttled back to the safety of the bus. I sidled in next to Cesar in the door frame, and he passed me my camera without taking his eyes off the corner. "Cesar," I whispered, as a young Brit in blue shorts and a grey Liverpool sweatshirt strode out for his photo, "This is fucking nuts." Cesar said nothing. He watched the kid, who was jumping up and down at the cliff edge. The bouncing made me nauseous with worry, so I turned to Cesar again.

"What were their names?" I asked, "The names of the women?"

"Try and get me mid-air!" shouted the Brit to his friend with the camera. Cesar watched stone-faced, not responding.

I realized I had crossed a line, and immediately regretted the question. Shamefully, I turned away, back to watch the Brit, who had inched over and was now sitting on the ledge, dangling his feet off the thousand-foot drop. "Look!" he cackled, "Doesn't it look like I'm about to fall?" He swung his legs.

"Sorry Sabine," Cesar's voice moved through the air thick and smooth, like a spoon cutting into cold whipping cream, "I can't remember their names."

"Look at me!" leered the kid, "I'm gonna fall!" He put the back of his hand to his forehead dramatically, "I'm gonna *die*!"

≈ ≈ ≈

Sabine Bergmann grew up in Northern California and studied Earth Systems at Stanford University. In Bolivia, when she wasn't busy risking her life, she worked for a local farmer's aid organization. Currently she serves as a Peace Corps Environmental Volunteer in the Dominican Republic.

❧ ❧ ❧

Shiva and Sadhus at Pashupati Temple

The author peers into lives very different from his own.

HUNDREDS OF GRAY-BEARDED SADHUS, BABAS, GURUS, yogis, and other varieties of holy men come from all over India and Nepal to Pashupati Temple on the outskirts of Kathmandu each February. They come to celebrate Sivaratri, the day of Shiva's birth. How do they demonstrate their devotion to Hinduism's wildest divinty? By smoking copious amounts of *ganja*. Though hashish is illegal in Nepal, charitable organizations set up distribution centers on the outskirts of the temple, and dole it out free to the holy men on this holy day.

I explained Sivaratri to my friends in North America like this: "It's like Christmas—the birth of God—but with hundreds of Santa Clauses going to the Vatican and getting stoned."

The festival lasted for a week, building up to the day of Sivaratri itself, when it seemed everyone in Kathmandu came to Pashupati to worship. The temple got so packed, more than one thousand police were on duty for crowd control before dawn.

I woke up at six in the morning, something I don't do at home in Washington, D.C. on a regular basis. Already the queue to the temple was backed up to the front door of my hotel—Dwarika's—a good kilometer and a half from the entrance to the main temple. It would take these devotees six hours to make it inside to deliver their offerings and receive their blessings. But everyone stood patiently. They seemed excited, cheerful even, in the early morning darkness.

Fortunately, I had made friends with a young Nepali named Aristu who had a festival grounds pass. He had been helping his mother who was working at one of the guru tents inside Pashupati all week. The pass allowed us to sidestep the queue and walk straight to the entrance to the temple grounds. We were not really jumping the queue, since I was not lining up to enter the holy of holies—only Hindus are allowed inside the inner courtyard. Aristu flashed a pass at armed guards, and we slipped inside.

I had met Aristu a few days earlier on the forested, shrine-studded hilltop that rises next to Pashupati. He was a bio-chemistry student, nineteen years old—the same age as my own son, back in America. He told me that his whole family had become quite religious recently. They all venerated his mother's guru and practiced yoga. He himself, as a student of science, believed "only 50-50." Keen to practice his English, he offered to be my guide on Sivaratri.

Aristu lived amid the rice fields on the far side of Pashupati—a rural area rapidly disappearing as new homes and paved roads filled the valley. Soon the temple grounds will be surrounded by city on three sides, with its back against a golf course and the airport.

"Twenty years ago, my father tells me, the cry of the wolf could be heard here at night," he said.

Half the hilltop has been preserved as a forest behind a tall iron fence. Some three hundred tiny deer race through the trees. Aristu told me the park was created in honor of Siva, for according to the legend (from the *Nepalamahatmya* and the *Himavatkhanda*) Siva came to this hilltop ages ago in order to escape the wearying company of the gods at Varanasi. He disguised himself as a golden deer, and joined the local herd. His wife Parvati, knowing his identity, joined him secretly in the form of a doe. As temple literature coyly describes it, the divine couple "frolicked" here for some time until the other gods tracked them down. In the scuffle to retrieve the recalcitrant Siva, they seized him by the shining horn on his head. It broke into pieces. One of the pieces took the shape of a lingam, and was buried at the spot where the main temple stands today. On it, four faces of Shiva as the god Pashupati have been carved. This is the statue all the people of Kathmandu have come to worship on Sivaratri.

Tradition says the lingam was discovered where the temple now stands when a cowherd found his cow repeatedly dripping her milk onto a certain spot. The local villagers dug up the spot, and uncovered the sacred phallus. The first shrine was built on the site supposedly in the third century. However, historical records indicate it was rebuilt with a golden roof in 1140 A.D. by King Shiva Deva III. But an earlier inscription from 605 A.D. declares that King Amshuvarman was favored by his touching of Pashupati's feet. This gives historical legitimacy to the idea that Pashupati may have been the tutelary god of the rulers of the Kathmandu valley from ancient times.

The name *Pashupati* means "Lord of the Animals." This is Siva's earliest manifestation, and remains one of his most important throughout the Hindu world. Seals and vessels from the prehistoric Indus Valley Civilization (4500-1900 B.C.)

depict him as a cross-legged, horned god with matted hair and erect phallus, flanked by beasts and serpents. This prehistoric version of Pashupati is believed to be connected with nascent forms of yoga. According to early scriptural references, the early followers of Pashupati were yogis—long haired, god-intoxicated ascetics who covered their bodies with ash.

In the second century B.C., a formal Pashupati sect took shape. It was founded by the ascetic Laukulisha, who supposedly died while performing harsh austerities. Siva entered his resurrected corpse and he became a leader of the ascetic devotees of the god. He founded a "City of Siva" that drew more than ten thousand yogis, and forged them into a cohesive sect that endured for over two thousand years. At the heart of the sect was the notion that human civilization covered up the true non-dual nature of reality. And so their yogic practices sought to free one from all social conventions. They let their hair and nails grow to stupendous lengths. They covered their bodies in ash, or else wore tiger skins, or went completely naked. Some even masturbated in public. And so they became known as the Order of Lunatics.

As centuries passed, the Pashupati yogis evolved into three sub-sects: The *Kalamukhas*—named for the black streak across their face that marked their death and renunciation—were the mildest sect, for they also practiced moral virtues. The *Kapalikas* abandoned all social and moral codes. They carried with them a bowl made from a human skull from which they ate and drank. They lived in cemeteries, among the dead. Most extreme of all, the *Aghoris*, the "Non-terrible," deliberately violated social taboos. They covered themselves in filth, slept on garbage, ate their own excrement, even the flesh of corpses.

"The process is a ruthless one," says one scholar of the path of the Pushapati sects. "It requires the individual to abandon all these things which men most cherish, and to strip, layer by layer, the veils of ignorance, conditioning, and delusions which separate his awareness from the immortal soul. True insight and inspiration, a new awakened sense of magic and wonder is the start of the journey to the Eternal. Without this, it is not possible to escape from the world of relativity."

Pre-dawn, Aristu and I entered the temple grounds, still a kilometer from the temple, but mashed by the crowd. Strands of tiny, bright, multicolored lights (Christmas lights, I would have called them) flashed along the fences and tree tops. For an hour we shuffled forward in the dark like some massive zombie army. As we neared the main temple, Aristu flashed his badge once more. We hopped a few cords, left the line to the temple, and found ourselves for the first time in open space.

As dawn broke, we crossed the bridge over the Bagmati River. The ghats leading down to the water's edge blazed with cremation pyres. So many people receive their last rites here that the river is clogged with the silt of ashes. All week I watched workmen, knee deep, shoveling out the accumulated sludge, trying to get a bit of a flow back into the river. Prolonged drought had turned the Bagmati into a fetid trickle that dribbles through the city. It picks up more sewage and trash than it does water. You know when you are near a bridge in Kathmandu—it stinks. You have to hold a scarf or a sleeve to cover your face in order to breathe.

On the far bank of Bagmati, we climbed the stairs up the hill to a viewpoint overlooking the golden-roofed pagoda in which the four-faced lingam rests. Around the shrines and stairways the holy men have made their camps. Tiny, smoky fires glowed orange before the makeshift altars of talismans and icons. The *Trisulas* (iron tridents), the sacred weapon of Siva, were planted firmly in the ground around the camps. The men cupped their hands and sucked the sweet smoke from their *chillims* (chillum pipes), chanting and chatting with their comrades and curious onlookers. A haze of *ganja* hung blue in the morning air. Teenage boys seemed keen to join in the sacred act, though Aristu for one said he had no intention of getting high.

I was riveted by the human artwork—how each Sadhu marks himself with ash and paint. Vermillion and bright yellow triangles on the forehead, or stark white lines. Some have let their hair grow long and wild. Mustaches twirled at the ends or drooping over the mouth like a walrus. Dreadlocks coiled round and round the heads of others like a massive frizzy turban. They remind me of prehistoric cave painting come to life. Indeed these men seem like something out of time—inhabitants not of the twenty-first century, but of Shiva's timeless realm.

Aristu ushered me through a door in a walled compound next to the stairs. Past a series of shrines we found the courtyard where more than a hundred more Sadhus gathered. My young guide pointed out to me the various types. Among the saffron robed Sadhus, we spotted ascetics who sat near naked, but for a loincloth, their bodies covered in ash, their hair wound around their heads in matted dreadlocks. Two men wore black robes and black turbans. Aristu told me they were eaters of corpses. He said one of them lived in a hermitage in the cliffs farther up the river. People were afraid of him. So, the more extreme of the Pashupati sects still do exist, I thought. I looked at the man. He had a gray beard, neatly trimmed. His black robe was clean. He sat alone, looking down, with long iron tongs of some kind resting on one shoulder. He appeared thoughtful, self-contained.

In another corner of the compound a naked man stood in the center of the group. His disheveled hair dangled down to his ankles. He wore dozens of strands of prayer beads round his neck that looped down and somewhat covered his genitals. I kept expecting these extreme practitioners to have the faces of maniacs. But this naked man, when he turned and I saw his face, had the sweetest, kindest expression. Although his peers seemed to honor and revere him, he seemed almost bashful, looking down, and grinning like a child at play.

To me it is amazing to see men like this, so out of step with modern times. But, then, Siva's devotees have always stepped away from their society. They were Lunatics right from the beginning. I tried to talk to some of them. Aristu was too shy to translate. Some knew a few words of English. Some encouraged me to take their picture and then hit me up for a donation. For one ragged pair who had made a pilgrimage from Bihar, I bought a package of biscuits, which they then shared with me in easy silence. Others offered to share their *chillims*, which I declined, being too much a creature of my own space and time.

Four months later I had the fortune to visit Kathmandu again and went to Pashupati with two Nepali journalist friends, one of whom had studied in Benares and written extensively about Pashupati and its holy men. With them as my interpreters, I entered the compound where the Sadhus were staying. It was dusk, and a prayer ceremony was taking place on the banks of the Bagmati River. *Bhajans* (spiritual songs) and the twang of a sitar could be heard in the night air. The music was punctuated by a band of monkeys jumping back and forth on the compound's tin roof, beating out their own cacophonous rhythms, and screeching to each other now and then.

About thirty holy men sat around the compound, some readying themselves for sleep, others clustered in conversation. We found a group of three sitting on a raised stone circle, willing to talk with us about their lives.

Bharati Baba was a Naga Baba, a Siva devotee from Benares. He had a long black beard and slender body—easy to notice from his naked chest—covered with several necklaces. He wore a large saffron turban with a huge orange *tika* mark on his forehead. His feet sported white athletic socks, something foreign to his yogic body, which may have been donated by a foreign visitor like me. My interpreters told me that though he was the youngest of the group, he was in fact the most senior Baba in terms of attainment. There was, I found out, a very clear pecking order in the world of Sadhus.

Pancha Das was in his fifties, and had been a Baba for twenty years. He followed the God Ram. He wore nothing but a white dhoti wrapped around his waist and a single necklace–the most minimalist garb I had seen on a Sadhu.

Hanuman Baba—named after Hanuman the monkey God—was a sixty-year-old Nepali farmer who had left his wife and children at age forty-five to become a Sadhu. Despite his Santa-like gray beard, his yellow robes and white stripes marking his forehead, he was the junior Baba of the group.

I asked first why they came to Pashupati for Sivaratri.

"It's the festival of the Babas," said Pancha Das, "so lots of high level Babas come here. It's where we get to meet them and learn from them."

"Also, because the high Babas come, a lot of lay people also visit, so we all benefit. So it's really good for the junior Babas like us," added Hanuman Baba.

"Why do you dedicate your life to God?" I asked.

There was a lot of chatter which I did not understand. I first thought there would be different answers from them. However, in the end I learned that there was agreement in their answers. They all said that the sacred music has something to do with their decision to become a Baba. Music has the power to enchant and apparently all the three Babas were drawn to the devotional songs called *bhajans*.

Pancha Das said he was thirty and married when he left his village and family. For him, the path of a Sadhu was a means to rid himself of the bad karma which he had accumulated in this and past lives. He said his present life was devoted to prayer in order to improve his future lives.

Bharati, the Naga Baba, said that he was only ten years old when he dedicated himself to Siva. Being a Sadhu was the only life he can remember.

"What's the most difficult hardship being a Sadhu?" I asked.

"No problems!" said Pancha Das.

"God provides everything," said Hanuman Baba.

"Solitude is the hardest part to handle," said Bharati. He looked me straight in the eyes. There was no self-pity there, but also no sugar coating. Perhaps this is enlightenment: the simple ability to just tell the truth about your life to yourself and others.

"And what's the most beautiful thing about this life?"

Pancha Das replied, "Life itself is wonderful. Even when we are in the mountains, we never go hungry. God provides. God finds someone to support us with food or whatever we need."

"For example?"

"Tonight God sent the three of you to talk with us!" said Pancha Das (this was a subtle hint that we were expected to make a donation in exchange for this conversation).

Another sadhu named Hanuman Das wandered over to our group. He was barely five feet tall, wearing a big white turban that turned out to be mostly hair. He told us he was over one-hundred years old. To prove it, he took off his turban and displayed his matted hair which fell all the way to the flag-stone floor. We expressed admiration for his advanced age.

"It's because we are vegetarian," the old man said, "and dedicate our lives praying to God. That prolongs our lives. Watch this!"

He grabbed his right foot and bent it up to touch the back of his ear, balancing neatly on the other foot. He looked around at the group, pleased at our astonished response. Satisfied that he had made his point, he coiled his hair back up into his turban, and wandered off into the night.

I resumed my questioning of the others:

"Why do you choose to stay here, at Pashupati?"

"Because this area belongs to God. He takes care of everybody," said Pancha Das.

"And it brings people, who make donations. So God takes care of everybody," added Hanuman, making another broad hint that we visitors had a cosmic duty to fulfill.

Bharati Baba added that Pashupati is one of the twelve Pindas—sacred sites of Siva: "So we come to pray here. It's also the only site with a five faced Siva linga in the whole world."

"Five faced? I thought it was four faced?" I asked my journalist friends. They explained that the lingam has four faces—one on each side. But the faceless top which faced the sky was also considered a face—the highest and most abstract face of them all.

I continued to question the Sadhus.

"In our modern society life seems to move awfully fast. But you Sadhus seem to have stepped out of time. What's it like for you, not to be part of this modern world?"

Bharati Baba was quick to respond, "Modern people need cell phones to talk and planes to travel. But if you meditate for twelve years, you can go into a trance and see the whole world."

"When we journalists look at the world, we see problems—political, environmental, and social. What do you see?"

This generated strong discussion among the Sadhus and my friends. Eventually they translated the response: "Politics and economics just don't exist for us. When we see 'the world,' we see sinners, criminals, and greedy people. So it doesn't take up much of our attention."

"When you look to the future, what do you see?"

Pancha Das replied enthusiastically: "A lot of joy—joy in the name of Siva."

Hanuman jumped in: "We have given our lives to the devotion of Siva. Whatever comes, we accept it in the name of Siva."

Bharati Baba didn't say anything. I think he was finished with us sinners. I interpreted the look in his eyes to mean, "The future? That's just a stupid question."

❧ ❧ ❧

Tim Ward is the author of What the Buddha Never Taught, Arousing the Goddess: Sex and Love in the Buddhist Ruins of India, Savage Breast: One Man's Search for the Goddess, *and the soon to be released* Zombies on Kilimanjaro, *an account of the journey he took with his son to the top of Africa. He travels to Nepal on a regular basis as a communications consultant for international development organizations. You can find him online at www.timwardsbooks.com.*

❧ ❧ ❧

Into the Underworld

Life is built on mysterious shifting sands.

I LOOK OUT THE PLANE'S WINDOW AT THE EARTH BELOW, THE sun raking hot and brutish across the Argolid plain. Old, weathered hills, brown, scrubbed, smoothed down by eons of pelting rain, but mostly by the sun: that unrelenting light with the power to wear down, to weather…to patinate.

The sea comes up suddenly, jarring—turquoise, violet and emerald layers swarm the suede coastline. The enormous metal carcass banks over the Saronic Gulf, gliding over the seaside villages south of Athens on its approach to the airport, a pink sheen dusts their whitewashed veneer. The sun is setting; a wedge of moon illuminates a purple eastern sky. I know to expect these extravagant sights, yet under my breath, like a tormented child rocking herself to sleep, I am muttering familiar words to myself, over and over.

I hate this place. I hate this place. I hate this place.

A knot tightens in my stomach. Greece and I are engaged
in a battle, and it is my destiny to search for myself in this
landscape, to stand on these slippery rocks and feel the earth
inhabit me. I want to be that conduit, that Persephone, that
mistress of the in-between. I can feel the water…it is trans-
mutable; plasma. I can touch that rock and hear its ancestral
sound. For reasons I'm not sure I'll ever understand, I have
chosen to return—again and again—to a land that I hopelessly manage to both hate and love.

The writer Lawrence Durrell tells a story that captures the
quintessential paradox of Greece—it warns the uninitiated
that this is not a postcard destination; is a place with a seamy
underbelly, dirt under its fingernails, and voices in the wind
that are not always benign.

An acquaintance of Durrell's was backpacking one afternoon, the story goes, in the mountains of Corfu, in search
of a plant specimen on the central ridge of the island. He
stopped to enjoy the view from a famous outlook when he
found himself suddenly surrounded in a white mist, which
had risen off the sea. He described it as an emanation with a
distinct outline; inside he heard the cries of seagulls and the
calling of human voices. The experience was so terrifying that
he grabbed his belongings and fled the scene, panicked. A few
months later, he was found dead, having fallen from a high
apartment building in Athens, the phone, torn completely off
his apartment wall, still clenched in his hand.

Such tales betray the soul of Greece. It is a place that, if you
are not prepared, will tear back your skin and expose your
soul to the elements. If you survive this baptism by fire, you
are eternally addicted to this numinous, often unforgiving
and utterly seductive earth.

Mythology has a way of creeping into modern terminol-
ogy, and the root of the word panic is found in Pan, the god
of the noonday sun. It is the idea of something scary making
its way into your waking life, the way shepherds are known

to fear the arrival of the cloven-footed god as they doze under the olive groves in the mid-afternoon. Beware, they say. Pan will get you. I know it is true, because he found me in an Athenian apartment, one September morning in 1976.

The sun slants through the shutters, thickly shellacked with dust. My view through the balcony window is a tangle of ugly concrete buildings stacked on the slopes up to Mount Imitos, barely visible beyond a jungle of television antennas and clotheslines.

Flying out over New York harbor a few months before, on July 4th, I celebrated my own independence day by leaving behind all that was familiar to study in Greece. But now I am second-guessing my decision.

The director of the program has a motto: "drop kick me Jesus through the goal posts of life," and her curriculum resembles a version of Outward Bound. Instead of leaving you alone in the woods with a book of matches to see if you survive, she sent me to live on a remote island with no knowledge of Greek, and now I've been dropped into the wilderness of Athens for the rest of the year. In these initial months since my arrival, the everydayness of life here is still so foreign, so strange—I wonder if I will ever get used to this place.

It seems like any other day, the sun rising like a yellow smear over the concrete of Athens, reflecting acid orange off the rooftop water heaters. I lie under the rough blanket and listen to the sounds outside my door—I am next to the kitchen and can hear my roommate, Paki, opening the refrigerator, scooping yogurt into a ceramic dish and sliding it across the table.

It starts slowly, insipidly. A crawling sensation of terror, making me break out in a sweat—I feel as if I'm being pulled into the floor. The sensation of dread increases, my pulse racing, wondering what will happen to me. Will I evaporate in this room? Will I run screaming into the streets? The balcony—I am five floors up. What if I fell off? I hear the call of the vegetable vendor far below, his three-wheeled cart making its way up the street behind the apartment, a megaphone on the roof. "Fresh vegetables, come buy, eggplant, peppers, tomatoes…" the voice intones in a raw, blunt stab. Car horns honk, a woman calls out from a balcony, "*Boree…*" she says to a woman across the street. "*…could be…*"

This psychological descent began, a few weeks before, with an actual journey underground. A few friends and I had dined at a favorite downtown taverna, famous for its enclosed patio and densely trellised arbor, offering an oasis from the chaos of the surrounding city. There, beneath the filth of the streets, the sounds of traffic and the cats climbing blood red bougainvillea, splattered like a mob hit against the brick-walled courtyard, I had an experience that changed my life.

After downing a couple of tiny copper pitchers of retsina—the resin tinged wine specific to Greece—I stepped out in search of the ladies room. The waiter told me it was "down there," and pointed to a hole in the floor. For some reason I hesitated, glancing around at the packed tables of the lunch-time rush hour before peering down the winding stairwell leading into a crepuscular doom.

At the bottom I was faced with a long corridor. Breathing in a mixture of damp earth and cooking oil, I crept down the hallway, my hands touching the moist stone walls for guidance. When I got close to the end, I heard a voice in the darkness.

"Do you want to see something interesting?"

My heart jumped; I stopped, too terrified to answer.

"It is very interesting. Do you like to see?"

Do I like to see? "What?" I finally said, in a pathetic lamb's bleat.

"Come here. I show you."

I walked slowly towards the voice, aware of an ambient light flickering softly like a nighttime ritual about to happen.

Suddenly I felt like Persephone in the Underworld, wondering where her mother went. There was Hades, my waiter, standing next to a large underground clearing, pointing to something. I leaned in closer for a look.

"See—there." Pause. "What you call it in English? A grave?"

I was stunned. Standing right before me, a few feet away, was an upright piece of marble. White, lonely and sacred, it was about five feet tall and projecting directly out of the earth.

"But...how did it get here? I mean, why is it here?" I fumbled over my words, too entranced to be frightened anymore by the fact that I was in a foreign country in a dark basement, alone with a strange man who was now holding my hand.

"Here—I show you," he responded innocently, pulling me closer to the object. We stopped at a respectful distance, but I could see the engravings on the face of the stone, clear as day.

"It was not placed here...it has always *been* here. You see," Hades said, animated, his white teeth flashing in the veiled light, and his voice lowering, at once excited and at the same time tinged with an edge of awe, "we are standing in a graveyard."

All at once, as if Zeus himself hit me with a lightning bolt, I got it. We were thirty feet below the modern Athenian street level, and I was standing in the middle of a Roman cemetery. This was the stuff they couldn't teach you with slides in the darkness of a university lecture auditorium. The ancient still lived here—thinly paved over by the present—and reached out for our understanding and awe, centuries and millennia later. A streetcar rumbled overhead, sending dirt off the ceiling joists, falling on my hair in a gritty benediction. I had lost track of time as well as the fact that Hades was squeezing my hand even harder.

"You like?" he whispered.

Suddenly, right there and then, I knew what I wanted to do with my life. The decision to become an archaeologist emerged from that singular moment under the streets of Athens. The landscape groaned under the weight of millennia of archaeological levels, but the atmosphere itself was also replete with layers—a heady intersection of both panic and wonder, where gods and mortals cross paths—and nothing could be more intoxicating than being face to face with something so unavoidably ancient.

As a child, I had been haunted by a recurring dream of being pulled into the earth, taken away from everything and everyone I knew and loved, to a place I did not recognize. And now, just like those nightmares, a spectral hand had reached up from the bowels of the earth, wrapped itself around my ankle and yanked me down. Like Persephone, I must have ingested some unseen pomegranate seeds: because it would become my destiny not only to make this place my home—but to learn to see in the dark. I gathered up my best possible answer.

"I like," I answered, giving his hand a presumptive squeeze. "I like very much."

I live out the following months in a blur of ancient marble, smoke, cacophony of traffic, people and language. The landscape is nonetheless perfect in a sort of surgical sterility: bone white marbles etched against Kodachrome blue skies, turquoise seas, half moon slices of beach. Not much green anywhere, just the sharp corners of Pythagoras' geometry living in the rocks, the staccato cypress slicing cliff faces, the hard edge bracing day and night. Yet the landscape speaks to me: I hear its voice in the stadium of ancient Olympia, whistling through the trees surrounding the sanctuary of Asclepius, and in the water lapping at the tip of Attica, reflecting the slender columns of the Temple of Poseidon in a miasmic ripple of sapphire and ivory.

Eventually, winter arrives, and the Athens skyline melts

into a flaccid gray smudge, the streets of downtown thick with the aroma of roast chestnuts. The rains come and we wade through the streets of our neighborhood in waist deep water. Over time I return, again and again, to a favorite spot on the Acropolis hill overlooking the Theatre of Dionysus, and as I recline against a marble drum, the rigid flutes penetrating my back, I feel as if I am downloading history. Scanning the city around me—a concrete river cascading from the heights of Lycabettus hill to the glittering shores of the Aegean in the distance—I think of Dionysus and his opposite, Apollo, and realize it's no coincidence the ancient Greeks worshipped deities representing both the logical and illogical...the atmosphere of this place remains infused with their essence.

One evening, towards the end of our stay, Paki and I are drinking on the rooftop of our apartment. After a couple of farewell toasts, she impulsively launches her glass into the air, and as it flies over the edge of the building, a missile catching the late afternoon sun, I think of Durrell's suicidal backpacker, phone in hand, placing a call that would never connect. As close to the edge as I have felt myself in the past months, I can't imagine performing such an erratic act, but still I understand: this place makes you a little crazy. Even though it will soon be time to return to the States and my own life, I know one day I will be back...as much as it frightens me, Greece also is implausibly alluring. Now, more than ever, I want to dig in this earth, to be that conduit, that Persephone, that mistress of the in-between, and search for myself in this landscape.

I listen for the sounds of screaming, terrified that her salvo has killed someone on the street far below. Gratefully, there are no wails, no sirens, just the sounds of seagulls having made their way inland, and the late November wind coming off the top of Mount Imitos in the distance...balding, imperious, and looming over my apartment with a wordless immensity.

≫ ≫ ≫

Amanda Summer Slavin is an archaeologist and writer. For the past 25 years she has returned to the Greek island of Ithaka, where she started searching for the palace of Odysseus in 1984 with a team from Washington University. Her work has appeared in the New York Times, Islands *magazine and other publications. Even though she has traced the odyssey of history's most famous male adventurer, she enjoys stories about women who have found transformation through travel.*

❧ ❧ ❧

Eternity

In the beginning was the word.

I LIE IN A BAMBOO CABIN ON THE PACIFIC EQUATOR, dumbfounded by the crash-upon-crash-upon-crash of breakers. I cannot see the swells approaching shore, but I sense their even rise—which have so often elevated and then lowered me—I sense their rise higher at the precisely appointed line and then they topple forward and come down with unbelievable sounds: the crashing of great swords; the faintest echo of colliding galaxies; the hiss of hurrying electrons; the sound of acres of sliding metal.

Some waves pound the sand like cannonballs, but these are just side-shows. The essence out there is in the rush, the slide; the billion-billion white noise of eternity; the sand-grinding of the ocean ashore. There is no code there, it seems, only particles in motion, but I fall into the sense that I know nothing at all.

The moment passes: Not true: I know something now, I know that these crashes and hisses are important. They preceded all humanity and they will succeed all humanity. I may never understand them, I think, but if I don't listen for messages in there I am a fool.

The next day, five fathoms under the gray surface of the Pacific, as I glance at my air pressure gauge, I am halted by another sound: a low whistle that has twisted through miles of water, a low whistle blending into a short, uprising moan. Whale. I breathe the word through my mouthpiece and it roils up and away in silver bubbles. I deflate my vest to kneel on the sandy sea floor and I listen.

Another low whistle, whorled by current and salt and thermocline, but unmistakable. It trips my mind like a switch, putting me right back in the cabin. Whales, I think, dumbfounded, their sound preceded all humanity and will succeed all humanity and though it's time to turn around and swim back in, you had damned well better commit their sounds to memory.

But back in the cabin I cannot reproduce the sounds in my mind. They have already been smashed away by fish-trucks, barking dogs, and the rumblings of the cat-food factory on the beach. It's O.K., I think, I heard it. I can find recordings. And if I don't, so what? I don't have to hear that twice.

~≈ ~≈ ~≈

Cameron M. Smith is an explorer and writer based in Portland, Oregon, where he is a member of the writing group The Guttery. He has written about his expeditions for many books and magazines. An active scuba diver and paraglider pilot, he is slowly retiring from ice cap expeditions in order to explore the lower stratosphere in a specially-constructed balloon and capsule. You can follow his expedition and writing projects at www.cameronmsmith.com.

Acknowledgments

Introduction by Pico Iyer published with permission from the
    author. Copyright © 2011 by Pico Iyer

"The Way of the Mist" by Cameron McPherson Smith
    published with permission from the author. Copyright ©
    2011 by Cameron McPherson Smith.

"Fire and Water" by Erika Connor published with permission
    from the author. Copyright © 2011 by Erika Connor.

"One Day, Three Dead Men" by Marcia DeSanctis published
    with permission from the author. Copyright © 2011 by
    Marcia DeSanctis.

"How I Promised Anusha the Smile" by Kevin McCaughey
    published with permission from the author. Copyright ©
    2011 by Kevin McCaughey.

"Ain't Ready for No Man" by Katherine Jamieson first
    appeared in the 2010 edition of *poemmemoirstory*, published
    by The University of Alabama, Birmingham. Published
    with permission from the author. Copyright © 2010 by
    Katherine Jamieson.

"The Memory Bird" by Carolyn Kraus first appeared in
    The Alaska Quarterly Review, Fall 2009. Published with
    permission from the author. Copyright © 2009 by Carolyn
    Kraus.

"Camel College" by Matthew Crompton published with
    permission from the author. Copyright © 2011 by Matthew
    Crompton.

"Lanterns of Fear" by Gary Buslik published with permission
    from the author. Copyright © 2011 by Gary Buslik.

"All in the Same House" by Bill Fink published with
    permission from the author. Copyright © 2011 by Bill
    Fink.

"Femme in the Vosges" by Mieke Eerkens published with
    permission from the author. Copyright © 2011 by Mieke
    Eerkens.

About the Editors

James O'Reilly, publisher of Travelers' Tales, was born in Oxford, England, and raised in San Francisco. He's visited fifty countries and lived in four, along the way meditating with monks in Tibet, participating in West African voodoo rituals, rafting the Zambezi, and hanging out with nuns in Florence and penguins in Antarctica. He travels whenever he can with his wife and their three daughters. They live in Palo Alto, California, where they also publish art games and books for children at Birdcage Press (birdcagepress.com).

Larry Habegger, executive editor of Travelers' Tales, has visited almost fifty countries and six of the seven continents, traveling from the Arctic to equatorial rainforests, the Himalayas to the Dead Sea. In the 1980s he co-authored mystery serials for the *San Francisco Examiner* with James O'Reilly, and since 1985 has written a syndicated column, "World Travel Watch" (WorldTravelWatch.com). Habegger regularly teaches travel writing at workshops and writers' conferences, is a principal of the Prose Doctors (prosedoctors.com), and editor-in-chief of Triporati.com, a destination discovery site. He lives with his family on Telegraph Hill in San Francisco.

Sean O'Reilly is editor-at-large for Travelers' Tales. He is a former seminarian, stockbroker, and prison instructor who lives in Virginia with his wife and their six children. He's had a lifelong interest in philosophy and theology, and is the author of *How to Manage Your DICK: Redirect Sexual Energy and Discover Your More Spiritually Enlightened, Evolved Self* (dickmanagement.com). His travels of late have taken him through China, Southeast Asia, and the South Pacific; his most recent non-travel project is redbrazil.com, a bookselling site.